The Ordering of Time

Out of the Boundless [*aperion*] the World arises from whatever is the genesis of the things that are;

    into this [Boundless] they must pass away according to Necessity,

    for they must pay the penalty and make atonement to one another for their injustice according to *the Ordering of Time*.

Anaximander[1]

---

[1] Trans. Patricia J. Cook, *Dictionary of World Biography*, vol. I, ed. Frank N. Magill (Oxford: Routledge, 2003), p. 69; my emphasis. I am indebted to Professor Cook for this translation and for any insights in this volume that might prove worthy.

The Ordering of Time

Meditations on the History of Philosophy

George Lucas

EDINBURGH
University Press

Edinburgh University Press is one of the leading university presses in the UK. We publish academic books and journals in our selected subject areas across the humanities and social sciences, combining cutting-edge scholarship with high editorial and production values to produce academic works of lasting importance. For more information visit our website: edinburghuniversitypress.com

© George R. Lucas, Jr., 2020, 2022

Edinburgh University Press Ltd
The Tun – Holyrood Road
12(2f) Jackson's Entry
Edinburgh EH8 8PJ

First published in hardback by Edinburgh University Press 2020

Typeset in 10/13 Meridien by
IDSUK (DataConnection) Ltd,

A CIP record for this book is available from the British Library

ISBN 978 1 4744 7855 7 (hardback)
ISBN 978 1 4744 7856 4 (paperback)
ISBN 978 1 4744 7858 8 (webready PDF)
ISBN 978 1 4744 7857 1 (epub)

The right of George R. Lucas, Jr. to be identified as the author of this work has been asserted in accordance with the Copyright, Designs and Patents Act 1988, and the Copyright and Related Rights Regulations 2003 (SI No. 2498).

Contents

Preface and Acknowledgements vi

    Introduction: Injustice in the Margins of Time and History   1
1. Ordering Time: Thinking with the Presocratics   8
2. 'The Tragical History of Doctor Beneke'   21
3. Philosophy's Recovery of its History   29
4. Three Rival Conceptions of the History of Philosophy   47
5. Art, Philosophy, and the Shapes of the Past   62
6. A New Methodology for Philosophy   81
7. The Critique of Enlightenment and the Question Concerning Metaphysics   98
8. Scientific Revolutions and the Search for Covariant Metaphysical Principles   125
9. 'People without a Name'   136

Bibliography   156
Index   165

Preface and Acknowledgements

This book is written for, and to a large extent about, old friends and philosophers, brilliant men and women, many of whom are no longer with us. It reflects what I have learned from them about philosophy, as well as what they and others, deemed to be merely ordinary journeymen by their peers (rather than inhabitants of Olympus), have nevertheless contributed to our knowledge of philosophy and of our place in the world. But primarily it is about philosophy as a collaborative exercise, a social (rather than purely individual) phenomenon that nonetheless celebrates supposed individual achievement and all too often ignores the rest. It is a critique of the selection process by which some are lifted up while others are ignored or cast down. It is a measurement of tragedy as well as of achievement, of how much we may have lost, as well as how much we believe ourselves to have learned. This book thus offers a challenge to our Darwinian faith that only the best and brightest rise to fame and recognition or that only their efforts are rightly celebrated and preserved.

This book offers a reconsideration of the *fin-de siècle* anxiety at the close of the twentieth century regarding the death of philosophy and its transformation into something else, . . . or, perhaps, into nothing at all. Philosophers at the time sensed the end of the analytic consensus that had dominated that century, but they did not perceive what the next moves might constitute. They turned to the history of philosophy for answers, but they left only unresolved questions. We have quickly moved on to philosophy and technology, applied ethics, evolutionary epistemology, and the philosophical challenges inherent in artificial intelligence and neurophysiology. But the ruins of that late-century conversation about philosophy's future lie strewn and unaddressed in its now-recent past. As a new generation of philosophers, with charming naïveté, now begins its own rediscovery of the importance of history,[1] this work invites a reconsideration and reformulation of the challenges remaining from that earlier era.

The work on this project began more than three decades ago, as a National Endowment for the Humanities Summer Institute for college and university faculty that I organised in 1990, 'The Philosophical Uses of Historical Traditions'. Over the first decade thereafter, most of the chapters were initially written as refereed colloquium papers or invited as symposium presentations for the main programme at meetings of the Eastern and Pacific divisions of the American Philosophical Association, as well as refereed journal articles or chapters in various books stemming from that initial experience. I am indebted to more friends and colleagues than I can possibly name for their support, timely criticism, and good suggestions regarding that work, then and since. The principal sources of inspiration for these essays came from the invited guest lecturers in the NEH seminar, including Alasdair MacIntyre, Lynn Joy, Jerry Schneewind, Martha Nussbaum, Arthur Danto, John E. Smith, Stanley Rosen, and Donald Phillip Verene. More than subtle traces of their ideas and influences will be evident here.

I benefited greatly in organising that seminar, and beginning my own thoughts on this topic, during a Fulbright research leave the preceding year at the Katholieke Universiteit in Leuven, Belgium, during which I had leisure for the first time to develop in nascent form the ideas that are presented here. I was honoured (along with Martha Nussbaum, Richard Hare, and Newton Garver) years ago with an invitation from Jaako Hintikka to serve as an invited plenary speaker at the seventeenth annual Wittgenstein International Symposium in Kirchberg am Wechsel, Austria, which permitted me to develop the thesis presented specifically in Chapter 7 – namely, that Wittgenstein, Whitehead, G. E. Moore, and others ultimately turned against the project of Cambridge analytic philosophy that they had been instrumental in launching – and to explore the significance of that apostasy for our understanding of the history of contemporary philosophy. Later that year (1994), I was honoured to receive the Pergamon Prize, awarded biennially by the Elsevier Science Foundation (United Kingdom) for the outstanding published essay on the history of European ideas. The encouragement was much needed, for the essay

---

[1] See Stephen Nadler, 'The History of Philosophy, pp. 39–48. Available online at www.apaonline.org/default.asp?page=presidents (accessed 15 December 2019). See also Daniel Garber, 'What's Philosophical about the History of Philosophy?', pp. 129–46.

in question was a deeply critical study of hermeneutics and the work of Hans-Georg Gadamer, which ironically earned the ire of his most ardent disciples in the United States but the ultimate praise and approval of their master, whose work it dismissed as a kind of elaborate and exotic fraud. That essay was also selected in blind review as a lead symposium paper at the Eastern Division programme of the American Philosophical Association in Atlanta in 1993, where it likewise drew the ire of the Gadamerites. Gadamer's own response finally appeared, shortly before his death, in the abridged version of that essay published in his volume of the Library of Living Philosophers, in which he began by remarking, 'I read Mr. Lucas's contribution with excitement and, whether he believes it or not, for the most part with agreement.' He went on to recommend beginning the discussion with Anaximander, rather than Plato or Aristotle – a suggestion I have taken to heart in this book.[2]

The invitation to deliver the annual Powell Lectures at Linfield College near Portland, Oregon, in the spring of 1998 provided the opportunity to begin the process of gathering this work into a unified collection for presentation there. Unfortunately, the ensuing years provided little opportunity to return to and complete the project, and it remained largely frozen in time at the end of the last millennium. It was at least another decade before I could return to the original project, aided by my election in 2016 as president of the Metaphysical Society of America.

In the meantime, however, I had all but given up on the project, on account of two excellent books published explicitly on this same topic, one by Randall Collins and one by Jorge E. Gracia – the latter, somewhat ironically, in a series that I edited.[3] All of this was, of course, in addition to extensive work on this general topic by Richard Rorty, Charles Taylor, Peter Hare, Donald Phillip Verene, and a host of other very eminent figures. Who on earth would be interested in anything further that I might have to say?

My only excuse now is that, with the passage of time, I came to believe that my treatment had some differences from theirs, as well as some observations and conclusions that might independently prove of interest. I do not, for one example, aim at a global theory encompassing the philosophy of other cultures (as does Collins), but I offer only a commentary upon philosophy in Western Europe and America after the Enlightenment. Nor do I attempt the sort of archival and classificatory, descriptive work that

---

[2] See Gadamer's 'Reply to George R. Lucas, Jr', pp. 190–1.

[3] Jorge E. Gracia, *The Sociology of Philosophies*, and Gracia's earlier and quite different account, *Philosophy and Its History*, a volume in the SUNY Series in Philosophy, ed. George R. Lucas, Jr.

establishes this thesis of philosophy as a community activity. In addition, the claim I make (alongside many others) that philosophy is unintelligible apart from its history merely (according to Gracia) serves to classify my view as one of two mutually exclusive kinds of attitudes that he describes: namely, as an 'historicist' view, rather than (like Quine) an incompatabilist. Readers of Leo Strauss, however, will recognise that this label is pejorative in a manner that Gracia does not intend: namely, denoting someone who merely reduces original ideas to their relativised historical context, which is not at all my orientation or intention. In brief, and in contrast to these other accounts, mine is a normative commentary on what philosophers do and how they behave, versus how they characterise themselves and others in their writings. But I leave those distinctions to be illustrated in the chapters that follow and let readers themselves judge whether there is anything unique or of value to be derived from them.

Finally, this book itself is dedicated to Jerome B. Schneewind. I originally intended it to be finished, and for it to be presented to him, upon the occasion of his retirement from teaching at Johns Hopkins University in 2003, as well as to mark the conclusion of his service (as a past divisional president) for three very critical and formative years as chair of the board of officers of the American Philosophical Association – which (again, at that time) had itself just concluded celebrating a century of service to the academic and scholarly community of the United States.

That was a significant moment because, absent Schneewind's judicious leadership at that time, the forces of marginalisation and fragmentation that I discuss in this book threatened to bring that organisation itself to near ruin. For those of us in the philosophical rank and file, for whom the lively conversations and enduring friendships and professional associations this organisation fostered, its loss or diminution would have constituted a genuine tragedy. Looking back now, two decades later, I am delighted to observe that the philosophical society he salvaged at that time is now healthier and more diverse than ever. I am likewise delighted that I may still have the opportunity to present to him this small token of my esteem while we are both still around.

My own specific and personal debt, however, is somewhat more complex than this testimonial would suggest. The ideas in this book, for example, strike me as little more than amplifications or further explorations of hypotheses Schneewind himself advanced in essays and discussions over the years with respect to the historical development of modern moral philosophy in particular.[4] This discussion encompasses several of

---

[4] Most especially in Schneewind's *The Invention of Autonomy* and in his subsequent *Essays on the History of Moral Philosophy*.

the hypotheses he first advanced, and descriptive historical accounts he first offered, for the differing interests and preoccupations of moral philosophy over time. I have learned much from him, and without his gracious support (which I had absolutely no right to expect), I doubt I would have survived in this profession long enough to bring this project to conclusion. I can only hope the result will not prove an occasion for him to regret his many acts of kindness and generosity.

The author wishes to acknowledge the *Review of Metaphysics* for permitting revision of portions of my 2016 Presidential Address for the Metaphysical Society of America, originally published as 'Anaximander and the Ordering of Time: Metaphysics Viewed from the Margins of History', *Review of Metaphysics* 70: 3 (March 2017), pp. 529–49.

The Index for this volume was prepared by Ms Joan Caywood (Cambridge, MA).

For J. B. Schneewind

Introduction: Injustice in the Margins of Time and History

There are, of course, numerous, perhaps infinite, ways to narrate the history of philosophy. Each attempts to provide insight into both what the activity known as philosophy is and what lessons we have learned over the centuries from its pursuit.

When one refers to perspectives on this (or any topic) 'from the margins', one might reasonably suppose in the present climate of opinion that yet another version of this narrative is to be presented, as seen through the eyes of those who have traditionally been excluded from the activity in question or whose contributions to it or attempts to participate in it fully have been ignored, perhaps on account of their race, class, or gender. Philosophy's history, seen from the margins, might thus represent an attack upon the mainstream Eurocentric, logocentric, phallocentric, or otherwise self-centred or privileged narratives that have long dominated our understanding of this topic.

While I have been grateful for, and have benefited over the years from, the retelling of philosophy's narrative by those long excluded or by representatives of those whose cultural contributions did not often count or were not fully recognised in the more traditional renderings of the history of philosophy, it is not my project in this book either to emulate their example or to otherwise follow in their footsteps. This work is not itself intended to offer another cultural critique of philosophy, nor is it yet another attack upon the validity of philosophical reasoning. I am neither prepared nor qualified to argue for the greater significance of marginalised peoples, cultures, or genders to the larger story that is philosophy. Nor, in light of the outstanding work in this vein by so many others, more qualified, would my contribution to this cause prove all that useful.[1]

Nor, it needs be said, do I intend, by speaking from 'the margins', to further the interesting project of Derridean deconstruction by offering inverted, unorthodox, or otherwise idiosyncratic or perspectival readings of familiar texts in ways that yield new and wholly unfamiliar interpretations of them. The work I am undertaking is in fact less about individual texts than about their authors and about the nature of the self-reflective activity in which many of them earnestly believed themselves to be engaged. Even further, the project is less about distinct individuals than about groups, clusters, schools, movements, disciples, and traditions that together constitute the history of human thought as a communal enterprise. Philosophy glorifies the creative individual genius but itself occurs only as the collective discourse of some community.[2] There are ways of shuffling the deck, rearranging the groups and clusters and the individuals that each such community contains, that result in strikingly different insights on what philosophy actually is, as opposed to how its most celebrated practitioners represent it as being.

I recognise that this way of posing my project may seem unnecessarily cryptic. By way of a clarifying illustration, perhaps the most famous and familiar recent example of this reshuffling is the case of Nietzsche. At his death, over a century ago, relatively few scholars were familiar with his work, and those who were did not take it very seriously. The philosophical scene[3] in Western Europe in 1900 was dominated by the grand, majestic, speculative evolutionary cosmology of Professor Hermann Lotze at Leipzig. Older readers are probably familiar with this irony, while many others, younger, will have to scramble to their encyclopaedias in order to discover who Hermann Lotze even was.[4] They will be shocked and puzzled, when they do, at how what they will undoubtedly regard as such unintelligible nonsense ever enjoyed widespread acceptance, let alone almost global dominance prior to World War I. Our smug and comfortable conventions about the historical process will assure all, however, that justice was eventually done, nonsense swept aside, and the worthier, 'world-historical' figure (Nietzsche) eventually (and inevitably?) elevated to his 'rightful place' in the philosophical pantheon.

It is my central thesis in this book that Anaximander was, in fact, the first philosopher to harbour grave doubts about the remorseless working of this historical process. In any case, I want to examine the kind of questions that would arise if we were to reconsider instances like this familiar example. Might we not legitimately wonder at the differences between the two radically different narratives of philosophy's proper activity and its historical route to that activity: the one told in 1901 (with its account of who is 'hot' and who is 'not'), and the one we tell ourselves now, in the year 2020 and beyond? What are we to make of those differences? What account of truth, or methodological legitimacy, or intellectual and philosophical authenticity are we to apply to justify our narrative now, as opposed to theirs then? How confident dare we be that we, in the presumably privileged later historical perspective, have arrived at the more authentic interpretive stance? Our complacent self-confidence in history's ability to select, in a kind of Darwinian struggle, the best and brightest intellectual achievements and their creators seems (to me, at least) open to grave suspicion.

Here is another example of reshuffling the deck, championed, but (so far as I know) never fully developed, by a prior president of the Metaphysical Society.[5] If we look at how the history of philosophy has been narrated in the West, including the fate of the two philosophers cited above, we might note that there is a kind of axis, centrally presupposed in most such narratives generated from the 'inside' of Western culture, that extends from the flourishing of Greek culture in the ancient period to the flourishing of the Enlightenment in Europe, predominantly and preeminently encompassed within German-language philosophy. That is not entirely an accident, since the enterprise of philosophical history really gets its start with German scholarship and its weighty historical self-consciousness (as Nietzsche himself complained).[6] What then could possibly be wrong with casting one's self, as a culture, as the legitimate heir and culmination of all that you and your cultural neighbours in the European Enlightenment period acknowledge as the best and brightest legacy of the ancient world? Or, in any case, what more might we expect of a culture's collective self-consciousness?

The problem, of course, lies precisely in seeing *what gets omitted or marginalised* in this narrative. There is, of course, another way of drawing this axis (no doubt there are many). Like the Mercator projection of the Earth's sphere onto a flat plane, moreover, the redrawing casts the principles and elements into a wholly new light, in a radically altered relationship. One might, for example, dismiss the Greeks as minor figures (as they are depicted, for example, in the famous Hellenistic bath mosaic in the Rhinesche-Germanische Museum in Köln), and focus instead on Roman and Hellenistic culture as the source of the legacy and philosophical patrimony to be preserved. Cicero, Seneca, and other 'rediscovered' (and currently quite popular) Stoic philosophers become cast in this narrative as the flowering of ancient culture, and their legacy is borne not by the familiar medieval and early modern philosophers of the ponderously theoretical German-axis narrative but by the likes of Dante, Cervantes, Nicholas of Cusa, and the subsequent figures of the Italian Renaissance, like Giambattista Vico and Pierre Gassendi, for whom history, rhetoric, and literary expression (rather than logic and formal analysis) constitute the proper elements of philosophical methodology.

That in turn feeds into the kind of question that Jerome Schneewind so brilliantly tended to pose: in this instance, how 'modern' (as distinct from medieval and ancient) philosophy *ever even gets started*. How, for example, does this business of individualism and personal liberty ever get going or catch on?[7] What was once settled dogma in this respect has now become highly problematic. *It matters* whether you start the modern story with Descartes (a scientist and mathematician who wrote books and treatises in his native tongue as well as in Latin) or with Francis Bacon (who wrote, by contrast, in the rhetorical form of aphorisms, once practised by Heraclitus and later favoured by Nietzsche) or (as Schneewind himself does) with Montaigne (who pioneered the form of the literary self-reflective essay). Each beginning generates a very different subsequent historical narrative, with contrasting emphases on what counts and who matters, on what the proper methodology and mode of expression of science and philosophy might constitute, and thereby ultimately issues in vastly different conceptions of what proper philosophical enquiry itself actually is.

The project of philosophical analysis as practised today, for example, has roots extending back for millennia in the effort to develop a precise if technical philosophical vocabulary out of a common vernacular by Aristotle, as well as in the methodological reductionism of Descartes, perfected in the logical atomism of Bertrand Russell. Francis Bacon is, by contrast, something of an enigma: likewise emphasising experience and induction, but expressing himself in pithy, Nietzschean-like aphorisms that are more oracular than precisely analytic in character. But if Montaigne is taken as paradigmatic, it is but a short journey (for example) to Marcel Proust, or Virginia Woolf, and to our current fascination with philosophy *as* (as well as *of*) literature and poetry generally. Here we would be following the example of Richard Rorty in ultimately turning our backs on Plato and his deep and abiding mistrust of these alternative forms of discourse, opening ourselves instead towards an antispeculative philosophical conversation devoid of any ground or foundation.

In our own time, we have witnessed the recovery of interest in what philosopher Martha Nussbaum and educational historian Bruce Kimball[8] variously identify as an 'oratorical' tradition in ancient philosophy and liberal learning, the Roman civic tradition of Seneca and Cicero, as distinct from the more abstract, analytical, and contemplative project of the Greeks. Here philosophy is seen more as a public and practical activity, as engagement in civic life and a preparation for leadership, than an aloof, god's-eye, disinterested, and disdainful dismissal of culture and community.[9] We have yet to ask ourselves, however, what happens to our overall picture of philosophy and its history if we take this public emphasis seriously and extend it forwards in time to rewrite our historical narrative of the present.

The point here is to notice that we are not arguing about facts: we are working with the same historical data, and we are even telling the story from inside the same broad cultural tradition. All the above narratives are explicitly Western, Eurocentric, logocentric, and male dominated. Yet even so, what different accounts they yield!

In other words, we need not descend into a caustic, post-Enlightenment cultural or ideological critique to grasp the problem I am describing. Feminist scholars and ethnic critics of philosophy's hegemony do not have a monopoly on critical discourse in this vein, even if they helped open our eyes to the need for this kind of cross-examination. We need not necessarily follow the Roman historian Tacitus and wallow in Western culture's unique tendency towards self-loathing and uncritical glorification of the Other in order to fully engage in self-reflection and constructive self-criticism. We can, instead, follow Nussbaum's exemplary method of defending, interpreting, and drawing contemporary inspiration from that classical tradition, replete with its many acknowledged flaws and lacunae.

As I hope to illustrate in the chapters that follow, the history of philosophy is fraught with the normative moral judgement that Anaximander offers with a measure of what must be identified as *prophetic anger*. Grave injustice is inevitably done, without rational explanation or justification, and seems almost unavoidable and unremediable. It is my hope that this book, and the historical portrait it offers, will address this ongoing tragedy and perhaps stem somewhat the loss to oblivion – at the very least, by calling attention to it.

In particular, I will hold that Hegel's final vision of a complete, Pythagorean 'master narrative' (as Alasdair MacIntyre terms it)[10] is finally a *normative* conception, pointing us towards what we, as philosophers, properly should be about: like archaeologists or forensic scientists, uncovering the past, and like forensic scientists and theologians, redeeming it and rectifying its inexplicable injustice. Anaximander and Heraclitus will seem, by contrast, much more like ineffectual art critics, commenting on the demise and the sorry state of art itself, but ultimately doing little otherwise about it. Both offer a description of philosophy in the world as we find it, one in which our efforts, and sometimes our conflicts with one another as philosophers, stand condemned.

Confession of these sins, however, is the requisite first step of redemption, absolution, and the rectification of injustice. Philosophy, in the middle of its third millennium as a mode of discourse distinct from mythology and religion, is sorely in need of such redemption.

Notes

1. By contrast, this *was* my explicit exercise in reviewing and extensively updating and revising the coverage of philosophy in reference works (including Grolier's *Encyclopedia Americana*, whose editorial oversight I inherited in the mid-1990s from J. B. Schneewind). With the help of Schneewind and my long-time colleague and friend Lucius Outlaw at

Vanderbilt University, we were able to forge a much broader and multicultural conception of philosophy and – virtually alone among general introductory reference works on this topic – to commission essays from some of the world's leading scholars that offered a variety of narratives from African, Asian, Islamic, and feminist perspectives that gave the novice some larger insight into the breadth and depth of philosophical reflection as a human and cultural (rather than strictly male or Western) activity. But this is *not* my principal task in this book.

2. This is a view of the social, rather than individual, nature of philosophy, which, as mentioned in the Preface, is meticulously documented in Randall Collins's magisterial work, *The Sociology of Philosophies*. While my work bears some comparison to his, it will become apparent that the approach taken is quite different, and that, in fairness, my own initial work on this general topic predated the publication of his seminal work in any case by at least a decade. Still, it is evident that my claim that philosophy is a social enterprise that fits poorly within the emergent 'culture of disciplines' that it helped to bring about was greatly strengthened by this important social scientific study.

3. Patient readers will come to see that I intend the deliberate use of this descriptor drawn from popular culture and aesthetics, one that is jarring and somewhat offensive when set against our conventional understanding of our activity as philosophers.

4. But cf. his surprising influence on Peirce and American pragmatism, as well as on the formation of personal idealism or 'personalism', much of which influence is now being rediscovered. See David Sullivan, 'Hermann Lotze' in *The Stanford Encyclopedia of Philosophy:* plato.stanford.edu/archives/win2014/entries/hermann-lotze

5. This is Donald Phillip Verene's insight, not mine. It is implicit in his organisation and presentation of materials in *The History of Philosophy*.

6. Nietzsche in fact lamented this 'bad' historical consciousness in German scholarship, and he thought it an impediment to true philosophising. See *On the Advantages and Disadvantages of History for Life*.

7. J. B. Schneewind's central question driving his historical commentaries and reading selections in *Moral Philosophy from Montaigne to Kant*, two volumes.

8. Bruce Kimball, *Orators and Philosophers*. Martha Nussbaum finds particular inspiration for this public, oratorical, civic tradition embodied in the thought of the Spanish 'outsider' in the Roman empire, the Stoic philosopher Seneca, and uses this to construct a remarkable reconception of philosophy's responsibility for civic education in a contemporary setting that is as multicultural as ancient Rome: see Martha C. Nussbaum, *Cultivating Humanity*.

9. The central thrust of the work of yet another of prominent MSA president, John Lachs; see also the mission of the Society for Philosophy in America (SOPHIA), a group that Lachs founded, and the discussion of liberal education, human rights, and individual capacity-building by Martha Nussbaum: *Cultivating Humanity*.
10. See Alasdair MacIntyre, 'Epistemological Crises, Dramatic Narrative, and the Philosophy of Science', pp. 453–72.

1 Ordering Time: Thinking with the Presocratics

Let me begin by setting out what I believe philosophy (including especially metaphysical enquiry as first philosophy) to be and what it will require for its future practice. There are three topics to highlight in this respect:

1. The theme of 'thinking with' the presocratics.
2. The long-standing quest for unmediated experience that initially motivated the reversion to the presocratics during the twentieth century.
3. The discovery of Anaximander's denunciation of the injustice inherent in the flux of such experience, especially as this pertains to the subsequent history of philosophy itself.

Each segment aims to flesh out an underlying notion of *philosophical thinking* itself as consisting fundamentally of an engagement with and redemption of historical experience.

Thinking *with*: The Origins of Philosophy in Myth and History

First, let me say a bit more about the theme of 'thinking with' the presocratics and why I wish to focus on the preposition *with* in particular, instead of the more conventional *about*. I do this deliberately in order to emphasise a way of doing philosophy that is grounded in its history and in the contributions of its predecessors, without limiting it merely to discourse *about* that history and those predecessors – at least, not exclusively. Thinking *about* the presocratics, for example, is what eminent scholars like Philip Wheelwright, Kirk and Raven, and W. K. C. Guthrie do.[1] Some eminent philosophers do not value that kind of historical scholarship. When W. V. O. Quine offered his condescending distinction between those who *are* themselves philosophers, and others who merely examine its history, I think he had this distinction, and such scholars, in mind.² Quine mistakenly believed, however, these were the only two options possible and, furthermore, that only the first constituted genuine, original knowledge rather than merely mucking about in the past.

Quine apparently did not envision the possibility of a third alternative, in which philosophers, authentically engaged in *doing* philosophy, pursue their philosophical enquiries primarily through *engaging* with its history.³ It is this distinction between thinking *about* and thinking *with* that I especially want to champion in this work as a way of doing philosophy and, particularly, of engaging in metaphysical reflection. Heidegger asserted that philosophy was the human enterprise of 'called thinking' – namely, allowing the thing(s) to be thought about to *call forth or elicit* the activity of thinking as an openness towards Being.⁴ Yet Hannah Arendt asserted that 'thinking itself is dangerous', and she accused both Heidegger (her mentor) and Adolf Eichmann (her most famous research subject) of having *failed to think*. This lapse was the essence of the banality of evil.⁵

It is with such rich resonances in mind that I hope to call upon us all to *think with* the presocratics, specifically about the origins of philosophy and metaphysics itself in myth and history. Eva Brann observed that Parmenides, in his *Proem*, claimed that thinking (*nous/noein*) and being (*esti/to eon*) were one and the same,⁶ thus demonstrating that logic (Quine's first love) and metaphysics as 'first philosophy' at least, are finally inseparable. Brann herself offers, I believe, a perfect illustration of the difference between merely thinking *about* the presocratics and thinking *with* them. This is especially apt since, in her book on Heraclitus as well, she characterises these historical first philosophers of having substituted rational accounts for myths of origin – searching for first principles that are intelligible rather than inscrutable – and so of having thereby stood at the boundary of myth, history, and the historical origins of philosophy as metaphysics.⁷

Scholars in history and classics, like the famous historians of Greek thought listed above, by contrast, intentionally think *about* the presocratics – about *what* they said and *when* (or even *whether*) they said it, as well as about how it was received, understood, and transmitted by their audiences. They treat such topics as factual investigations only. Employing the terminology of F. H. Bradley and A. N. Whitehead, I would say that, by design, historically inclined philosophers choose to remain externally related to the topics or subjects of their investigation – at arm's length, if you will, from what they are thinking *about*. Their objective is to get at the history, get it clear, and get the ideas of particular classical figures in philosophy correct (or correctly translated). It is no part of their task or intellectual obligation, by contrast, to enter into some kind of internal, subjective, transformative relationship with their subject matter, let alone to engage in the kind of dialectical discourse and reflection that characterises philosophy as (in Heidegger's terms) 'called-thinking'.

Fields of academic scholarship, such as classics, thus do not aim primarily at engaging in a philosophical dialogue with earlier thinkers, nor to think *with* them, let alone to be themselves somehow transformed and inspired through their own encounters with the past nor propose to re-engage and reformulate the thoughts or the edifices of ideas earlier historical figures may have contributed. We might claim that academic and disciplinary scholarship of these kinds is methodologically precluded from engaging internally, inspirationally, and transformatively with their subject matter. It is not what they are supposed to do, nor is this how they are to behave responsibly as custodians and stewards of the past. So intellectual history and the history of philosophy (both topics very dear to me personally) consist in the examinations and analyses of the history of ideas and of the chronicles of the lives and adventures of those who formulated them. But they do not – again, by custom and design – entail Heidegger's called-thinking: that is, they do not require thinking *with* their subjects of enquiry. They only think *about* them.

Quine may thus have been right, in that very limited sense, in refraining from calling these activities 'philosophy'. But he was quite mistaken to disparage the history of philosophy itself on so limited an account of its wider significance. This is an important point that I hope to demonstrate in the chapters that follow.

The Presocratics and the Postmodern Quest for Unmediated (Primordial) Experience

For the present, let me ask readers to hold in mind my brief opening sketch (in the Preface) of alternative histories of philosophy as we turn next to the specific mission or goal that apparently fascinated Husserl and Heidegger when they first blazed the path I am encouraging us now to follow and attempted to re-engineer the course of modern philosophy and (in Heidegger's case) draw our attention towards the presocratics in the first place: the quest for direct, unmediated experience.[8]

What would it be like to have direct, unmediated, entirely theory-free experience of one's own self, immersed in its immediate life-world, without carrying the burden of theory, or even suspecting what it might mean to be theory laden? Indeed, would we, or even *could* we, wonder about that very immersion itself, about its nature and effects, wholly absent some prior (*a priori*) beliefs about it that would provide us with the root concepts and key vocabulary in which to explain it? What, indeed, would it be like to be wholly lacking even a vague awareness of what a theoretical construct itself might be, other than some vague rejection of past prior accounts of experience in terms, say, of myth, poetry, or the will of the gods (as we credit the presocratics with having been the first in history to achieve)?

Here I would like to pay further tribute to several distinguished philosophers (who also served as past presidents of the Metaphysical Society of America) who have taught us all a great deal about this topic over the years. The late Edward Pols, for example, spent his own career examining what he termed 'direct realism' as a way around the highly abstract theory-ladenness of much post-Kantian epistemology – both idealism (which he rejected) and the epistemological gymnastics (which he detested) of later critical realists, including Ralph Barton Perry and A. N. Whitehead, attempting to explain how they were *not* 'idealists'.[9]

Donald Phillip Verene, whose work in this vein I cited above, through his many fascinating reflections on myth and imagination in Vico, and their reprise in the literary works of James Joyce,[10] argued over several decades that this question regarding primordial experience also fascinated Vico, infusing Vico's accounts of the first imagined quaking response of the human subject to the sound of thunder (an image captured and repeated by James Joyce, who makes this primordial event the opening of *Finnegans Wake*). That 'first word',[11] the beginning of language, on Vico's account, is an imitation of what the subject directly experiences, absent the slightest understanding or comprehension. And so, as Eva Brann likewise describes Heraclitus as having revealed: the *logos* itself begins with the first *logoi*, gradually gathering them together so as to order the world intelligibly.

This was what Heidegger wondered, in particular, apparently inspired by his teacher Husserl's conception of the *epochē* : can we 'open ourselves' to experience in order somehow to 'know' what is hitherto unknown without any underlying assumptions about what it is that we are knowing? Husserl and Heidegger held that in bracketing the *epochē* (or in called-thinking) we render ourselves open to disclosure, to a shining-forth (*Erscheinung*) of Being itself. Such attitudes or stances constitute forms of pretheoretic, unmediated intuition – very similar, perhaps, to the sort of direct knowing of Ed Pols, or the *fantasia* of Vico, on Verene's account.[12]

We find strikingly similar proposals regarding unmediated experience put forward around the same time as the rise of phenomenology in Europe: by the classical American pragmatists, and by Charles Sanders Peirce and William James in particular. Indeed, we find all of these disparate thinkers on both sides of the Atlantic in a similar historical period, moving towards the view that Experience (Peirce's category of 'firstness') precedes its Ordering (mediation, 'thirdness'), which lies in its Naming

(Vico's encounter, Peirce's 'secondness'), which in turn allows Experience to be rendered intelligible. We might say, in a kind of mytho-poetic sense, that the birth and history of this recent preoccupation with a metaphysics of experience mirrors the birth and history of those mythical first philosophers, and their rival interests as well, over a similar duration of historical time.

While the *logos* of Heraclitus may constitute the first explicit account of this ordering principle, Brann argues (correctly, I believe) that credit is due to *all* the presocratics–physicists–materialists to some degree for this achievement. None were 'materialists' in the trivial sense in which they were categorised by Aristotle, but each was searching instead to discern and name the underlying ordering principle of things, rather than simply describing the things, stuff or substance, of experience itself in a physical sense. In this sense, absent that principle, even ignorant of it, almost by definition their experience was 'unmediated' in the sense required by Heidegger, for each of these first philosophers or presocratics would have been obliged, constrained, or limited by their initial collective ignorance as humanity's first wise men, or thinkers, to be open to the call of Being.

Pragmatists, like William James in America, in contrast to the newly emerging phenomenologists in Europe at the same period, however, thought that a newborn baby, rather than a methodologically trained phenomenologist or a presocratic philosopher, should be taken as the proper exemplar of unmediated experience. Peirce, as noted in passing above, characterised 'firstness' as unmediated, unanalysed experience utterly lacking in order or differentiation, in an account that is strikingly similar to Husserl's *epochē* (but only after the phenomenologist teaches herself to 'bracket' in an eidetic or phenomenological reduction), while James famously labelled such primitive experience a 'blooming, buzzing confusion' (more along the lines of the decidedly nonconceptual *hyle*, the flux of sense-impressions constituting raw experience for Husserl).

Scholars of each of these figures, to be sure, may rightly worry that I have oversimplified, truncated, and even butchered or mangled their individual accounts in order to disclose what I take as the broader commonality of their respective quests to get at things-as-they-are-in-themselves before we superimpose our presuppositions and theories upon them.[13] But this summary account of a common quest to attain and to ground knowledge in unmediated experience is *not* a 'night in which all cows are black'. There are some distinctions to be upheld in this account. Sensory impressions, Husserl's *hyle*, or Russell and Moore's sense-data, for example, were likewise the foundation of Anglo-European analytic epistemology during this period. But while *everyone* around this time seemed to be concerned, to some degree, to 'avoid metaphysics' (by which they usually meant the lapse into Hegelian idealism in particular), none were so tunnel-visioned and proscriptive as positivists. If a nonjudgemental 'openness to Being', or perhaps James's infant (immersed helplessly in a raw and disorganised sensory flux) constitutes one pole on a continuum of self-conscious attitudes, its opposing pole is what I might characterise as 'dogmatic epistemology', in which the ordering principles sought in and for experience come to function instead as rules for *excluding* various kinds of experiences from consideration altogether that do not conform to these rules. Such experience is dismissed merely as nonsense or nothing.

Intelligibility, as Heraclitus first discerned, is essential to deriving knowledge from raw, unmediated experience. But stipulating what counts as knowledge, as the positivists did, simply cuts off sources arbitrarily, based upon a rule or system of rules that cannot be justified or derived. So experiencing colour patches and shapes, and cognising them as a 'coin' or 'tabletop', as G. E. Moore did, counts and is verifiable, falsifiable, and therefore veridical. Insights allegedly derived, however, through prayer or meditation or through an attitude of 'openness' to, say, the beauty of Nature are, by contrast, utterly without significance (nonsense) or, at best, private and wholly subjective emotive states with no genuine perceptual veridicality or cognitive content.

This is not Socratic 'love of wisdom' or the 'wonder' in which philosophy begins for Aristotle. Neither is it the same spirit of enquiry and openness encountered either in phenomenology on one side of the Atlantic or of classical pragmatism on the other. This attitude of contempt was, instead, a rather peculiar, perverse kind of simple-minded, mean-spirited pinheadedness. It is tragic to look back on the period just prior to World War I – as we have been inadvertently engaged in doing while compiling the new Whitehead Critical Edition – and realise that it was a period during which an international collaboration towards a new philosophy of experience was under way across the Atlantic that was subsequently cut off by war and brutally crushed in a tsunami of bitterness and recrimination, fomented by an anti-intellectual school of philosophy determined to stamp out and eradicate competition and, in the process, inadvertently cause philosophy itself to all but grind to a halt for the ensuing century.

Anaximander: The Ordering of Time, the Injustice of History, and the Task of Philosophical Thinking

Thus far in the opening pages of this book I have revisited many of the primordial, mytho-poetic first accounts of, and preliminary rival hypotheses concerning, experience in the raw and its underlying principle(s): flux and becoming (the 'flux-gibberish' of Heraclitus that William Desmond discusses);[14] undifferentiated Being and the decided absence of non-Being (Parmenides); a material 'mixture' of some sort with opposite forces as agent of mixing (the love and strife of Empedocles); or initially with the Ionians, one above others of the materials mixed: water (Thales); air or vapour and a principle of condensation and rarefaction (Anaximenes); *nous* or Mind (Anaxagoras); the 'Logos in the lightning' (as Philip Wheelwright characterised Heraclitus).

All or most of these accounts had antecedents in mythology: 'in the beginning was water, the formless void, and the Spirit of God moved over the face of the water'. And in a strangely similar sense, the contemporary quest for unmediated experience and direct intuition is likewise a history shrouded in myth. Peirce's recognition of 'firstness' demonstrates this, because it is strongly coupled in his case to the necessity of turning raw experience into knowledge through mediation that (he recognised) places the cognising subject 'at arm's length' from raw experience, as the price paid for knowledge. Finally to know, to cognise, to understand, is to stand at a distance from the Real.

What turns out to be, in its own right, this myth of direct intuition or of unmediated experience, fails to encompass this essential feature of the necessary ordering of experience. As Whitehead tried to explain in his theory of 'symbolic reference' (i.e., perception in the mixed modes of causal efficacy and 'presentational immediacy'), the primordial flux of sensory data experienced by subjects, even after bracketing and a phenomenological reduction,[15] is always the back end of a chain of events whose complexity (and therefore distance or 'thirdness') is itself dependent upon the nature of the 'organism' (in Whitehead's unique, generalised meaning of that term). Whether for a rock, a jellyfish, or a late nineteenth-century aesthete, unmediated experience and openness towards Being is invariably, of necessity, that 'grey upon grey' of a shape of life that has itself already grown cold. Understanding and wisdom, as Hegel so eloquently and tragically realised in the case of the human subject, is that Owl of Minerva that spreads its wings only at the coming of night. Philosophy can accomplish its business of understanding the world, but it cannot itself change that world – since, by then, the world thus understood has already perished.[16]

Here, finally, is why I represent all these metaphysical ruminations as fundamentally stemming from a reflection upon Anaximander. I would claim that he was the first to introduce a normative quality into this discussion, to which I would like to give consideration in conclusion: justice (or rather, its absence) exhibited in this flux of becoming, this issuing forth of a finite limited Being from the *Aperion* or Unbounded, and its retreat once more into oblivion. *Dike*, 'justice', actually means something more akin to 'righteousness' than the more impersonal distributive notions of equity, fairness, and giving each his or her due. Justice is also a character trait, like integrity. But however we understand 'justice', it is not its presence but its decided absence, according to Anaximander, that characterises 'experience'. What can this mean, and how can it be so?

Our parents first teach us, when we, as children, object to certain sets of circumstances or social arrangements, that 'life is not always fair'. Is that it? Fatalism? So it goes, *que sera, sera*: whatever will be will be? Or is there something else beyond resignation – perhaps *anger*? To Parmenides's claim, '*It* Is!', Anaximander in effect responds, 'And *It* is corrupted, rotten to the core!' *Aperion* is not some vague abstract possibility field: it is the totality of what could be, but is not. But *why* is it not? There is more than simply no answer to this question. There is a recognition that Existence and Experience cannot simultaneously encompass all possibilities, to be sure. But the unpleasant deeper truth is that what is chosen and exemplified, in this account of experience, is not chosen or exemplified for any compelling or self-justifying reason. There is no rational justification for what is, instead of what might be or have been: rather (Anaximander seems to say), what *is* 'commits injustice against its opposite', banning it to nonbeing, hogging the ontological stage, monopolising experience, starring itself, casting itself in the lead role, not on account of moral worth, or value, but at best, arbitrarily, and at worst, as a monstrosity of injustice, since *what is* crowds out *what might be* (even if the latter were found to have more worth, more justification, more claim to be real, than what actually is). In the process, what is (or, at least, might be) better and more worthy is denied its chance, deprived of its opportunity to excel before all is swept away in oblivion.

Whitehead benignly supposed that Process always involved the creation of Value. Anaximander seems to claim precisely the opposite: that process is not merely destruction but that, even worse, what is created crowds out what is often of as much value as, or more value than, itself. Process exhibits injustice; its issue is not 'value' in any normative sense but is the misery and the suffering that we cling to desperately nonetheless. Who, confronted with such an account, would not recoil in anger, would not cry out in protest, would not characterise existence itself as the fundamental commission of injustice against its opposite, and would not rage, with Dylan Thomas against the darkness that condemns all, finally, to oblivion?[17]

Anaximander introduces a dimension of moral outrage into experience: he is as angry (as are we, when children) that the world can offer no better account of itself than our parents do when they shrug off our recognition of moral unworthiness and injustice: 'Life isn't always fair!' But who made that rule, and why must it be so?

Our own experience of Experience sustains this moral outrage. Anger is the proper attitude towards this injustice, and moral outrage is the proper response to hogging the limelight and dominating the limited stage of Being. Doing so crowds out others with as much or greater claim to the limelight, at least if justice is the measure of all such things. Experience, according to Anaximander, is characterised chiefly by the absence of justice. It necessarily entails, he says, the commission of injustice, as well as the recognition that though it is so, it need not be and should not be. There is no *logos*, no principle of intelligibility, in this particular *nomos* of Anaximander. There is only frustration and rage.

This conclusion is not as shocking or self-contradictory as it seems. If philosophy begins in or emerges from mythology generally, as we have borne witness, then so does this particular philosophical attitude. It is *de rigueur* to think of the presocratics as dreamers and as contemplative, calm, wise, and otherworldly (think merely of Pythagoras or of the ancient parable of the wise man gazing at the stars who falls into a hole in the ground – who turns out to be Thales). But then think of the Hebrew prophets, of Amos and Jeremiah in particular: anger is a reflective attitude as well. And the philosophically equivalent response is to generalise from the focused specificity of the ancient Hebrew prophets towards their own particular people and god, to the universe generally. It is the move towards generality and universality, objectivity, that is the initial philosophical move, not the absence of normative judgement or emotion. Anaximander is our first philosophical prophet, our existential moralist, raging at the dying of the light.

If our anger and outrage are now properly aroused, perhaps it is time to seek their proper subject, and to practise philosophy itself within the margins of history. Those who are marginalised (for example, through Schleiermacher's 'new' ordering principle of reclassifying Aristotle's 'first wise men' instead merely as 'pre'-Socratics) experience anger at their marginalisation, their diminution, and perhaps are entitled to be angry – especially if Anaximander is correct, that no sufficient reason can be given for *why* they are relegated and treated thus.

In this opening chapter, I have attempted to sketch alternatives to the standard way of narrating philosophy's history as part of the development of Western culture, emphasising voices and themes inside the culture that are nonetheless marginalised as minor, unimportant, unrecognised, or forgotten figures and movements. Hegel (himself largely marginalised for much of the past century) argued in the final pages of his *Phenomenology* that philosophical insight, 'absolute knowing', consisted of a complete recollection and simultaneous re-enactment of its history, holding all the partial pieces together in a kind of divine insight. In my account, by contrast, most of philosophy's history consists of what Whitehead euphemistically termed 'perishing' and consequent 'negative prehension': conflict, strife, forgetting, and loss to oblivion. The historical process that is philosophy's narrative resembles more the strife that Heraclitus celebrated, and even more the tragic and aimless process that Anaximander critically narrated in his fragment on 'injustice' and the 'ordering of Time', than it does the Pythagorean memory exercise that Hegel championed. As such, it is fraught with the normative moral judgement that Anaximander offers with what can only be described as a measure of prophetic anger. Grave injustice is inevitably done, without rational explanation or justification, and seems almost unavoidable and unremediable.

Hegel's final vision of a complete, Pythagorean 'master narrative' (as, again, MacIntyre termed it) is finally, instead, a *normative* conception, pointing us towards what we, as philosophers, properly should be about: like archaeologists or forensic scientists, uncovering the past, and like forensic scientists and theologians, redeeming it and rectifying its inexplicable injustice. Anaximander and Heraclitus, as I noted earlier, seem much more like ineffectual art critics, commenting on the demise and sorry state of art itself, but ultimately doing little otherwise about it. Both offer a description of philosophy in the world as we find it, one in which our efforts, and sometimes our conflicts with one another as philosophers, stand condemned.

Whitehead appears to offload the task of redeeming Experience from its inevitable injustice onto the Consequent Nature of God. I think that is a mistaken impression for which he himself is culpable, but that, in any case, Hegel (and Pythagoras) have got this much right. *Metaphysics is, finally, the recollection and redemption of history and the rectification of injustice.* It is a task that falls to us and cannot be shuffled off on 'God', or some abstract and impersonal notion of Absolute Spirit. Absolute 'knowing', (a more accurate understanding of Hegel's concluding phrase) entails a full recognition and confession of these sins as the requisite first step in the redemption of history and the rectification of injustice. Philosophy, poised at the onset of its third millennium as a mode of discourse distinct from mythology and religion, is sorely in need of its own redemption, through finally recognising and willingly shouldering this important task.

Metaphysical thinking in particular is, finally, the redemption of history and the rectification of injustice. In that unique and indispensable metaphysical sense, we are all 'called to think'.[18]

Notes

1. Philip Wheelwright, *The Presocratics*; G. S. Kirk, J. E. Raven, and M. Schofield, *The Presocratic Philosophers*; W. K. C. Guthrie, *A History of Greek Philosophy, Vol. I.*

2. The distinction appears in several places, e.g., Quine, *Pursuit of Truth*; and much earlier as an offhand quip (of the sort for which Quine was famous): 'Mr. Strawson on Logical Theory', pp. 433–51.
3. G. R. Lucas, 'Refutation, Narrative, and Engagement', pp. 104–23.
4. Heidegger, *What is Called-Thinking*? That is: the objects of thought call forth or compel your thinking about them, and not vice versa.
5. See Hannah Arendt, *Eichmann in Jerusalem*. So this 'thinking with' or 'called-thinking' is apparently an important dimension of authentic human experience that we neglect at our peril. For Arendt of course we are all storytellers by nature, and the history of philosophy is a 'story'. In *The Human Condition*, for example, she writes, 'He who acts never quite knows what he is doing, that he always becomes "guilty" of consequences he never intended or foresaw, that however disastrous or unexpected the consequences of his deed he can never undo it, that the process he starts is never consummated unequivocally in one single deed or event, and that its very meaning never discloses itself to the actor but only to the backward glance of the historian who himself does not act' (Arendt, *The Human Condition*, p. 181).
6. Eva T. H. Brann is senior tutor and dean emeritus at St. John's College (Annapolis, Maryland), the original 'great books' school, and a renowned scholar of Plato and the presocratics. See her keynote address for the 2016 annual meeting of the MSA: 'Presocratics, or First Philosophers?', pp. 435–51. Brann (and, she notes, Plotinus) translate *to gar auto noein esti te kai einai* (Diels-Kranz, *Die Fragmente der Vorsokratiker*, 3, 8, cited in Brann, *The Logos of Heraclitus*) as 'For it is the same to think and to be.'
7. Eva Brann, *The Logos of Heraclitus*.
8. Current work on the new Critical Edition of Whitehead situates Whitehead for the first time squarely in the midst of this re-engineering and reorientation of philosophy to experience in his critique of theory-laden scientific reasoning about it. See Paul Bogaard's introduction to the first volume of *The Harvard Lectures of Alfred North Whitehead, 1924–1925*, devoted to *The Philosophical Presuppositions of Science*, ed. Paul Bogaard and Jason Bell (Edinburgh: Edinburgh University Press, 2017).
9. Edward Pols, *Radical Realism*. See also my account of Pols and this historical dispute in *The Genesis of Modern Process Thought*. I failed at that time, as I believe Pols failed as well, to recognise that Whitehead was trying to move in a very different, Continental–American (rather than British) direction in regard to fashioning a unique metaphysics of experience that, like a good 'master narrative', would wholly absorb and replace the narrow, stale English dispute between realism and idealism. I discuss this larger project in a bit more detail below.
10. Donald Phillip Verene, *Vico's Science of Imagination*, *Vico and Joyce*, *Philosophy and the Return to Self-Knowledge*.

11. 'bababadalgharaghtakamminarronnkonnbronntonnerronntuonnt-hunntrovarrhounawnskawntoohoohoordenenthurnuk!' This 100-letter word signifying a thunderclap precedes the famous opening, 'riverrun, past Eve and Adams, from swerve of shore to bend of bay, brings us by a commodius vicus of recirculation back to Howth Castle and Environs'. The thunderclap is repeated ten times in the book, the last consisting of 101 letters, signifying the commodious vicus (Vico) of recirculation (cyclic history).
12. *A propos of* Verene's interest: James Joyce, during this same historical period, experiments with attempts to portray the inward experience of that flux at the beginning of an individual's life, in his first novel, *Portrait of the Artist as a Young Man* (1916). This is explicitly Joyce's attempt to document the preconscious organism going through socialisation, development, and self-realisation. It's interesting where he ends up as a Self – he yearns to become a creator. Salvation is in the creative imagination (he wants to be a 'priest of the imagination') and fulfilment. 'Welcome O life! I go to encounter for the millionth time the reality of experience and to forge in the smithy of my soul the uncreated conscience of my race.' And the manifestation of that is his capacity to tell stories. Joyce used mythology also to tell the story of human consciousness – Daedalus, Odyssey, and so on. And his version of 'wonder' was the notion of epiphany with its sacred overtones.
13. This, I think, was the point of Whitehead's otherwise puzzling project to 'recur to pre-Kantian modes of thought' of which I was earlier extremely critical: see Lucas, *The Rehabilitation of Whitehead*.
14. See Desmond's essay: 'Flux-gibberish: For and Against Heraclitus', in which he, like Vico and Joyce, not to mention Hegel and Nietzsche, engages in 'ventriloquising' with the presocratics, examining the various senses of 'flux', and reflux as 'watery words', signifying cyclical recurrence and circadian rhythms that Joyce, in particular, offers up in his own rendition (*Finnegans Wake*) of the 'old, tired river, Effluvia', flowing to the end of its journey, returning to its source, emitting a kind of 'moaning' sound.
15. Unless, I suppose, that 'reduction' is finally a transcendental deduction regarding the necessary background features for the possibility of experience (Whitehead) or *Erfahrung* (Kant).
16. But is it not possible that Heidegger in particular is onto something? Daniel Dahlstrom thinks so, and he said so in his MSA presidential address in 2011 ('Negation and Being'), and William Desmond's glorious lecture at that same meeting in Boston illustrated itself what a metaphysical disclosure or 'shining forth' might be like, in terms of an authentic revelation or disclosure of Being. Brann does likewise, in discussing the way dialectic, reflection on the ruminations and aphorisms

of history's earliest thinkers, might afford such a disclosure. Sean Kelly and Hubert Dreyfus depict the whole of philosophy's history as this kind of Heideggerian revelation in *All Things Shining*.

17. 'Though wise men at their end know dark is right, / Because their words had forked no lightning they / Do not go gentle into that good night'. This is the less-often quoted, but (for this chapter) more relevant second stanza, from Dylan's *The Poems of Dylan Thomas*.

18. Towards the end of the 2012 movie about Hannah Arendt's remarkable life, written and directed by Margarethe von Trotta, Heidegger's character says to his former mistress, during her final visit with him: 'Liebchen, I meant no harm, I knew nothing about worldly affairs. I am merely a philosopher', begging her forgiveness and understanding. But he hardly ever otherwise portrayed himself as what, in this moment, he surely was, a partially educated, brilliant bumpkin, far out of his depth. Better to be surrounded in mysticism, lost in the 'beyond' and its *paraousia*, than mired in the unpleasant reality that one has proven, as most of us do, to be incapable of withstanding what Kant called 'the strife among the faculties'. Overcome by *willkur*, forsaking the simple demands of judicious *Wille* and Reason, Heidegger himself, we might conclude, *failed to think*.

2 'The Tragical History of Doctor Beneke'[1]

The dialectic of [consciousness] is nothing else but the simple history of its movement or of its experience, and [consciousness] itself is nothing else but just this history.... Consciousness ... is always reaching this result, learning from experience what is true in it; but equally it is always *forgetting* it and starting the movement all over again.... The consciousness which is this truth has this path behind it [but] has *forgotten* it ... it merely *asserts* that it is all reality, but does not itself comprehend this; for it is along that *forgotten path* that [each] immediately expressed assertion is comprehended. (G. W. F. Hegel, *The Phenomenology of Spirit* (1807))[2]

Shortly after publishing his *System of Logic* (London, 1843), John Stuart Mill wrote to a colleague: 'I am reading a German professor's book on logic – Beneke is his name – which he has sent to me after reading mine, and which had previously been recommended to me by Austin and by Herschel as in accordance with the spirit of my doctrines.'[3]

This is an astonishing observation. According to the conventional understanding of the history of European philosophy during the first half of the nineteenth century, German thought was thoroughly dominated by Hegelian idealism. Dissent from this dominant tradition, to twenty-first-century observers, seems virtually indistinguishable from it as found during the 1830s and 1840s, for example, in Feuerbach and other 'left-wing' Hegelian social philosophers quarrelling about the hegemony of the Absolute or in Schopenhauer's self-styled romantic and speculative 'Kantian' protest against the stifling right-wing Hegelianism characteristic of German academics. The positivist 'spirit' of Mill's empiricism and logic of induction is equally alien to all of these movements and should hardly have inspired the sympathetic interest of a German academic philosopher during this period.

Still less should we expect that a German philosopher would have arrived independently in the early 1840s at results that Mill himself would be led to describe as 'in accordance with the spirit' of Mill's own work. The rise of antispeculative frustrations in Germany, leading to the grounding of subsequent philosophical investigation in the verifiable deliveries of experience on analogy with the newly emergent natural sciences, are developments associated with neo-Kantianism and positivism only after 1865, supposedly under the twin influences of Mill and Auguste Comte.

In contrast to this received view, Beneke's own unfortunate career might well be of immensely greater significance than his current modest footnote immortality would suggest. His work demonstrates that as early as 1820, German philosophers were already growing disenchanted with absolute idealism and speculative metaphysics. Beneke's thought anticipates by several decades the subsequent cultural rejection of grand speculative system-building in favour of an expressed desire to return to Kant and to an experientially grounded theory of knowledge. His troubled career provides decisive evidence that a philosophical revolt was already under way in Germany fully a half-century before such sentiments were to become the common coin of the 'new' philosophical reform movement known as neo-Kantianism.

The received accounts of the history of neo-Kantianism, in marked contrast, date it with the appearance of Otto Liebmann's *Kant und die Epigonen* in 1865 (containing the famous declaration, 'Also muss nach Kant zurückgegangen werden!'), and Friedrich Lange's three-volume *Geschichte des Materialismus* in 1866 – works whose uncharacteristic interest in positivism is taken, in turn, to stem from the growing influence of John Stuart Mill and Auguste Comte on a generation of sceptical and disillusioned German philosophers in the 1850s. This is obviously not quite right: German philosophers could not possibly have understood, let alone welcomed, the work of Mill and Comte unless they were already harbouring serious doubts of their own concerning idealism.

Who, then, is this 'Beneke', whose book on logic, written even before Mill's own, is presumably of sufficient resemblance to commend it to Mill's interest?

Friedrich Eduard Beneke was born in Berlin in 1798. He studied theology at Halle and subsequently wrote a doctoral dissertation in philosophy in 1820 in Berlin, where he attended Schleiermacher's lectures. In the same year he published *Erkenntnislehre nach dem Bewusstsein der reinen Vernunft*, arguing that traditional formal logic should hereafter be grounded more centrally in the growing scientific understanding of human psychology. Clothing himself in the twin mantles of authority of Kant and Locke, Beneke also argued, against the 'presuppositionless' philosophy of the dominant Hegelian idealists, that perception must play a central role in the problem of knowledge. *Erkenntnislehre*, which Beneke in this work conceived of as a new and autonomous scholarly discipline, bears unmistakable similarity to the term, presumably introduced for the first time into German philosophy only much later, *Erkenntnistheorie* – the theory of knowledge, or epistemology in its current sense.[4]

Such views did not earn favour for their author. Despite publishing a number of journal articles and ten additional books, including a two-volume outline of his psychological theory, Beneke was able by his thirty-fifth birthday to obtain a position only as an unsalaried assistant professor. Arnulf Zweig suggests that Beneke's work incurred the displeasure of the 'entrenched Absolute idealists', including Hegel himself, all of whom found the work of this young upstart not so much flawed in the details as unphilosophical overall and – in the words of an 1833 memorandum denouncing Beneke to the Prussian Ministry of Education – 'quite devoid of principle'.

Beneke's critics thus managed to persuade state authorities for a time to deny Beneke even the licence to teach without salary, and they persistently frustrated his attempts to secure a decent permanent situation. His career did not progress until well after Hegel's death; even then, the suspicions about his alleged materialism and relativism and his avowed renunciation of systematic *a priori* philosophy impeded the reception of his work in Germany. During his own lifetime, a handbook of the history of philosophy decried 'the birth of this sensualist in a German city' as 'plainly a mistake'. Beneke suffered from poor health and, under circumstances never fully explained, he disappeared on 1 March 1854; his body was found in a Berlin canal two years later.[5]

The name of Friedrich Beneke never figured subsequently in a central way in the history of philosophy, either as that history was written from the perspectives of several recognised periods in the nineteenth century or as that history has since been interpreted from the standpoint of major periods in the twentieth. Beneke is, at best, a minor figure of little importance who has been all but forgotten. Even today, he dwells only in the margins of history.

In *The Rise of Neo-Kantianism*, however, a German social historian, Klaus Christian Köhnke, recollects and comments on Beneke at some length and with a thinly disguised sense of moral outrage. In particular, Köhnke argues that Beneke's thought was of immensely greater significance than his current modest footnote immortality would suggest. Beneke's work as early as 1820 suggests that many German philosophers were already growing frustrated with absolute idealism and speculative metaphysics and signals the beginning of a larger cultural rejection of this mode of philosophising on behalf of an expressed desire to return to Kant and to an experientially grounded theory of knowledge. Indeed, Köhnke seizes upon Beneke's troubled career as evidence that such a discussion was under way in Germany fully a half-century before sentiments such as these were to become the common expression of the philosophical reform movement known as neo-Kantianism.[6]

The exchange with Mill, moreover, is taken by Köhnke with an understandable sense of cultural pride to indicate that the Germans, after all, did not require the intercession of an English reformist and a French eccentric to teach them the bankruptcy of unrestrained abstract speculation carried out in the name of pure, presuppositionless Reason. Instead, Beneke's writing proves that German philosophers were quite able to come to this insight on their own.

Beneke had also objected that philosophy suffered, during the early part of his century, from an anarchy among competing 'systems'. Indeed, things became so thoroughly muddled in German thought by mid-century that Beneke's contemporary, Christian Hermann Weisse, subsequently called for what would be the first pan-German philosophical congress (held at Gotha in September 1847) to overcome this fragmentation and work towards a 'historical reorientation' of philosophy. In June 1846, Weisse drew up for the Gotha Congress a proposal that described the then-current state of philosophy: 'Alone and molelike, most of us go digging along our own passageways, and have cause to fear an ill encounter if we disturb the mineshafts of others.'[7] Moles in their mineshafts are persistent little beasts, and Weisse's characterisation of the frustrations of philosophy in the mid-nineteenth century, as we will observe in later chapters, would not be far from the mark in the early twenty-first century.

In the second pre-phase of neo-Kantianism, according to Köhnke, academic philosophy in Germany was all but destroyed in the political repression following the abortive Revolution of 1848. Citing the impossibility of pursuing a livelihood in a discipline in which the merest hint of deviation from sterile and unproductive orthodoxy was regarded as subversion, Köhnke calls attention to the resulting and dramatic collapse of enrolments in university philosophy courses (as well as in law courses) following the revolution. These shifts were accompanied by a sharp increase in enrolments in theology and the natural sciences, and Köhnke observes that the most important figures in the subsequent rise of neo-Kantian philosophy – Dilthey, Helmholtz, Lange, and others – did not actually take their degrees in philosophy itself but in theology, medicine, and physics. Driven into the bosom of the natural sciences, and into a university culture that increasingly emphasised the methodological distinctiveness of isolated disciplines, the rediscovery of Kant, in effect, permitted philosophers a rapprochement with science and a safe place in the academy without caving in utterly to positivism and materialism, as illustrated in Helmholtz's address for the Kant Memorial in 1855. It was precisely this corrosive climate of philosophical bickering against which Beneke had complained, in which original work would be ignored, if not suppressed, and the best minds driven from this to other fields, in which unfettered expression and freedom of enquiry had some hope of prevailing.

Beneke specifically complained that philosophy therefore represented the last field of human knowledge to adopt the standpoint, increasingly evident in his day, of 'scientific' disciplines within the university setting, according to which each distinctive discipline would be defined by a common agreement among practitioners on the basic methodological principles of its practice. From the perspective of the late twentieth century, Beneke's analysis of the historical development and differentiation of a culture of disciplines in the academy seems remarkably far-sighted and visionary, as does his specific proposal that *Erkenntnislehre* constitutes the new scientific methodology that philosophy itself should henceforth adopt. Philosophy did, of course, eventually and inevitably adapt itself to this emerging culture of disciplinary-based enquiry. The extent to which anything recognisably philosophical and reflective can survive in such a culture, however, is a question with which we continue to wrestle.

The tragedy, and the moral injustice, is that Beneke evidently did not possess the egoistic and financial resources of, say, an Arthur Schopenhauer, nor did his work have the kind of broad public appeal that Schopenhauer enjoyed in his own time as a self-styled apostate from the ranks of academic philosophy. Thus vulnerable, Beneke was brutally and unfairly suppressed in his lifetime by his intellectual enemies. As a result, he was all but forgotten in the subsequent history of thought. In light of his accomplishments, however, the whole prior history of neo-Kantianism and positivism – or, rather, our understanding or interpretation of that history – now seems radically oversimplified, truncated, and misconceived, necessitating the kind of thorough recollection and reconstruction that Köhnke, in his intriguing book in the early 1990s, proposed to provide.

I simply wish, decades later, to file an *amicus curiae* brief in support of Professor Köhnke's moral outrage and historical judgement that, in this case, a grave injustice was done by his contemporaries and immediate successors to the life, work, and reputation of an original, brilliant, and far-sighted philosopher. Unfortunately, the history of philosophy is littered with such examples, so much so that I will maintain that the history of human thought is largely constituted out of such injustices. Dr Beneke's sad case is an example of the sort of relentless, remorseless, unceasing process that Anaximander's mysterious fragment narrates: an endless cycle of strife, opposition, and loss to oblivion, in which each successive dominant intellectual movement or consensus serves to suppress and marginalise the contributions of those who do not neatly fit. This perpetual cycle of injustice that is the history of philosophy generates what (with Anaximander's assistance) we term in this book 'the ordering of time'.

To return to our case study of Beneke: there are multiple ironies in this particular historical account of loss and of resurrection. Despite the subsequent evolution of institutions designed to protect academic freedom of enquiry and expression from the kind of abuses described, for example, one cannot help but observe that the intellectual descendants of Beneke succeeded (even if unwittingly) in avenging themselves on the intellectual descendants of Hegel for much of the next century, resorting to tactics not unlike those practised so egregiously by his enemies on Beneke himself, and often with similar results. Thus, the twentieth century, just like the nineteenth, is littered with the disappointing and often failed careers of distinguished scholars whose chief failing seems to have been their unwillingness to subscribe to the intellectual consensus of the moment. I have long argued, for example, that R. G. Collingwood and Alfred North Whitehead have suffered a wholly undeserved fate not unlike Beneke's during the twentieth century.[8] Indeed, the ruthlessness with which totalitarian tactics are often employed in these perpetual culture wars within disciplines of the humanities during the twentieth century might lead an observer to cast such affairs as successive incarnations of the historical principle that Hegel himself first enunciated in the *Phenomenology*: each intellectual fad or fashion asserts itself as the truth, 'the reality', forgetting the path by which it ascended to this position of 'absolute' self-consciousness.

If I am correct in this dismal assertion about philosophy's central role in what we now term 'culture wars' or the Darwinian struggle for survival and supremacy among disciplinary cultures, then it follows (and indeed, I will attempt to show) that philosophy as an activity, and its history, are both markedly different from what any of us suppose. Our sense of the hagiography of the most notable figures in that history is, for example, open to suspicion. Far more significantly (since the majority of contemporary philosophers do not concern themselves overly with the classical canon and its membership), our sense of what counts as meaningful contemporary thought and philosophical methodology is likewise impugned. We have no basis upon which to rest the smug self-confidence that we, as a practising community of intellectuals, 'know' who is doing the 'best' work or of what counts as the measure of excellence in this self-confident judgement.

Even more significantly, such case studies as above, and such a perspective on philosophy from its margins, calls into question what the proper role and function of philosophy itself is and how it should be carried out. I will take as evidence for this claim the disputes of the past two decades: the eroding of the analytic consensus among English-speaking philosophers, the rise of 'applied' and practical philosophy and ethics, the reintroduction and subsequent fascination with so-called Continental philosophy, forays by leading philosophers like Rorty and Nussbaum into literature as philosophy, or the retreat of leading philosophical figures like Arthur Danto from the weary practice of philosophy itself into the realm of art and art criticism. Preeminently, I will maintain, the sense of injustice and confusion about what philosophy is, and how it ought to be pursued, is captured in the return of philosophy to an interest in its history, after almost a century in which such interests themselves were deliberately and forcefully relegated to the margins of present practice.

Lynn Joy, in her fine book on Gassendi published in this same series conceived by Schneewind,[9] demonstrated precisely what we had ourselves experienced by the end of the twentieth century in the gradual historical turn of Gadamer, Rorty, and others, a turn that stemmed directly from the dismal results of a century of positivist experimentation in philosophy. As I read the larger lesson of her book, and the present case study, there is a fundamental but oft-forgotten historical principle of philosophy itself that, in every historical epoch, works something like this: intellectual foment, crisis, and disillusionment almost always necessitate a return to the historical tradition that philosophy itself is, in search of new inspiration for addressing philosophical *aporiai* in the present.

Let us then proceed to examine the most recent examples of this historical turn, in the hopes of shedding light upon how we ought to think of philosophy at present and how we might profitably practise or pursue it in the future.

Notes

1. In deliberately purloining the original title of Christopher Marlowe's 1592 play, I should probably borrow the complete title, which includes the phrase, 'of the life and death'. For it is of the life and death not of Faustus but of an obscure German philosopher upon which I would like us to reflect. To my mind, his tragedy is every bit as dismal as that of the famous fictional scientist – except that it is not myth but authentic history.

    Now, some 30 years after this chapter was first published, Beneke's mysterious death in 1854 has become the subject of a German-language mystery novel, while the victim himself is at last beginning to receive the attention he deserves in the history of analytic philosophy.

2. Hegel's *The Phenomenology of Spirit*, pp. 64, 141.
3. Quoted in Klaus Christian Köhnke, *The Rise of Neo-Kantianism*, p. 51. This is volume 20 in the series 'Ideas in Context', edited by Richard Rorty, J. B. Schneewind, Quentin Skinner, and Wolf Lepenies.
4. Köhnke, *The Rise of Neo-Kantianism*, p. 44.
5. Arnulf Zweig's original article of two columns (approximately one page) on Beneke is in the earliest edition of *The Encyclopedia of Philosophy*, ed. Paul Edwards, vol. I, p. 278. The memorandum from Karl Rosenkranz to the Prussian Ministry is cited at length in Köhnke, *The Rise of Neo-Kantianism*, p. 46. Beneke is cited briefly in two other articles in this first edition of the *Encyclopedia* devoted to psychology and psychologism, in marked contrast to his treatment in more recent editions.
6. This case, and these observations, serve to illustrate the divergence of my approach to understanding philosophy from that of Randall Collins in *The Sociology of Philosophies*. On the one hand, if his general account of philosophy as necessarily a community enterprise is correct, then Beneke's fate is explicable in a descriptive sense. He attracted no disciples, had no 'students', and thus failed to generate the following or participate in the discursive community necessary to a philosopher's survival. Yet the tendencies of which he first wrote ultimately prevailed. It is my point that his fate was neither accidental nor justified. He was suppressed, and his contemporaries might legitimately be charged with having conspired in something approaching second-degree homicide. This normative dimension and judgement of history is entirely absent from Collins's account.
7. Cf. Köhnke, *The Rise of Neo-Kantianism*, pp. 62–3.
8. See, for example, my comments in *The Rehabilitation of Whitehead* (1989), and in 'The Seventh Seal', pp. 104–16. I also take up this problem in my discussion of Wittgenstein and the rise of Cambridge analytic philosophy, later in this book.
9. Lynn Sumida Joy, *Gassendi the Atomist*. Volume 4 in the series 'Ideas in Context', edited by Richard Rorty, J. B. Schneewind, Quentin Skinner, and Wolf Lepenies.

3 Philosophy's Recovery of its History

From a time dating back at least to the first appearance of Diogenes Laertius's classic *The Lives and Opinions of Eminent Philosophers*,[1] the *history* of philosophy has served as a useful pedagogical and heuristic introduction to the *discipline* or *practice* of philosophy. In the modern academy, in addition, the history of philosophy customarily serves dutifully alongside courses in Western history, art history, and the history of literature to provide students with a more general introduction to the broad intellectual heritage of Western civilisation.

Increasingly during the early decades of the twentieth century, however, the history of philosophy came to be portrayed as a bloodless procession of quaint, outmoded ideas and arcane disputes offering little in the way of insight, guidance, value, or significance for the practice of *contemporary* philosophy. Often without realising it, philosophy teachers and textbooks portrayed the history of philosophy as a captain's log of the difficult and perplexing voyage to present privileged, and finally settled, perspectives on significant philosophic issues.[2] Once the student passengers on this voyage had arrived at their desired destination and the proper contemporary philosophical perspectives had been fully appreciated, then the historical voyage itself – like the pedagogical ladder of Ludwig Wittgenstein or the mythical raft of Mahayana Buddhism – served no further useful purpose. Indeed, in some accounts, the history of philosophy is depicted as a bleak and infertile landscape, littered with the failed attempts of 'false philosophies' and with what Bertrand Russell described as the decaying lumber of antiquated metaphysical systems.[3]

The majority of academic philosophers, of course, do not overtly disparage the value or efficacy of introducing students to philosophy as a discipline, nor do they object to the custom of defining for such students the intellectual heritage of Western civilisation, by means of historical illustrations and accounts describing what past philosophers had thought and done. Nonetheless, it seemed increasingly plausible throughout the twentieth century – until quite recently, in fact – to regard the history of philosophy as in some sense optional for the essential understanding of what philosophy is, at least as we have come to practise it today.

The history of philosophy has been increasingly regarded as comparable to the history of mathematics or of physics, in this sense: the history of philosophy is no more essential to the understanding of philosophy as currently practised than the history of physics or of mathematics is regarded as essential to an understanding of the practices of mathematics or of the physical sciences at present. Thus, just as it seemed feasible to function as a fully competent and proficient physicist or mathematician without knowing more than the barest rudiments of the history of science, so – admittedly to a lesser degree – it has become acceptable to embark on the analysis of questions in applied medical ethics or linguistics, or to construct models of memory and mental representation or of psychological concept-formation in the newly labelled 'cognitive sciences', without necessarily making reference to prior historical developments in ethics, metaphysics, and epistemology.

This internal disciplinary perspective on the history of philosophy would strike scholars from other disciplines as strange indeed! The widespread conventional or popular image of philosophy, after all, is invariably framed in terms of anecdotes drawn from its history: the peripatetic teacher Socrates; the pious and scholarly proponents of faith and reason Maimonides and St Thomas Aquinas; the despised and forsaken lens grinder and solitary apostle of Stoic wisdom Spinoza; the brilliant but eccentric Renaissance genius Vico; or the obscure, abstruse, unintelligible 'professional' academic philosophers on the Germanic model, such as Kant and Hegel. Colleagues in literature, classics, or history might wonder how philosophers ever came to abandon these familiar images of their lives and vocations as humanists and sages.

As R. G. Collingwood complains,[4] the impulse to jettison the familiar historical image of the philosopher as sage came chiefly in the twentieth century from philosophers like G. E. Moore and Bertrand Russell in England, as well as from leading members of the Vienna Circle at around the same period in Europe, including Rudolf Carnap, Moritz Schlick, and Hans Reichenbach. These philosophers rejected the historically grounded view of philosophy in favour of a new vision for their profession, grounded more centrally in the newly emerging culture of disciplines within the modern university. This new vision of philosophy, moreover, was strongly influenced by awareness of the special prestige accorded to the natural sciences and technological fields within what Alasdair MacIntyre terms 'this peculiar academic division of labour' within the university,[5] as symbolised by the culture of disciplines.

This academic division of labour within which we currently dwell is itself a comparatively recent historical phenomenon. It constitutes, in fact, the legacy of Alexander von Humboldt's vision in the mid-nineteenth century of a modern scientific university concentrated upon graduate study and research, comprising specialised schools, academic departments, and increased intellectual specialisation. Von Humboldt viewed scholarship in much the way that Adam Smith, decades earlier, had portrayed the emergence of the modern industrial economy. Scholarly effort must be seen as an organised effort to produce a product. Surprisingly, the activity was not teaching or education, nor was its envisioned produce wisdom, learning, or the stewardship of human knowledge. The university was no longer a place in which students would come to drink at the fountains of learning, and so be refreshed. The university was instead to be seen as a modern factory, with technical expertise and disciplinary specialisation enabling its workers (primarily its faculty, rather than its students) to produce new knowledge.

Quite obviously, something considerable is gained in this reconceptualisation. This is a liberating vision for scholars in physics, chemistry, biology, or geology, establishing boundaries and methodological ground rules for enquiry and superimposing a sensible management plan on their pursuit of knowledge at the frontiers of these discrete bodies of knowledge. When one compares the intellectual vigour, the forward-looking and forward-thinking robustness of German universities at the end of the nineteenth century, and the rapid spread of this conception to centres of higher learning in London, Baltimore,[6] and beyond with the stale, sterile, and unimaginative atmosphere of university life that Goethe and Hegel initially encountered in many of those same institutions scarcely a century before,[7] one cannot but be impressed with the growth and transformation of what we have since come to call the 'knowledge industry'.

Something, however, is also sacrificed in this conception. Students, and the activity of teaching them, is a decidedly awkward intrusion on the new main business of university life. Students of the natural sciences, insofar as they may be inaugurated into their disciplinary profession as apprentices in the laboratory, will come to occupy a useful niche in this new arrangement that will yield benefits for them in the form of gradual membership in a learned guild. But teaching as a distinct activity, and any concern for the broad and deep liberal learning of students, must be viewed as, at best, *babysitting*, a decided distraction from the scholar's main task of immersing oneself ever further in one's discipline and in the pursuit of new knowledge through productive research.

Philosophy, in particular, subsists very uncomfortably in the midst of the resultant culture of disciplines that von Humboldt's vision of the modern research university ultimately brought about. That discomfort only increased, moreover, as the earlier non-discipline or parent discipline of philosophy witnessed, time and again, essential parts of itself slough off and reconstitute themselves as separate and independent disciplines, only to turn upon the original parent discipline and declare it of no further usefulness or of only historical interest. Not just physics and biology and mathematics were lost to philosophy in this manner, but even more essentially the ill-titled social sciences – political science, sociology, economics, and psychology, each so profoundly and inherently philosophical in both methodological orientation and cultural justification – went on to achieve this disciplinary independence.[8]

While they thus unwittingly robbed themselves of their essential philosophical heritage, these new disciplines tended more tangibly to present the newly conceived 'discipline' of philosophy with a kind of existential crisis by appearing to leave it without a unique subject matter or methodology of its own and hence devoid of justification of either place or stature within the modern university. As a result, during the 170-year interval from the first publication by Immanuel Kant of his *Critique of Pure Reason* in 1781 to the appearance of Hans Reichenbach's highly influential book *The Rise of Scientific Philosophy* in 1951, one can trace the steady development of a strong impulse towards purging philosophy once and for all of speculative and historical concerns. We can now appreciate that this familiar agenda was not independently motivated by selfless normative notions of what philosophy ought to be but rather was driven by the desperate and powerful desire to establish philosophy itself as a pure, well-defined, thoroughly respectable discipline within the larger emerging culture of disciplines in higher education generally.

In order to achieve this radical disciplinary transformation, moreover, it proved necessary to engage in a special kind of apologetics: in effect, to establish and maintain that philosophy *itself* was in possession of a clearly delineated (though hitherto poorly understood) subject matter and a shared methodology, both of which were now properly to be seen as the domain of technical specialists (analytic philosophers) rather than speculative dilettantes and avocational dabblers.

The course of this disciplinary transformation required that what had already transpired in physics and chemistry must now occur in philosophy as well. Chiefly, the history of the discipline (philosophers now argued) would henceforth be seen as largely irrelevant to its new content, focus, and methodological consensus. At best, the history of philosophy, like the history of physics or mathematics, proves to be relevant only in Reichenbach's *negative* sense of showing the irremediable defects of historically prior views of the proper philosophic vocation, and of providing simultaneously a background chronicle of the slow course of progress by early scientifically minded philosophical pioneers trudging relentlessly under the banner of Galileo and Descartes towards ultimately true, definable, and verifiable perspectives on legitimately philosophical (rather than pseudo-philosophical) problems.

Scholars who became overly infatuated with the narrative of this journey itself – scholars like Collingwood, Foucault, Gadamer, Smith, or MacIntyre – would hereafter be politely relegated to a secondary status as mere historians of the discipline, rather than being classified as philosophers proper (as we saw Willard V. O. Quine so clearly attempt). That, at least, was better than the fate envisioned for Vico, St Thomas, Hegel, Bergson, Schelling, Whitehead, Dewey, William James, and C. Lloyd Morgan, let alone others whose modest but essential contributions to their culture enjoy a degree of footnote immortality or whose names have altogether slipped beneath the turbulent seas of world history. In the popular view, such lesser and even unknown figures had always constituted a harmless cottage industry in philosophy. The new official disciplinary record, however, could no longer tolerate their presence. Richard Rorty rather shockingly endorsed Reichenbach's earlier attempt to consign the works of all of these historical figures to the flames for having *failed* to perceive 'the philosophic discoveries immanent in the science of their time' and accordingly for having 'developed, under the name of philosophy, systems of naïve generalisations and analogies'.[9]

How, we might ask, could philosophers as a community come so quickly to turn their backs not only on philosophy as traditionally practised but also on their own historical legacy? Whence this hatred and denigration of history? The atmosphere of urgency, I contend, stemmed from an underlying concern that philosophy would receive respect and stature as an academic and professional discipline only by achieving success in the delineation of problems that would fall solely within its professional or disciplinary purview, in a manner in which the older perennial philosophical questions regarding the best form of political order, the highest good for a human life, the conflict between duty and desire, the foundations of logic, and the significance of individual mortality apparently did not. Moreover, achieving the status of a discipline in the university required that professionals in the discipline engage in the effective analysis and solution of these new problems solely within the boundaries of a clearly determined subject matter that did not significantly overlap the territories of rival disciplines like physics, biology, history, or psychology – areas of study with which philosophy had been so thoroughly intertwined at least through the late Renaissance.

In fairness, the proponents of the new philosophy faced an array of political and intellectual pressures building in the academy at this time, not wholly of their own making – political pressures that are still much with us, of a sort that critics like Collingwood perhaps did not fully recognise. These growing academic constraints on the pursuit of teaching and research in higher education were certainly less 'Fascist' (as Collingwood characterised them in his *Autobiography*) than they were insidiously bureaucratic in stressing efficiency, progress, and quantitative productivity in the most mundane sense imaginable. For what we would today term 'assessment' in the university – the specific enumeration, the attainment, and ultimately the quantitative evaluation of such precise and measurable disciplinary goals and objectives – had become the *raison d'être* of a rapidly expanding managerial, administrative class overseeing the organisation and operation of the modern university. 'Herr Heidegger', the Rector at Freiburg allegedly remarked in exasperation in the spring of 1927, 'we simply *must* have a manuscript'.

The new conception of philosophy as a distinct, methodologically precise discipline offered certain definite advantages in coping with these pressures when compared to its predecessor historical model. The disciplinary claims of contemporary philosophers – whether in symbolic logic, in language analysis, or in conceptual elucidation and the dissolving of puzzles and paradoxes encountered in other fields – seemed at once more precise and less pretentious than the objectives sought by the earlier systematic, synoptic, and historical purveyors of what Edmund Husserl (yet another proponent of philosophy as a scientific discipline) disparaged as merely 'eine *Weltanschauung*: a matrix of beliefs and intellectual commitments attained through a vague, diffuse, and illusive search for' wisdom and truth. The new philosophy, like the new technological model of the sciences, offered its overseers the chimera of measurable progress and realistically attainable results. Results, in turn, justified risk, growth, retention, and the kind of expenditures of funds (not to mention the justification for acquisition of further funds) requisite to the continued maintenance and operation of the sort of organisation a 'university' had increasingly become in the technological society.

While my account relies on broad allusions to organisational and political features within educational institutions,[10] most readers will have long since discerned obvious parallels between this specific transformation, attempted self-consciously within philosophy, and the now-familiar account of the revolutionary transformation from a 'pre-paradigm state' to a 'normal science' in Thomas Kuhn's *The Structure of Scientific Revolutions*.[11] So stark are those parallels, in fact, that we might now plausibly say, with the benefit of hindsight and liberal use of Kuhn's conceptual categories, that the 'new philosophers' early in the twentieth century desired nothing less than that philosophy itself should achieve in this century and in this culture the status of a 'normal science' in Kuhn's sense and hence emerge at last from the chaotic immaturity inherent in preparadigm, prescientific fields. The history of the discipline would gradually lose its prior normative significance. The well-defined journal article would replace the book as the medium of research and scholarly communication, while classroom textbooks would reflect the emerging methodological consensus to be imparted to novices in the discipline. Each of these historical innovations (now associated by Kuhn with the usual development of a disciplinary *science*) was stridently urged and repeatedly defended over a period of decades by proponents of the new philosophy in conscious analogy with demonstrable developments in their sister disciplines in the natural sciences, long before Kuhn's illuminating analysis had itself entered the historical picture.

Philosophy and the Recovery of History

Ironically, it would seem that precisely the opposite results issued from these attempts. Whether these intentions of earlier generations of philosophers in the twentieth century are portrayed as nobly misguided or (following Collingwood) as nefarious and destructive, it remains undeniably the case that philosophy, at the close of the twentieth century, resembled more than ever what Kuhn himself describes as a *pre*paradigm science. There is no agreed-upon method, subject matter, or set of definable problems in the field. Adherents of different philosophic methods and traditions often cannot even communicate across the boundaries of the various resulting subdisciplinary communities now grouped within philosophy proper. Journals have proliferated in response to the fragmenting of the earlier fragile philosophic consensus; no one journal or group of journals can any longer claim legitimacy in the profession as a whole. One result is that the book has once again replaced the scholarly research article as the preferred means of communication. And, most importantly, the fact that they share a history is now the *only* thing that the rival camps have in common.

Beyond these massive failures, there were often more immediate and irritating deficiencies noticeable even to the triumphalist visionaries themselves. For example, the decidedly hostile antihistorical attitudes of early realists, positivists, and early analytic philosophers often tended to produce superficial, unflattering, and historically inauthentic caricatures of earlier philosophical viewpoints. If we require in ethics, for example, that every historically prior approach to moral theory be classified as either teleological or deontological, we inadvertently suppress or downplay approaches to morality that stress the cultivation of virtues within a moral community – richly informative and complex elements of morality clearly evident in Aristotle, Hume, Kant, and even in J. S. Mill, but conspicuously absent from 'the attenuated and impoverished discipline that modern philosophical ethics has become at the hands of most of its modern practitioners', as Alasdair MacIntyre complains.[12] In metaphysics and epistemology, Berkeley's idealism is liable to be indistinguishable from Hegel's, and both can be confused with something either completely different or decidedly less sophisticated, such as the Advaita Vedanta nondualism of F. H. Bradley or the Christian idealism of A. E. Taylor, respectively.[13] In textual analysis, obscure or neglected passages of Aristotle's corpus are combed meticulously in a search for 'publishable' logical or linguistic infelicities. Indeed, in the approaches to the history of philosophy that have been prevalent until quite recently, it is not uncommon (as Arthur Danto once perceptively complained) to find a treatment of Plato written as though 'he to whom the whole of subsequent philosophy since is said to be so many footnotes, were in effect a footnote to himself, and being coached to get a paper accepted by *The Philosophical Review*'.[14]

The most dramatic development to occur in academic philosophy in the Anglo-American tradition during the twentieth century has been the decisive collapse of this earlier consensus regarding philosophic method and subject content characteristic of positivism and subsequent logical and linguistic (or 'analytic') philosophy. This collapse or demise occurred gradually, and it was slow to be recognised by professional academic philosophers. Again with the benefit of hindsight, we can now locate the beginnings of this unravelling of this methodological antihistoricism and the undoing of the analytic consensus with the publication in the field of logic of Quine's own sceptical essay 'Two Dogmas of Empiricism', disparaging the analytic–synthetic distinction; in epistemology with the publication of Thomas Kuhn's aforementioned monograph *The Structure of Scientific Revolutions*; and perhaps also in the corresponding rise to prominence of studies in the sociology of knowledge signalled in Berger and Luckmann's essay, *The Social Construction of Reality*.

The recognition of a kind of crisis in confidence in professional philosophy burst full on the scene, however, with the appearance of Richard Rorty's brilliant and controversial book *Philosophy and the Mirror of Nature* in 1979; almost immediately followed a decisive refutation of the ahistorical and antiliterary analytic consensus in moral philosophy by Alasdair MacIntyre in *After Virtue* (1981). Rorty's work, though it provoked outrage among many philosophers, went on to stimulate a renewed interest in pragmatism and its relationship to hermeneutics in European thought. More generally, Rorty's characterisation of philosophy as 'edifying conversation' prompted a vigorous renewed interest in the history of philosophy, and especially in the reinterpretation of classical texts and figures in the Western tradition.

MacIntyre's work likewise effected a dramatic sea change in the customary modes of thought of two generations of self-styled 'professional experts' in so-called applied and theoretical ethics by exposing the impoverished and truncated intellectual foundations of rationalistic, calculative decision theory advocated by economic utilitarian theorists and deontological, legalistic 'rights' theorists in moral philosophy. His work also spawned a renewed interest in the teaching of historical figures in ethics (Aristotle, Hume, Aquinas, Marx, and Nietzsche), as well as of literary–moral traditions ranging from Sophocles, Dante, and Cervantes to Jane Austen. These developments, in turn, prompted a renewed and vigorous enquiry into the role played by culturally and historically conditioned narratives in the natural and social sciences, as well as in literature and art.

Collectively, such revolutionary developments have made an impact on the profession of philosophy, as well as on the customary teaching of philosophy, in a number of ways. Under the aegis of philosopher John E. Smith at Yale University, canons of membership and inclusion in the profession were dramatically transformed by the rise of a pluralistic movement in the American Philosophical Association, stressing the importance of European philosophy, non-Western traditions, indigenous American philosophy, and a return to the importance of the history of philosophy. Kant, Locke, and Hume have since been joined, in the two decades following this bitter philosophical divide, by previously neglected or disparaged philosophers such as Hegel, Vico, Husserl, Heidegger, Kierkegaard, Dewey, and Whitehead in philosophy curricula from Harvard, MIT, and Chicago to Berkeley, Stanford, and UCLA. A kind of Hegelian hysteria of *ungluckliche Bewusstsein* took hold of philosophers in the 1980s and 1990s, who, at virtually every professional gathering, engaged with depressing regularity in obligatory acts of ritual self-flagellation in seminars announcing 'The Death of Philosophy' and featuring the work of Rorty, MacIntyre, Foucault, Lyotard, and Derrida, set against the brooding Nordic background of a philosophical *Götterdämmerung* suggested by Nietzsche and Heidegger. Critics and proponents of such changes alike came to refer to this collection of diverse directions and postmodern currents in philosophy as 'post-analytic philosophy'.[15]

Philosophy, History, and Other Disciplines

What seems transparently obvious, in light of those developments in philosophy since around 1980, is that philosophers, as members of a discipline in the academy, still remain deeply troubled and decidedly ill at ease with their relationship to their history. It is as if the disease that

Nietzsche complained of in Germany – the obsession with history, the bad historical consciousness that constituted one of the *disadvantages* of history for life – has come to consume philosophers everywhere. Philosophers seem concerned about being perceived as antiquarian or anachronistic, being classified by their peers *merely* as intellectual historians, and the like. In itself, this phenomenon of historical consternation in philosophy is not likely to prove interesting to those who are not themselves members of this particular academic discipline.

But suppose that the very consternation and conflict over history itself is somehow symptomatic of a deeper malaise? I have suggested that the conflict over the understanding and the role of its history in the recently defined 'discipline' of philosophy is itself a function of philosophy and philosophers having first come to see themselves, and indeed wanting to see themselves, as one among many disciplines in the modern university. Towards what sort of understanding of the present state and the future of philosophy might this historical–sociological observation then lead us? And how ought philosophy in the future relate to the other disciplines in the modern university?

Once again I recur to the elegant historical reconstruction of the conflict between late Renaissance humanism and the rise of the modern notion of a purely quantitative, mathematical, and ahistorical conception of the natural sciences offered some years ago by Lynn Sumida Joy. She provides an important insight on our present dilemma. Late Renaissance philosophers like Gassendi (on whom Joy primarily focuses) disagreed sharply with Galileo, Descartes, and other proponents of modernism, not only in distrusting their confident application of mathematical principles to events in the physical world but also by opposing 'the views that philosophy, science, and history are autonomous academic disciplines'. Gassendi, Joy informs us, rejected in particular 'the Cartesian assumption that the central problems of science and philosophy can be articulated independently of a historical understanding of the places they occupy within their respective scientific or philosophical traditions'.[16]

Gassendi, as we know, lost that argument. Joy portrays the ironic difficulty that modern scholars now face in knowing how to classify Gassendi – is he, for example, a philosopher, a historian, a scientist, a mathematician? Yet somehow, we sense, these questions are not correctly put. History is not a problem for Gassendi in Joy's account; rather, history is seen by this Renaissance scholar as the prior normative background for the studies we now classify as 'disciplines' in the natural sciences.

What does this example of Gassendi's losing struggle against antihistoricism in the late Renaissance, however, teach us in the twenty-first century?

History becomes a problem, I suggest, only when one accepts the academic division of labour proposed at the dawn of modern science and modern philosophy by Galileo and Descartes. In this division of labour, history itself becomes one discipline among many, or else it is perceived as integral to some of the new disciplines and irrelevant to the others. The *disciplinary division itself* forces the question: which disciplines are primarily narrative and historical, and which are, by contrast, quantitative, mathematical, and nonnarrative?

This question, in turn, does more than engage us in idle taxonomy. Precisely in the course of modern history, it has become more and more a badge of honour, a mark of prestige, to be ranked in the quantitative, 'scientific' classification. It is here, ever since the triumph of Galileo and Descartes, that knowledge is seen as certain and growing, that progress is being made, that problems are being solved, that work is being done. While there is seemingly no end to the stories one might tell or the historical tales one might weave, the scientific disciplines offer the realisable goal of knowledge, of genuine discovery, and of progress. It follows that, where possible, the practitioners of each resulting discipline will want, in due course, to declare independence from their history in behalf of science, to effect the famous modern divorce between *questio juris* and *questio facti*, between subjective value judgements and objective facts, between uncertain interpretive narrative historical accounts and the certitudes of nomological explanation.

We have been examining, in the special case of philosophy, the consternation that arises within *any* discipline when – despite strong desires and vigorous programmatic attempts by adherents of the discipline – this divorce proves impossible to effect. If the historical analysis of this situation that I have offered is correct, it further implies that some of the other academic disciplines share with philosophy this consternation over the role of history in their profession, while others (in which such a divorce from historical narrative and tradition would not seem the least desirable) would not appear to share in this consternation.

To test this implication, let us, on the one hand, consider the academic departments and disciplines in the modern university that encompass literature, languages, and the fine arts. There is not, so far as I know, the same degree of consternation among artists, art critics, or art historians – or, *mutatis mutandis*, musicians, music critics, and music historians – regarding the histories of their respective enterprises as one finds among philosophers about theirs. Histories of literature and of fine arts are understood as significant, as fascinating in themselves, as worthy of study for their own sake by scholars in these fields and as worthy of being presented, taught, and interpreted to students in these fields. Histories of art, music, or literature chronicle evolutionary developments and record radical discontinuities, breakthroughs, and periods of stagnation and creativity, all of which offer a narrative, a saga, that collectively purports to answer questions such as what is art, or music, or literature, or poetry; what does it mean to be an artist, a musician or composer, a writer or poet; and what roles do art, music, literature, and poetry play within the larger scheme of human cultures? So far, so good.

It would be fatuous to suggest that there are no controversies here: surely there are. Which artists or periods, for example, ought to receive emphasis in the canon or doxography of art history? Smith, the traditionalist, thinks that literature declined after Milton and Shakespeare, while Jones, the modernist, believes that the literary enterprise only flourishes in the work of Austen and Woolf. Jones, in addition, holds (*contra* Smith) that only bourgeois pedants and young, upwardly mobile professionals listen to Pachelbel or Bach, while Wagner – or perhaps Schoenberg, or Shostakovich – denotes the transition to genuine sophistication in taste.

But these controversies over individual aesthetic preference are generally taken as merely that: the historian of art, music, or literature does not seem to be haunted by these aesthetic disputes over historical preferences in anything remotely resembling the sense philosophers are. These controversies mask a kind of underlying peaceful consensus regarding the sacred canon tradition, and the histories of these activities and interests are seldom portrayed by any save the most tendentious, opinionated bigot as establishing a record of 'progress' in the field from ignorance and quaintness to sophisticated, deeper, and richer understandings in the present.

In art history, for example, one notes the development early in the Renaissance by Alberti and others of techniques for expressing perspective and dimensionality on a two-dimensional canvas, without necessarily denigrating medieval iconography as having somehow rested upon a mistake or as having been thereby 'repudiated'. The transition from Baroque to classical styles of composition and performance in the work of Mozart, or from classical, in turn, to Romantic in the later work of Beethoven, is not taken to 'repudiate' or 'refute' all that has gone before, nor does it imply that predecessors were quaint, ignorant, or incompetent idiots. Rather, such histories record both gradual evolution and radical discontinuities, innovations, and resulting transformations of outlook and practice, none of which repudiates their predecessors except perhaps in Hegel's famous sense in which the flower refutes or 'repudiates' the bud, or the fruit the flower: that is, by replacing or succeeding, by absorbing and transforming.

To borrow a phrase of Collingwood's: *what a lunatic idea of history it would seem* were we solemnly admonished that, after Mozart, we could never again listen to Bach or Vivaldi with a straight face, or that, after

Rembrandt, we must come to realise that the brothers Jan and Hubert van Eyck were little more than primitive exponents of preartistic form.[17]

My point is that such historical claims, which would seem prejudiced, idiosyncratic, or even nonsensical in the fine arts, are coin of the realm in the academic discipline of philosophy, as the earlier citations from Reichenbach and Rorty bear witness. But perhaps these comparisons merely demonstrate that there is no real or meaningful comparison to be made between philosophy and art, music, or literature, at least so far as all these take their place in the modern university's disciplinary culture. Let us then consider the opposite side of the disciplinary field as conventionally understood: the natural sciences themselves.

History does not constitute a problem in the natural sciences either, but for quite different reasons. According to Ian Hacking (who cites the views of contemporary scientists in this dispute), it is still the case that the history of science, perceived as a respectable scholarly amusement, plays no integral part in contemporary practices.[18] To ring a change on Whitehead: physicists have remained as blandly indifferent to their historical refutation by Thomas Kuhn as they have to their philosophical refutation by Hume, despite the convincing arguments of scholars like Collingwood, MacIntyre, and Joy that history is, after all, normative for these disciplines as well. Biology and chemistry customarily are not taught, and need not be taught, or practised, historically. The courses might be more interesting, the practitioners more enlightened and appreciative of their role as technically expert citizens in the *polis*, were such subjects approached in this manner. But hardcore cynics would still insist that this cultural improvement would not affect the technical ability of those who (in Hacking's phrase) get their 'license from the world' to develop a biodegradable pesticide, sequence DNA, or formulate the correct version of the 'standard model' (unified field theory) in physics.

It is in the social or human sciences, interestingly enough, that one finds the greatest parallels with the crisis of history in philosophy. Economics is a discipline that (in the words of American humorist James Thurber) 'amuses with its pretentions' yet is utterly lacking in the kind of methodological consensus characteristic of normal science on Kuhn's account. Today's Nobel laureate is likely, tomorrow, to be vilified as the antichrist. Despite a clear desire within the discipline to model itself after mathematical physics, economics as a discipline is still much more closely allied with philosophy, as some of its most astute quantitative practitioners, like Amartya Sen, have acknowledged. Indeed, Sen's recognition as recipient of the Nobel Prize in economics constituted a monumental refutation of those who denied that moral values or the interpretive stances of investigators should play a role in a fully mathematicised and data-driven discipline.

Similar stories can be told regarding the ambiguous role assigned to historical studies in psychology, in sociology, and in political science. Those disciplines are deeply divided between scholars who see the history as integral to the discipline and those who see the histories as 'pre-historic' prescientific tales of decidedly secondary import to the discipline. Political science is often portrayed as divided between those described by their critics as 'quantitative number crunchers' and the political philosophers and historians, described by *their* critics as armchair scientists or medievalists.

Hacking suggests that Kuhn's analysis has had far more impact on social scientists than upon natural scientists. MacIntyre confirmed this diagnosis in describing 'the ritual obeisance toward Kuhn . . . required in presidential addresses to the American Political Science Association – to license the theoretical failures of social science'.[19] This is so for several reasons.

First, most of those fields are beset from within by a host of methodological and conceptual controversies – but then, so are literature and the arts. Unlike the case with literature and the arts, however, there is an implicit *telos* in these fields – a yearning or perhaps a dogmatic lust for power that Dilthey's tepid distinctions fail to capture but to which Kuhn's conceptual analysis speaks with almost messianic forcefulness.

Kuhn's *The Structure of Scientific Revolutions*, in effect, offers an eschatological vision of disciplinary history in which the vagaries of history will be overcome and history itself may be transcended. The controversies to which I alluded above seem to be precisely (as they seemed also to be in philosophy) characteristic of the preparadigm state *of a science*. These very controversies with which philosophy and the human sciences are beset by their very existence seem to entail the promise, at least, of a 'normal' scientific state of the discipline, one unbeset by such controversies. This condition lies beyond some historical *parousia* (or perhaps apocalypse) yet to come, in which the discipline will rid itself once and for all of 'those idiots' who still haven't caught onto the proper methodology (whatever it may be), just as Descartes and Galileo finally rid themselves of Gassendi and his supporters.

Now, contrast that fervent eschatology with the 'normal' state of methodological controversy found within fine arts and literature. I know of not one single member of the Modern Language Association who envisions a day when he or she will not be at war with his or her colleagues over style and methodology. Such warfare is the lifeblood of literary scholars, who seem to have preserved the ancient wisdom of Heraclitus: that an end of strife would mean the end of their world. Tragically for philosophers and social scientists, by contrast, the eschatology of consensus promises a New Jerusalem: a stage of benign progress, achievement, and the final attainment of self-respect for practitioners of the discipline. Philosophers, in particular, cast themselves as the new Evangelicals of the present academic situation. The promise of the kingdom clearly motivated the iconoclastic and often ruthlessly arrogant and single-minded intellectual and academic agendas of the positivism of Mach, Carnap, and Schlick in the Vienna Circle, as well as of Collingwood's analytically inclined colleagues at Oxford (he termed them 'realists'). Through Reichenbach, Carnap, and others, this evangelical movement made its way into the academic institutions of the United States during the twentieth century and set about transforming those structures into their own image in the name of excellence and rigour, in a precise emulation of one of Kuhn's scientific revolutions.

The effects upon teaching and research and upon the role of philosophy and the regard for philosophers in the wider culture have, however, been quite different than expected. They have unleashed a divisive and destructive force of remarkable power, but of no lasting creativity or achievement, of the sort that Stanley Rosen identifies as the essential form of nihilism.[20] It is these dismal effects and this disappointing outcome that have been quietly repudiated by the prominent apostates from philosophy's own ranks, such as Rorty.

The Future of Philosophy and the History of Philosophy

In the conclusion of *Philosophy and the Mirror of Nature*, Rorty himself wondered whether 'a new form of systematic philosophy will be found which has nothing whatever to do with epistemology but which nevertheless makes normal philosophical inquiry possible'.

The term 'systematic philosophy' was used in that work as an acceptable euphemism for metaphysics or synoptic philosophy. Bearing this in mind, Rorty's interesting speculation has indeed come to pass in the recent development of a variety of new forms of systematic metaphysical enquiry, in a manner that few save Collingwood himself would have imagined possible, let alone acceptable, only a few decades ago. In many cases, this new systematic, synoptic, and non-epistemological metaphysical enquiry is espoused and practised by philosophers who had previously held such modes of enquiry to be infeasible or superfluous.[21] This resurgent interest has, in turn, fostered renewed attention to the classical metaphysical tradition symbolised by Aristotle, Aquinas, Spinoza, Leibniz, Hegel, and Whitehead, as well as by Collingwood, himself – figures who collectively emphasise the importance of, and illustrate the potential achievements to be won from, greater attention to philosophy's synoptic, systematic, and integrative task within historical cultures.

Most characteristically, however, the decisive end of the hegemony of what I have termed 'the analytic consensus' in philosophy is evidenced by the growing list of distinguished thinkers educated and sanctioned within that consensus – including Rorty, Putnam, Taylor, Hacking, Danto, and others mentioned at the outset of this chapter – each having subsequently come forward with almost evangelical fervour to call for a renewed dialogue with what Martin Heidegger liked to call 'the tradition'. For Heidegger believed – in common with Hegel, Collingwood, Smith, and MacIntyre – that philosophy *is* its history: indeed, as we have now reluctantly and painfully come to understand, the history of philosophy is nothing more nor less than (in the words of Hans-Georg Gadamer) 'that conversation which we are'.

Philosophy's problem with its history is a kind shared precisely with those other fields to which it gave birth. The practitioners of each desire to be seen, and perhaps more importantly to see themselves, as custodians of certain knowledge and some particular type of expertise, as keepers of some eternal flame, or perhaps as priestly stewards of the mysteries of God – and hence as deserving of special priestly status in modern culture.

The tragedy of this sad adventure – this narrative of priestly *hubris* – is that it represents the triumph of an inversion of values and priorities more to be feared (according to both Plato and Aristotle) than any other: namely, the elevation of *episteme* and unreflective *techne* – merely encyclopaedic and instrumental forms of knowing of the sort programmable in the algorithms of artificial intelligence (AI) – to a status in our culture that renders them more to be sought after than good judgement, practical sensibility, and wisdom for its own sake: *sophrosyne, phronesis,* and most of all, *sophia*.

The re-emergence of history after its forceful suppression and denigration in philosophy provides an important object lesson: that this 'discipline' of philosophy is no discipline and that this professionalised, eschatological, or ideological model of its activity is unworkable – that, indeed, such a conception forsakes the deepest values and the most cherished historical traditions of philosophy itself.

The neglect of this insight at the dawn of the twentieth century led to an extraordinarily barren and unproductive career for philosophy, a record of largely unintelligible solutions to problems of interest to virtually no one. Precisely the dissatisfaction with the arid and barren 'results' of philosophic pursuit in that century led to a recovery of history by philosophy at that century's end. Surely, in these early decades of the twenty-first century, that instructive episode will itself now serve as one of the most profound ironies encompassed within that living historical tradition that philosophy inescapably, ineluctably, and irreducibly is.

Notes

1. There are certainly earlier histories or 'doxographies' of philosophy than that of Diogenes, including Hermippus of Smyrna's *Lives* (third century BCE), and Favorinus's *Memorabilia*. The beautifully preserved 'Philosophers' Mosaic' dating from the beginning of the Common Era (displayed in the Köln Rheinische–Germanische Museum) testifies, even before Diogenes, to a widespread public acknowledgement of a kind of 'pantheon' of great thinkers, in which Plato, Aristotle, and Socrates figured prominently. Perhaps one would date this concept of 'teaching' philosophy through biography and history to Aristotle's historical accounts, e.g., in Book Alpha of the *Metaphysics*, or Xenophon's *Memorabilia*. I focus on Diogenes simply because of its strategic historical significance, evident in the widespread influence his work had on the teaching and transmission of philosophy in our culture and also because his work appears to signify an important transition from purely biographical accounts of great individuals, on the one hand, and partial and tendentious summaries of opponent's doctrines (as by Aristotle) on the other, to a genre in which both biography and an attempt at faithful doctrinal summary were combined for pedagogic, rather than for apologetic or polemical, purposes.
2. Witness, for example, Richard Rorty's claims about Aristotle and 'real essences', Leibniz and belief in God, or the 'correct' contemporary view that 'the mind is just the central nervous system under an alternative description'; cf. 'The Historiography of Philosophy: Four Genres', p. 49.
3. Compare Rorty's conclusion to *The Consequences of Pragmatism*, pp. 213–14, with Russell's attitude, evident forty years earlier, throughout Rorty's *History of Western Philosophy*.
4. Cf. Collingwood's *Autobiography*, pp. 27–31.
5. Alasdair MacIntyre, 'The Relationship of Philosophy to its Past', p. 31.
6. Johns Hopkins University was originally established as the first solely graduate research institution in the United States, based explicitly on von Humboldt's vision. Only in recent decades did it even begin to admit undergraduates.
7. Cf. Terry Pinkard's masterful account of this corrupt and infecund university culture in his magisterial biography *Hegel*.
8. Collins documents this process in early modern European philosophy in his *The Sociology of Philosophies*.
9. The quotations are from Hans Reichenbach, *The Rise of Scientific Philosophy*, p. 121; the endorsement by Rorty of at least the more radical of Reichenbach's negative historical assessments is found in *The Consequences of Pragmatism*, p. 214.
10. Bruce Wilshire comments at length on such developments in *The Moral Collapse of the University*.

11. Thomas Kuhn, *The Structure of Scientific Revolutions*.
12. MacIntyre, 'The Relationship of Philosophy to its Past', p. 32.
13. As, for example, in G. E. Moore's famous 'refutation' of idealism in 1903, in which the quotations cited are from A. E. Taylor's *Elements of Metaphysics* and the position refuted is at best marginally related to Berkeley's idealism and not at all relevant of the mystical monism of Bradley or to the 'objective' or 'Absolute' idealism of Hegel, with which Moore had no direct acquaintance.
14. Arthur Danto, *The Philosophical Disenfranchisement of Art*, p. 140.
15. Cf. the essays in *Post-Analytic Philosophy*, ed. John Rajchman and Cornel West. For a more intercontinental treatment of these issues, see *After Philosophy: End or Transformation?* ed. Baynes, Bohman, and McCarthy.
16. Cf. Lynn Sumida Joy, *Gassendi the Atomist*, Part II, chapter V, esp. pp. 103–5 for a summary of Gassendi's concerns over both linguistic and ontological incoherence inherent in the use by Galileo, Kepler, and others of mathematical demonstrations to model quite distinct physical processes. The quotations on Gassendi's opposition to disciplinary distinctions are found at p. 19.
17. Such arguments regarding the history of art were made during the pre-Raphaelite movement, but I maintain that this polemical treatment of the history of art did not ever constitute the norm for understanding art history, as it did for the history of philosophy.
18. Ian Hacking, 'Five Parables' in *Philosophy in History*, pp. 114–19.
19. Cf. Hacking, 'Five Parables' in *Philosophy in History*, pp. 117–19, and Alasdair MacIntyre, 'Epistemological Crises, Dramatic Narrative, and the Philosophy of Science', p. 464. MacIntyre updates this Kuhnian diagnosis of the social sciences in their debates over Kuhn and the 'end of ideology' in their fields in his Aquinas Lecture. Cf. *First Principles, Final Ends, and Contemporary Philosophical Issues*, p. 21.
20. 'Nihilism is fundamentally an attempt to overcome or to repudiate the past on behalf of an unknown and unknowable yet hoped-for future. The danger implicit in this attempt is that it seems necessarily to entail a negation of the present, or to remove the ground upon which man must stand in order to carry out or even merely to witness the process of historical transformation. . . . The nihilist invokes us to destroy the past on behalf of a wish which he cannot articulate, let alone guarantee fulfillment' (Stanley Rosen, *Nihilism*, p. 140).
21. These developments were both chronicled and characterised by the contributors to Robert C. Neville's anthology, *New Essays in Metaphysics*. Collectively the concept of metaphysics advocated in these essays follows closely the model first set forth by Collingwood in his *Essay on Metaphysics*, Part I, chapters 6 and 7.

4 Three Rival Conceptions of the History of Philosophy

In this book, I have thus far suggested that Anglo-American philosophy towards the end of the twentieth century could be characterised increasingly by the return to prominence and respectability of the history of philosophy. Historians of philosophy, Continental hermeneuts, and specialists in one or another historical figure might complain about this characterisation, arguing that *they* had never forsaken such interests or ceased to 'do' philosophy historically in the first place. Still, it is remarkable how prominent philosophers from Richard Rorty, Charles Taylor, and Arthur Danto, to Hilary Putnam, Ian Hacking, and Keith Lehrer – none of whom would have been classified in the historical camp twenty or thirty years before – came forward at various points towards the close of the twentieth century to declare a renewed interest in the historical figures and traditions of Western philosophical thought. Quine's earlier famously derogatory distinction between those who pursue philosophy 'proper' and those who merely engage in the history of philosophy had ceased to be taken seriously.[1]

The dating of this issue is hardly precise. The trend back to the history of philosophy by prominent American philosophers is usually taken to begin with Rorty's publication of *Philosophy and the Mirror of Nature* in 1979 and in the many works of his on this theme that followed. Others would point to the influence of Alasdair MacIntyre's *After Virtue* in 1981. But Charles Taylor had already signalled this emerging trend on the part of analytic philosophers with his publication of *Hegel* in 1975. Ian Hacking dates his own conversion from 'the commonplaces of a perfectly conventional training in analytic philosophy' to what he terms a 'historico-linguistic point of view' (informed by Michel Foucault) as occurring sometime after 1974.[2] Putnam was by this time deeply embroiled in the question of whether Aristotle was right or wrong about real essences, and henceforth he has seemed bent (as Edward Pols remarked) on 'transforming himself before retirement into the Compleat Continental

Philosopher'.[3] Keith Lehrer's fine work on the Scottish Enlightenment philosopher Thomas Reid and the widespread interest in Martha Nussbaum's *The Fragility of Goodness* (1986) constituted some of the other earliest episodes in this historical trend.

This renewed interest among leading philosophers in the philosophical uses of historical traditions invariably provoked greater focus on attendant questions of method: that is, to the quest for an appropriate historiography of philosophy and to the concomitant development of various philosophies of the history of philosophy. One of the more substantive contributions to this topic was Richard Rorty's highly tendentious essay in 1984, 'The Historiography of Philosophy: Four Genres'.[4] In reconsidering and building upon Rorty's earlier assessment, I propose to consider two competing attempts to formulate a philosophy of the history of philosophy that were advanced during that same period by Arthur Danto and Alasdair MacIntyre, respectively. I then add a third perspective in conclusion.

Refutation

In an eloquent collection of essays, *Connections to the World*, Arthur Danto portrayed the history of philosophy in sharp contrast to both the history of science and the history of art. The history of science Danto described as progressive, at least inasmuch as successors see themselves as building upon and advancing the discoveries and breakthroughs of their predecessors, all directed to a common and explicitly acknowledged goal of enhancing our knowledge of the natural world. Art history he argued, is a very different sort of entity: it consists of a series of experimental episodes – of what Danto characterised as *adventures* – with only a loosely connected narrative. Rather than recording progress towards a common goal, the successive episodes of art history simply exhaust themselves when the original inspirations and creative genius of the founders are gradually supplanted by imitation, stagnation, and a growing self-reflective preoccupation with the philosophical significance of the artistic movement itself. Ironically, on Danto's account, it is the growing philosophical self-consciousness of artists in a school, period, or movement that heralds the death of the movement. Like Hegel's Owl of Minerva, this philosophical self-analysis spreads its wings only when the daylight of genuine artistic creativity dissolves into the dusk of self-absorption that signals what Danto described in one essay as 'the end of art'.[5]

The history of philosophy, according to Danto, stands in sharp contrast to both of the preceding genres. Each successive episode in the chronology of the history of philosophy

Three Rival Conceptions of the History of Philosophy 49

seems to regard itself as a completely new beginning, which appears to require a corresponding complete repudiation of everything that came before. . . . It is characteristic of the great philosophical thinker to discover that everything that went before rested on *some hopeless and fundamental mistake*. So, the past of philosophy is kept alive by the need of those who mean to advance the subject to disengage themselves from their predecessors by some *monumental refutation*.[6]

Danto's view of the history of philosophy was unabashedly Cartesian and modernistic. Descartes provided the paradigm example of the philosopher attempting to disengage himself from his predecessors and repudiate past philosophical traditions in the quest for a new beginning, a new foundation for philosophical thought. MacIntyre warns us, however, of a certain Cartesian deception; namely, that by uncritically and unreflectively carrying over his knowledge and use of Latin and French, not to mention a host of tacit beliefs and background convictions inherited both from his culture and from many of his philosophical teachers and mentors, Descartes inadvertently saddled modern philosophy with a highly misleading account of what he had in fact accomplished.[7] Philosophers like Descartes who seem to embody Danto's formula for the history of philosophy often present us with spurious accounts of monumental refutations that were in fact no such thing.

Nevertheless, Danto is surely right that philosophers such as G. E. Moore, Bertrand Russell, Rudolf Carnap, and Hans Reichenbach – and in a quite different context, Edmund Husserl – all thought it plausible to follow Descartes's example. Each, that is, took pains to argue that his own thought represented a clean break from the past and a new beginning for philosophy, inasmuch as all previous philosophy had (again, in Danto's words) 'rested upon a mistake'.

Narrative

Danto's philosophy of the history of philosophy, however, failed to account for a number of other examples of philosophers engaging their own history. From Aristotle through Aquinas to Hegel, for example, one can trace a lineage in which the history of philosophy is appropriated by philosophical authors as representing a kind of progressively greater insight into the nature of things, more along the lines of Danto's thoroughly unreconstructed, pre-Kuhnian view of the history of science. The truth, as Hegel observed, requires more than merely an understanding of the whole. Truth also entails a rational understanding of the historical process by which what is actual came to be just *what* it is, instead of something else. To paraphrase the *Rechtsphilosophie*: what is historically actual can always be given a rational narrative – a description of episodes, each of which traces the interaction of human purposive agency and historically contingent events sufficiently for us to understand what took place and why.

This, in turn, is usually taken to be the hallmark of the historicist approach to the history of philosophy. Advocating the historicist position, Charles Taylor suggested that the truth of an idea lies in its genesis and in an understanding of its historical development.[8] Such understandings, finally, emphasise historical continuity: the Hegelian *Aufhebung* is not literally a negation or rejection but a superseding of the past moment – a 'sublation' that is a temporal transcendence of the past and simultaneously an inclusion of it. Since the philosopher's past is literally enfolded in each present philosophical position, there can be no such thing as a clean break, a new beginning, or a monumental refutation of what has gone before.

Richard Rorty, during the latter part of his career, argued that this philosophical use of the history of philosophy – what he termed, after Hegel, *Geistesgeschichte* – is really aimed at a kind of self-justification or legitimation of the philosophical concerns and outlook of the author of that history.[9] Thus, on Rorty's account, we were obliged to understand that philosophers like Hegel, Collingwood, and perhaps MacIntyre were all, through a reweaving of the philosophical–historical narrative, attempting to provide a warrant, a rational justification, and a satisfactory explanation of their own personal concerns and philosophical points of view through an appeal to history. This remains the case, even in the decidedly pessimistic and antiprogressive philosophers like Augustine, Vico, and Nietzsche.[10]

Rorty's account of *Geistesgeschichte* in fact offered a paradigm case of what, in those bygone days, he termed 'edifying conversation': the revelation and clarification of a philosopher's (or a culture's) ideological stance. That stance, however, was by nature radically subjectivised and relativised; it utterly lacked transcendental or cross-cultural resources for evaluating its adequacy, and it was subject to being found incommensurable with, and possibly even unintelligible from, the standpoints of its various rivals. In contrast to Rorty's strict limitations on the scope of the narrative genre, however, MacIntyre's analysis of the structure of narratives in both the history of philosophy and the history of science strongly suggested at that time that there *were* norms and substantive criteria of truth that could apply to and adjudicate between competing narrative justifications. Using Aquinas's interpretation of Aristotle's *Posterior Analytics* as a starting point, MacIntyre argued that – even without an imperialistic notion of 'timeless, transcendental, and absolute Truth' – one can adjudicate both rationally and cross-culturally between competing, and even seemingly incommensurable, narrative accounts of scientific and philosophical phenomena.

The superior historical narrative in science or in philosophy (on the MacIntyre–Thomas reading of Aristotle) is that narrative that can plausibly represent itself as a cumulative final state of perfected understanding by 'specifying, in part at least, the relationships between prior states of imperfect and partial understanding and that final state'.[11] That is, the true narrative engages all its rivals and all historically prior accounts, demonstrating thoroughly what each rival account entails, why its adherents would have come to hold it, and what problems or issues it addresses successfully, together with the salient issues or problems that the rival narrative is *unable* to account for, and why. The truth of a narrative is thus contingent upon its ability at any historical juncture to encompass all major previous and rival points of view in this manner. This in turn implies that the 'true' narrative account is always a 'master narrative': a totalising or summarising account that reveals its rivals and its predecessors as constituting a nested set of partial narratives converging towards the master narrative itself. Aristotle provides paradigmatic instances of this teleological narrative method in science and philosophy in his treatment of rival conceptions of the *summum bonum* in Book I of the *Nicomachean Ethics*, as well as in his historical account of causal explanation in Book Alpha of the *Metaphysics*.[12]

In contrast to Kuhn's thesis regarding the incommensurability of rival paradigms in the history of science, moreover, MacIntyre argues that the same teleological, nested-narrative structure is revealed in the triumph of, say, relativistic cosmology and quantum mechanics over Newtonianism. Each of these newest master narratives in physics, that is to say, is believed to be true by practising physicists insofar as each offers a fully intelligible account both of classical Newtonian successes in their respective branches of physics *and* of its shortcomings. By contrast, no such comprehensive account can be offered from the standpoint of Newtonianism, which can account only for its successes and *ex hypothesi* for the failures and shortcomings of its own historical predecessors and rivals – but not for its *own* current shortcomings and failures (which are simply unintelligible in its own terms) and certainly not for its rivals in the form of relativistic cosmology or quantum mechanics.

Such all-encompassing historical narratives do not merely constitute a rational justification from the point of view of the new theories, but in fact they provide a demonstration both of their continuity and commensurability with the old theory and of their explanatory narrative superiority to it. Furthermore, as this example illustrates, future theories or scientific paradigms will supplant present ones, not arbitrarily but only by in turn demonstrating *their* teleological narrative superiority (and hence, greater claim to truth) to currently reigning theories and paradigms, using precisely the same Aristotelian criteria outlined above. As the narrative structure is the essential component of any scientific revolution, MacIntyre concluded, the famous incommensurability debate is largely obviated, and science as well as philosophy is revealed as essentially, rather than contingently, historical and narrative in character.[13]

Reflective Engagement

MacIntyre's Aristotelian account of the role of historical narrative in science offered a new avenue around what had become a stifling and well-worn incommensurability debate in epistemology of science by the end of the twentieth century. Surprisingly, however, this account does not work nearly so well in providing an adequate philosophical interpretation of the history of philosophy.

But there remains one exception to Danto's Cartesian account of the history of philosophy that is still worthy of consideration. John Dewey once observed that a philosophical position is never so much refuted as simply abandoned. And, indeed, a historical record of almost casual abandonment in a quite undramatic sense defines the topography of the recent past, as well as of the more remote past history of philosophy.[14]

For example, whatever became of the early twentieth-century metaphysical versions of neo- or critical realism in America, or its counterpart, sense-data theory in Great Britain?[15] Who reads the evolutionary cosmology of Herbert Spencer, or of Spencer's American populariser, John Fiske, anymore, apart from a handful of scholars whose motivation is fairly described as purely antiquarian? In this same vein, whatever became of the *Microcosmus* of Hermann Lotze? At the beginning of the twentieth century, Lotze was the most widely read and discussed philosopher on the European scene. Are there any personal idealists left on that scene? And lest I seem merely to be picking on what Rorty labels 'weakened forms of idealism',[16] whatever happened to ordinary-language philosophy, which H. H. Price, writing in the very first issue of the (now venerable) *Philosophical Quarterly*, described as 'this potent and formidable deity which now rules the philosophic world'?[17]

Such movements, and countless others like them, were never even accorded the dignity of a decent burial in the form of a solid refutation, nor can we even claim for most of them the questionable fate of having been *Aufhebung*ised into some narrative Absolute. Far better, it might seem, to have your philosophical position examined and refuted – as was Sir William Hamilton's by John Stuart Mill – than to suffer the even

Three Rival Conceptions of the History of Philosophy

greater humiliation of simply fading away, like an old soldier, from philosophical consciousness into footnote immortality.

This final perspective on the history of philosophy is parallel in many respects to an anarchistic, antirationalist account of the history of science. Scientific theories, according to Paul Feyerabend, rise to prominence and then fade from the scene (as did their predecessors) more as a function of 'prejudice, conceit, [and] passion'[18] than of their rational or explanatory comprehensiveness. Luck, passion, and the cooling of passion and loss of interest – not logic or falsification – form the warp and woof of the history of science. Likewise, on my account of philosophy's history: philosophers propose their views with an inordinate, even arrogant degree of pomp and circumstance, but history disposes rather unceremoniously of all save a few. The vast majority of these philosophical systems, theories, and movements are never refuted or torn down. Rather, they are simply neglected or abandoned, like old unserviceable buildings. Their foundations gradually disappear beneath the debris of subsequent intellectual history unless and until some philosophical archaeologist spades them up again for his or her own purposes or stumbles across them warehoused in a library or museum.[19]

My perspective on the history of philosophy (like Feyerabend's perspective on the history of science) is strikingly similar to Danto's portrayal not of the history of philosophy but rather of the history of art. Like the history of art, the history of philosophy records a series of inconclusive episodes – or, perhaps more charitably, a sequence of 'Adventures of Ideas' – each exhibiting a common internal structure ranging from brilliant insight and originality to widespread interest and popularity, leading invariably to the kind of stagnation associated with imitative discipleship, scholasticism, and dogmatism, which lead in turn to decay and disinterest.

In *The Ancients and the Moderns*, Stanley Rosen suggests that 'modern philosophy begins with an attempt to . . . justify passion'.[20] Somewhat in contrast, I am arguing that all philosophical perspectives or movements, ancient or modern, are born in the passionate interest and engagement of their founders; they perish when it simply becomes the case that no one any longer cares about the issues or problems they address. If 'care' [*Sorge*] is the 'Being of *Dasein*', as Heidegger claimed, then it is all the more the 'being' and lifeblood of philosophical systems and authors. The Owl of Minerva takes its flight from the reigning movements in both art and philosophy when, finally, no one any longer cares.[21]

The Argument for Historical Engagement

None of the preceding perspectives can claim to be fully representative of the history of philosophy; philosophers and philosophical movements were found that exemplified each of the positions described. However, each of these three philosophical perspectives on the *history* of philosophy in turn defines and seeks to legitimate a specific attitude towards philosophy itself. And it is here, in their respective philosophies of *philosophy*, that disturbing and incompatible differences become apparent.

Danto's 'mistakes and refutation' version illustrates the tendency of some philosophers to disassociate from and denigrate the history of philosophy. This perspective encourages philosophers to engage in what Gilbert Ryle used to call 'philosophy without footnotes'. Those like Carnap, Russell, and Reichenbach who personify this view *did* tend to denigrate and to misunderstand the history of philosophy. Theirs was a report card vision of history, determining, from a privileged (some would say, presumptuous) perspective, just who got it right. Indeed, Reichenbach's portrayal of the history of philosophy as a series of 'pseudo-scientific answers' and 'naïve generalisations and analogies'[22] constitutes nihilism in Rosen's sense: a wholesale repudiation of the past 'on behalf of some unknown and unknowable yet hoped for future'.[23] Like disillusioned followers of some religious millennialist, philosophers are just now beginning to disabuse themselves of a century of disappointed eschatological expectations for their profession that originated with this view of their history.

In MacIntyre's radical revision of Rorty's *Geistesgeschichte* version, by contrast, history is canonised. Philosophy *is* its history, and present philosophical episodes of that history simply represent persistent attempts to weave and reweave the fabric of the past into a suitable garment for the present. The history of philosophy is literally (in the words of Hans-Georg Gadamer) 'that conversation which we are'. With the passing of millennia, however, that cultural conversation (like the lengthening chain of Marley's ghost) becomes increasingly burdensome.

And who, we often wonder, is allowed to participate in that conversation – and on what terms? Deconstructionists, and feminist and ethnic voices from the margins of authoritative traditions, often rightly complain (to paraphrase MacIntyre himself): whose history? Whose tradition? The history of philosophy on this second perspective threatens to issue in a totalitarian suppression of *la différance*, while the master narrative comes to represent the deadened oppressive weight of a thoroughly contingent and wholly unrepresentative past: logocentric, Eurocentric, onto-theocentric, phallocentric.

The aesthetic perspective on the history of philosophy that I propose sides with Nietzsche and Plato in holding that philosophy begins in *eros* as a kind of divine passion. My view allows that there may simply be more genuine instances of incommensurability between rival philosophical views than MacIntyre's narrative account of the history of science, as applied to the history of *philosophy*, would permit.[24] And, despite the long-standing analogy of philosophy with science in Danto, my view suggests

Three Rival Conceptions of the History of Philosophy 55

that there is nothing like the kind of 'progress' in philosophical positions, let alone on philosophic truth, that this analogy requires. Philosophical positions are never taken up or abandoned because they are, or cease to be, logically compelling. Rather, the life and death of a philosophical movement in history lies wholly in its ability to arouse the passionate interest or to compel the authentic engagement of adherents.[25]

Rorty, in *Philosophy and the Mirror of Nature* (1979), likewise made 'interest' a category for the analysis of historical transitions in philosophy. There is a large difference, however, between 'interest' as an expression of cultural or ideological fashion, on the one hand, and the *daimon* of Socrates, the *eros* of Plato, the 'wonder' of Aristotle, or, for that matter, the divine madness of Nietzsche or Van Gogh, on the other. Against the postmodern notion of interest as purely relative fashion and passing fancy, my perspective proposes the ancient notion of passionate engagement as the motivation for historical transitions in philosophy, as in art, music, or literature. In addition, my perspective on the philosophical significance of the history of philosophy corresponds more closely than do its rivals to *how* that history has, in the vast majority of cases, largely transpired.

Conclusion

What conclusions should we now draw from these alternative orderings of time in philosophy's history? A host of competing options are available for the use and interpretation of history, and these have long generated their own controversies and subdisciplinary divisions. Richard Rorty's generally tolerant and eclectic view would brand only the thoughtless doxography – what I earlier termed the 'bloodless procession of ideas and figures' – as a genuine abuse of historical traditions.[26] Charles Taylor joins MacIntyre and Collingwood in calling for a kind of contextualism regarding truth, and he advocates a post-Hegelian historicism, according to which our grasping the truth of an idea is wholly dependent upon our ability to recover and to understand its historical genesis and evolutionary development. In order to understand why the Cartesian foundationalism in epistemology that we are currently engaged in rejecting ever caught on in the first place, we must engage in the difficult activity of (in Taylor's words) articulating the unsayable, or, as the idea-archaeologist Michel Foucault put it, 'we must show that things "weren't as necessary as all that". . . . [We must learn to] breach . . . those self-evidences on which our knowledges, acquiescences, and practices rest.'[27]

At first glance, it might seem possible for the historicist, perhaps surprisingly, to forge an alliance with a deconstructionist like Derrida, who intends to burrow beneath the appearances of unity and continuity in a given historical text and thereby to overturn the veneer of arbitrarily superimposed conceptual orderings in philosophical or literary systems. The purpose of this project is at least in part to bring to light the kinds of tensions and discontinuities, the suppressed contradictions and paradoxes that every author and philosopher faces and must overcome in the eventual transformation of his or her living thought from the chaos of irrational and disordered *mythos* into the tidy conceptual categories of the written *logos*. Indeed, Derrida argues that his project embodies precisely the sort of complaint that one finds Socrates levelling against the newly emerging art of writing in Plato's *Phaedrus*.[28]

Both such approaches to history, however, stand in sharp contrast to the views of students and disciples of Leo Strauss, such as Stanley Rosen, for whom both Hegelian historicism and literary–textual deconstructionism constitute abusive, conceptually flawed, and inappropriately relativistic uses of historical traditions. From this perspective, there is no more advantage to be gained from Derrida or Collingwood than from the analytic philosopher's attempts either to ignore or to anachronistically co-opt history.[29] Indeed, Taylor's frequent admonitions to 'go back to genetic sources' sounds suspiciously like the attitudes of young Phaedrus himself, whom Socrates gently lampoons for his obsession with sources and details rather than truth.[30]

A way around the apparent impasse between historicism and the Straussian adulation of the timeless and transhistorical features of culture and tradition might be found within a broad and less dogmatic and less mysterious understanding of the techniques of hermeneutics. Such an understanding, however, would need to move us beyond the seemingly endless and utterly fruitless technical discussions of the fine-structure of distinctions (from Dilthey through Gadamer and Habermas) between *Erklärung* and *Verstehen* – that is, between the role of nomological or causal descriptive explanations in the natural sciences and the role of 'understanding' or historical narrative accounts in the *Geisteswissenschaften* or 'human sciences'.[31] The obsession with such issues tended to elicit and even encourage an unflattering portrayal of hermeneutics by analytic critics like Adolph Grünbaum,[32] who saw in such preoccupations merely the dogmatically self-justifying attempt to put the results of hermeneutical studies beyond the pale of evaluation and criticism. Even more importantly, however, in light of the interpretation of the essential role of historical narratives in the sciences as well as the humanities offered by MacIntyre, the belabouring of these dogmatic distinctions may prove to be utterly irrelevant.[33]

The deeper and more fruitful avenue of approach to hermeneutics, I suggest, lies in exploring the possible implications of Gadamer's suggestive comparisons between the role of interpretation in historically grounded philosophy and the sort of interpretation necessary in aesthetics or, in a different sense, in law and in theology.[34] Gadamer's instructive comparison of philosophy with legal reasoning and with theology in particular seems close to but not precisely on target in defining the philosopher's task in the wake of this new historical turn. Law, grounded in precedent, honours tradition but is not itself sufficiently reflective; reflection on the ground of law constitutes, instead, philosophy of law. Christian theology, which Gadamer has in mind (as opposed to Islamic or Hindu theology) often either is mired in dogmatism and unreflective traditionalism or else celebrates the *avant-garde* and freedom from tradition. Neither practice, I would argue, precisely captures through analogy the point that Gadamer intends to make.

An even more instructive and appropriate analogy is, I believe, suggested by the orientation and activity of the rabbinical scholar. The philosopher, like the rabbi, inherits and indeed is called to display a special degree of custodial or stewardly reverence for a long and richly self-reflective tradition. But he or she is likewise called upon simultaneously to apply, extend, extrapolate, and so contribute to that tradition – and in so doing, ultimately transform it – in the process of bringing the tradition to bear upon new and novel problems and in order to obtain the fresh insights without which the tradition and the culture whose conversation it is must necessarily wither and die.

Philosophy, if it is anything at all, is precisely this sort of thing – that is, *sophia* is the sort of simultaneous *arche* and *telos*, first principle and provisional final end (Aristotle's terminology for incomplete sciences in the *Posterior Analytics*) that Torah or Law is in the rabbinical tradition. Philosophy and philosophical reflection begin in the crucible of issues bequeathed by accumulated historical wisdom; yet, almost paradoxically, it is simultaneous wisdom, *sophia*, that serves as the end or goal of philosophical reflection. Philosophy, that is to say, is not a scientific pursuit of random novel insights or discoveries; it is, rather, a living tradition: reflective, discursive, and dialogical. It is that historical *milieu*, or what Whitehead might have termed the accumulated stream of causal efficacy, within which we stand not merely to view the world but also of necessity to engage it.

Notes

1. Quine's remark, apparently *viva voce*, is cited by Richard Rorty in *The Consequences of Pragmatism*, p. 211.
2. Cf. Hacking, 'Five Parables' in *Philosophy in History*, esp. pp. 109–13.
3. Edward Pols, 'Realism vs Antirealism', p. 733.

4. In *Philosophy in History*, ed. Rorty, Schneewind, and Skinner, pp. 49–75. The essay espouses a tolerant and broad-minded attitude towards the differing conceptions of the history of philosophy, while simultaneously caricaturing and dismissing a number of historical figures, views, and approaches to that history. Such evaluations, however, are apparently *ad hoc*, in that norms for historical discourse are *ex hypothesi* impossible to formulate.
5. The comparison with Hegel is no accident, but it became central to Danto's controversial thesis concerning the 'end' of art. Cf. 'Art, Evolution, and the Consciousness of History' and 'The End of Art' in *The Philosophical Disenfranchisement of Art*, pp. 187–210 and 81–115, respectively; see also a public television discussion, devoted to this thesis, regarding Danto's book, *Encounters and Reflections*: 'Bookmark' (6 May 1990). Hans-Georg Gadamer makes a similar point when discussing 'the hundred-eyed argosy that in Hegel's apt words is presented by art', which, when integrated into our self-understanding 'is no longer art, but philosophy'; cf. *Reason in the Age of Science*, p. 19.
6. Arthur C. Danto, *Connections to the World*, p. 3; my emphasis.
7. Cf. Alasdair MacIntyre, 'Epistemological Crises, Dramatic Narrative, and the Philosophy of Science', pp. 458ff.
8. Charles Taylor, 'Philosophy and its History' in *Philosophy in History*, esp. pp. 20–5.
9. Rorty, 'The Historiography of Philosophy: Four Genres' in *Philosophy in History*, pp. 56–61. *Geistesgeschichte* depends to a large extent upon two other genres that Rorty identifies: (1) historical reconstruction (e.g., Margaret Wilson on Descartes, or Charles Taylor on Hegel; the attempt to read and interpret a text or figure on its own terms in proper historical context); and (2) rational reconstruction (e.g., Jonathan Bennett on Spinoza, or Keith Lehrer on Thomas Reid; the process of trying to translate, without undue anachronism, the salient thoughts of a past philosopher into our own idiom). All three genres are legitimate, in Rorty's view, as distinguished from 'doxography', the reverential, bloodless and uninsightful rehearsal of the received canon of great men and their ideas.
10. Each of these philosophers read the history of philosophy as the dismal record of descent from an age of innocence or nobility into subsequent ages of decay, barbarism, and nihilism. Pessimistic narratives, unlike their neo-Hegelian progressive counterparts, however, seem to entail a certain disengagement from history through the claim that not only all past philosophy but also all recent and contemporary culture (again, in Danto's words) 'rests on a mistake'. Nevertheless, neither progressive nor pessimistic *geistesgeschichtliche* narratives entail anything like Danto's Cartesian project of refutation.
11. MacIntyre, *First Principles, Final Ends, and Contemporary Philosophical Issues*, p. 25. MacIntyre cites and makes use of Jonathan Barnes's

proposal to reconcile the differences in scientific method between what is set forth in the *Posterior Analytics* and what is actually practiced in the *Physics* and the biological treatises. According to Barnes, the *Posterior Analytics* is concerned with the *demonstration* of cumulative, acquired knowledge: the work instructs its readers on how to exhibit and teach knowledge already acquired, not on how to obtain knowledge. Jonathan Barnes, 'Aristotle's Theory of Demonstration' in *Articles on Aristotle*, vol. I.

12. *After Virtue* (1981) seems to focus on cultural and historical relativism and incommensurability. The subsequent arguments on this issue in *Whose Justice? Which Rationality?* (1988) are sufficiently unclear as to mislead Martha Nussbaum in a review of this work to accuse MacIntyre of having 'recoiled from *Reason*' in favour of a notion of social order and cohesiveness derived from Thomistic piety (cf. Nussbaum, 'Recoiling from Reason', pp. 36–41). MacIntyre was in fact proposing to abandon not reason itself but the relativistic notion of mere 'rational justification' in favour of this revised criterion of 'narrative truth' suggested by Aristotle and noted approvingly by Thomas. The issue is admittedly complex, and MacIntyre's argument is set forth somewhat more clearly in MacIntyre's Gifford Lectures, *Three Rival Versions of Moral Enquiry* and in *First Principles, Final Ends and Contemporary Philosophical Issues*, from which the preceding account is largely derived.

13. In addition to the works listed above, see MacIntyre's 'The Relationship of Philosophy to its Past' in *Philosophy in History*, and 'Epistemological Crises, Dramatic Narrative, and the Philosophy of Science', in which the positions on Kuhn, incommensurability, and the history and philosophy of science are explicitly developed.

14. Cf. Collins's interpretation in of philosophical change in *The Sociology of Philosophies* as, like Kuhn's account of revolutions, the death of the sustaining community for lack of generational interest.

15. The obituaries for early (metaphysical) realism and a host of other widely popular philosophical movements in America and Great Britain around the turn of the century are analysed in Lucas, *The Genesis of Modern Process Thought*, Part IV.

16. The phrase occurs in the conclusion of Rorty's *The Consequences of Pragmatism*, p. 214.

17. H. H. Price, 'Appearing and Appearances', pp. 3–19; the quote is at p. 7.

18. Paul Feyerabend, *Against Method*, p. 175: 'Science is much more "sloppy" and "irrational" [in its history] than its methodological image [would suggest] . . . the difference between science and methodology *which is such an obvious fact of [its] history* indicates a weakness of the latter, and perhaps of the 'laws of reason' as well. . . . Ideas which today form the very basis of science exist only because there were such things as prejudice,

conceit, passion; because these things *opposed reason*; and because they *were permitted to have their way*.'

    Cf. also the role of 'attitudes' in the rise and fall of Aristotelian physics in *Science in a Free Society*, pp. 53–70. For example, at p. 60, Feyerabend argues in effect that radical shifts in the scientific worldview occur in history 'because certain *changes of attitude* had also taken place . . . [which were] partly non-intellectual reactions to new historical circumstances'. He disputes the role of logic, argument, demonstration, and 'proof' in effecting such changes in attitude.

19. Cf. Ian Hacking's revealing account of the 'rediscovery' of Dresden porcelain: 'Five Parables' in *Philosophy in History*, pp. 104ff. It is remarkable, in fact, during the lengthy course of my own project, to have watched in the rear-view mirror as most of the major philosophical celebrities and debates have faded from currency, not because those debates were settled or the philosophers were found unworthy, but because a new generation of philosophers simply ceases to care about most of these people and issues.
20. Stanley Rosen, *The Ancients and the Moderns*, p. 14.
21. There is an untraceable sense in which this perspective on the history of philosophy is deeply indebted to a beautifully written essay by yet another past MSA president: George Allen, *The Importances of the Past*.
22. Hans Reichenbach, *The Rise of Scientific Philosophy*, p. 121.
23. Stanley Rosen, *Nihilism*, p. 140.
24. Feyerabend's cynical portrayal of the 'shrinking imagined context' of allegedly refuted scientific theories also challenges the adequacy of MacIntyre's Aristotelian account of commensurability in the triumphant master narratives forming the history of science. Cf. *Against Method*, chapter 15.
25. Here once again I am more in agreement with Danto in *Connections to the World*: philosophical views are oddities; they are not, like scientific views, natural kinds standing in experiential opposition to one another. Rather, they are (as a physicist would say) orthogonal to the world and its objects and states of affairs. The question, Danto asks, is 'whether philosophy is knowledge after all, if there is such a thing as philosophical truth – or whether, instead, philosophy is like a mood, a coloration of the whole of reality . . . [rather than] a separable part of the world'. Danto cites James, rather than Dewey, as the source of this insight. But the views advanced are similar to my own. Cf. Danto, *Connections to the World*, pp. 11–13.
26. Rorty, 'The Historiography of Philosophy: Four Genres' in *Philosophy in History*, pp. 65–7.
27. Michel Foucault, 'Questions of Method' in *After Philosophy*, p. 104.
28. Cf. Jacques Derrida, *Margins of Philosophy*.

29. Such claims are found throughout the essays in Stanley Rosen's book, *The Ancients and the Moderns* (1989), as well as in an earlier work, *Hermeneutics as Politics* (1987).
30. 'The authorities of the temple of Zeus at Dodona, my friend, said that the first prophetic utterances came from an oak tree. In fact the people of those days, lacking the wisdom of you young people, were content in their simplicity to listen to trees or rocks, provided these told the truth. For you [Phaedrus], apparently it makes a difference who the speaker is, and what country he comes from' (*Phaedrus* 275 b–c; Plato, *The Collected Dialogues*, p. 520). This passage occurs in the midst of Socrates's denunciation of writing, upon which Derrida is commenting. The passage itself, in dialogical context, also has (by implication) something rather interesting to say about the contemporary practice of 'celebrity philosophy'. I am grateful to Patricia Cook for several very pointed and helpful exchanges of views regarding this passage.
31. I tend towards Paul Ricoeur's view that the relationship between 'understanding' and 'explanation' should not be viewed simply as one of opposition; rather 'understanding precedes, accompanies, closes, and thus *envelops* explanation. In return, explanation *develops* understanding analytically.' Cf. *The Philosophy of Paul Ricoeur*, p. 165.
32. See Grünbaum, *The Foundations of Psychoanalysis*.
33. I offer a succinct account of MacIntyre's neo-Aristotelian formulation of totalising narratives and their role in scientific revolutions in 'Refutation, Narrative, and Engagement' in *Philosophical Imagination and Cultural Memory*, pp. 104–21.
34. See, for example, Gadamer's 'Hermeneutics as Practical Philosophy' in *Reason in the Age of Science*, pp. 94–7.

5 Art, Philosophy, and the Shapes of the Past

When I saw the Pendulum, I understood everything. . . . You see . . . even the Pendulum is a false prophet. You look at it, you think it's the only fixed point in the cosmos, but if you detach it from the ceiling of the Conservatoire and hang it in a brothel, it works just the same. . . . Wherever you put it, Foucault's Pendulum swings from a motionless point while the earth rotates beneath it. Every point of the universe is a fixed point. (Umberto Eco, *Foucault's Pendulum*)[1]

With my eyes shut I beheld a tuft of freezing seaweed splayed against a wet, perhaps ice-glazed rock somewhere in the universe, oblivious to its location. I was that rock, and my left palm was that splayed tuft of seaweed. (Joseph Brodsky, *Watermark*)[2]

The Infinite Horizon of Aesthetic Interpretation

In the National Gallery of Art at the Smithsonian Institution in Washington, DC, hang three studies of Waterloo Bridge in London, painted by the French Post-Impressionist Claude Monet. The bridge itself, located towards the end of the commercially navigable portion of the Thames, is thoroughly unremarkable: a standard Roman design in which the road surface is supported by an alternating series of piers and arches. Though not as familiar or popular as others of his works, Monet's studies of this bridge, painted when the artist was at the height of his career, are anything but unremarkable. Monet, among other things, was a phenomenologist with a paintbrush: he delighted in recording studies of the dramatically different appearances taken on by single architectural objects under a variety of conditions; two of his several and much more famous studies of the west facade of the cathedral at Rouen, for example, also hang in this gallery.

Temporal passage, transformation, and fleetingness are central themes in these works, undertaken in a crucial period after 1891, during which Monet largely abandoned work on human figures to concentrate on multiple studies, first of landscapes near his home at Giverny and then on architectural objects like the cathedral and Waterloo Bridge. As he embarked on these new experiments in 1891, Monet wrote, 'One must know how to seize the moment of the landscape on the very instant, for that moment will never return.' The cathedral itself is an impressive structure, almost like a cliff, exuding permanence and solidity. Monet's many portrayals of the cathedral, however, dissolve that permanence and atemporal solidity of the single structure into a multiplicity of distinct appearances; time creates, with light and shadow, many out of one.

His three studies of Waterloo Bridge, undertaken between 1903 and 1904, were included by Monet in an exhibition in Paris in 1904, entitled simply '37 Views of the Thames'. Here his paintings likewise portray this perfectly conventional structure at different times of day. The first painting in the series, as the gallery visitor encounters it, displays the bridge at sunset, barely visible as a coherent structure within complex patterns of shimmering, rose-hued light. The second study portrays the bridge at twilight. Here the structure and solidity of the bridge are muted in the softness of evening mists rising from the river below; the veiled edifice seems for all the world to be attended by silent, gaunt-robed priests; votive candles twinkle from some unseen altar, hidden within the dark background of the approaching night.

The third, and somewhat more familiar, painting in this series (as displayed in the Smithsonian gallery) was actually painted first: it portrays the bridge on a grey, cloudy afternoon. The bridge is stark, solid; it teems with industry. Several watermen row their heavily loaded skiffs between the piers; crowds of labourers move in both directions. The robed priests of the twilight are revealed as grimy industrial smokestacks; the votive candles have disappeared; the 'altar' that supported them is, in fact, a collection of forbidding factories. An aura of gloom pervades.

I find these three studies of Waterloo Bridge intriguing for a number of reasons. That a French artist chose to paint, in London, this particular memorial, is worth at least a moment's reflection. This was, after all, yet another chaotic period in French political history: Marie François Sadi Carnot, president of the Third Republic, was assassinated in 1894; in the ensuing xenophobia, and under the continuing threat posed by the Triple Alliance, all France reeled in the army's discovery of evidence of espionage and in the subsequent charges of treason levelled against a young gunnery captain, Alfred Dreyfus. Anarchists detonated bombs in cafes, university students demonstrated in the streets, the left and right accused one another of plotting coups; artists, as always in France, were in the middle of things, under constant suspicion by both sides, and a number (including Monet's friend, the novelist and journalist Émile Zola) were arrested. Monet, however, seemed utterly unaffected. He continued to paint and to bask in popularity and wealth, to the irritation of some of his friends and colleagues, who thought him perhaps too sanguine, too remote from the political turmoil they faced.

But do we find, after all, a political subtext in these works, perhaps a subtle resentment of the panorama of chaos to which England's victory, early in the century, had consigned its neighbour for the duration?

Quite apart from the political ruminations, there is the philosophical question, first raised in Book X of Plato's *Republic*, regarding the ontological standing of these images or *eikasia* of Waterloo Bridge in relation to the '*Brücke an sich*'. The first two studies suggest a beauty and romance that are decidedly lacking in the third, but the third would seem to be the appearance most related to the actuality, the stubborn fact, or the 'being', of the structure itself that the majority of non-artists would encounter. The actuality or being of the bridge, its ordinariness, might be said to constitute only one aspect of its reality, which would include at least the other two aspects captured by Monet.

Is Monet, in these three paintings, delivering a pictorial intimation of the central Heideggerian notion of the inexhaustibility of being? Like Heidegger's own analysis of the being of a Rhine River dam in 'The Question Concerning Technology', for example, the being of this bridge is perhaps also *not* limited to its actuality – to the bricks, stones, mortar, and geographical setting. Being, in Heidegger's well-known account, is not limited to what is disclosed, it also includes what is concealed. Perhaps we should say that the being of a thing consists in its brute facticity together with the infinite ensemble of its possible meanings or 'appearances' (*Erscheinungen*, in Heidegger's special sense of that term). The *chronological* order of Monet's paintings seems to move from what we might call the profane to the sacred, from the limited actuality or facticity to the inexhaustible infinity of being.

The Smithsonian curator, however, displays the paintings in reverse-chronological order. Are we to infer that the third painting, in this non-chronological arrangement, is to be taken, in effect, as a reinterpretation, perhaps a kind of deconstruction, of the romantic narrative offered in the other two? Perhaps the curator holds to the political reading of these works, displaying them so as to tease out and reveal the appropriately complex response by a French artist to an English memorial to its military triumph over France?

In this series of paintings, we are confronted with a number of 'texts'. The statements comprising texts, as Hans-Georg Gadamer informs us, individually and collectively represent *answers* to some set of *questions*:

Art, Philosophy, and the Shapes of the Past 65

One of the more fertile insights of modern hermeneutics is that every statement has to be seen as a response to a question and that the only way to understand a statement is to get hold of the question to which the statement is an answer.[3]

If Monet's paintings in this series are taken (in this instance) as the artist's own statements, then, in our encounter with them, we are moved to recover and to frame the foregoing questions in coming to terms with the paintings themselves.

In the end, the *visitor* raises the questions, to which the artistic display is made to yield up an answer or answers as the gallery visitor integrates these works into his or her own self-understanding. The interpreter's self-understanding may, in turn, range over everything from that visitor's thoughts on war and military history to the relationship between appearance and reality and the manner in which such 'philosophical' questions are explored by Post-Impressionist artists. But, as Gadamer notes, 'just as the artistic statements become integrated with ourselves, in the process of our self-understanding, when they are perceived in their truth, it is no longer art but philosophy at work'.[4]

Interpretation is thus interaction and enquiry; it is an immersion within a context in which one gradually becomes aware of the questions to which, in this case, these paintings and the mode of their presentation might represent answers. Such questions emerge from an almost infinite horizon of possible meanings, and they prompt a perpetual conversation about those meanings.

Aesthetic versus Philosophical Interpretation

What we have just done – or rather, begun to do – in our encounter with these art objects provides an apt illustration of the bold claim by the eminent German philosopher Hans-Georg Gadamer that 'hermeneutics *is* philosophy, and as philosophy it is practical philosophy'.[5] Interpretation, in Gadamer's account, is a kind of *praxis* characteristic of the human being's immersion in its *Lebenswelt*.

Although this interpretive activity is certainly 'practical', this chapter is intended to cast doubt upon the move to conflate hermeneutics and philosophy. Interpretation, after all, is an activity lying at the base of numerous preoccupations – art especially, but also poetry, literature, theology, and law (to name the most prominent on Gadamer's own list of influence and expertise). Hermeneutics, born in other disciplines, might be said to exceed the confines of philosophy alone. Likewise, in deference to colleagues engaged in logical or linguistic analysis, or immersed in the pursuit of cognitive science, we might wish to leave open the question of whether proper philosophical activity might include something other than interpretation.[6]

What is interesting is the manner in which philosophical hermeneutics relies so heavily on examples and experiences drawn from art and aesthetic experience. In his autobiographical reflections for the Library of Living Philosophers volume on his own thought, Gadamer recalls the dissatisfaction that younger German intellectuals after World War I began to feel with the stultifying 'methodologism' of neo-Kantianism and positivism. What appealed instead was the rich contextualisation of Husserl's phenomenological description and of 'life-philosophy' under the influence of Nietzsche. But, in Gadamer's own case, he adds:

> I myself simply could not ignore the fact that the experience of art had something to do with philosophy. . . . The price that the university philosophy [post-Hegelian, neo-Kantian, and positivist alike] had to pay for its failure to recognise this truth – was barrenness. . . . In my view then, and it remains my view, the task of reclaiming this truth about the relevance of art to philosophy is something our historical heritage has assigned to us.[7]

We are reminded of this as well by subsequent converts to hermeneutics, such as Richard Rorty, Mary Hesse, and even Martha Nussbaum, who, by the end of the twentieth century, came to this same view that Gadamer and his colleagues held close to the beginning of it: namely, that the analytical pursuit of rigour can often deceive and mislead, or just plain prove disappointing in its results. As Nussbaum now observes in *Love's Knowledge*, philosophers must learn hereafter to seek their insights in poetry and literature; she holds that there is something special, something superior, that transpires when philosophers (as contrasted with mere mortals) read and discuss such works.[8]

Even if we are a tad embarrassed at the subtle arrogance implicit in the latter claim, we may assent to most of the remainder of this thesis, that it cannot be other than helpful and profitable for philosophers to read good literature and contemplate great works of art. So that when Rorty reads Nabokov, or when Danto writes about the tradition of Chinese art, or when Nussbaum engages in a dialogue with the stories of Henry James or the writings of Marcel Proust and Virginia Woolf, or when we view the gallery portraits of Monet or cite passages from Joseph Brodsky and Umberto Eco, we are all at least engaged in the current fashion in the discipline.

But this lust of philosophy for the aesthetic consciousness, so reminiscent in many ways of the romantic philosophers of the early nineteenth century, misses something central to the definition and practice of philosophy itself. I want to argue that unlike art, philosophy is *essentially* related to its own past.

By this I do not mean to suggest that art does not have a history, nor do I propose to ignore the obvious fact that artists (if they wish to avoid mere imitation in lieu of genuine creation) are to a very real extent constrained in their exercise of creativity by what has transpired in that history. Rather, I mean to call attention to what I regard as a simple but easily misunderstood point of difference: that artistic creativity need not, and often does not, consist in a self-conscious dialogue between an artist, working in the present, and that portion of the record of past events that is the history of that art form or medium.[9] Poets may write odes on ancient artwork or on past poets, and sometimes some poets do so. Composers may celebrate influence by composing variations on a theme by an earlier composer or by weaving familiar themes from past compositions or from musical folk traditions into their own compositions, and sometimes some composers do this. But they need not; there would be nothing odd if they did not; there is nothing intrinsic to poetry, music, or painting that constrains it to be self-reflective in such a limited and peculiarly historical fashion. Rather, the engagement with or use of history in art is one of many options for potential creative expression.

This, in turn, stems from the fact that a creative activity like poetry is essentially a world-making activity, and in that sense a poet may be compared to a god. Gods fashion worlds from whatever they please – from something ready to hand or out of nothing. Philosophers, by contrast, do not create world*s*; rather, they propose to come to terms with *a* world, to understand the world as they find it – a historical artefact bequeathed to the philosopher by the past. Thus, in contrast to artistic creativity, philosophical activity always does consist in large part of a dialogue between the philosopher in the present and past philosophers or philosophical positions or issues.

Now, to be sure, a philosophical understanding of 'the past' constitutes one of the most essential aspects of Gadamer's thought, something that he felt had been profoundly misunderstood by philosophers before Heidegger. From Schleiermacher to Dilthey, hermeneutics had developed largely as a methodological approach for recovering the meaning of a text or historical artefact by reconstructing the *Sitz im Leben* within which it originated – by bridging the historical distance between historians, translators, or textual commentators on the one hand, and the historical phenomena they proposed to interpret on the other. This emphasis on method was intended primarily to establish historically grounded studies on a par with the natural sciences, principally by bracketing out the investigator's own cultural standpoint or 'prejudices'. The title of Gadamer's most famous and influential work, however, is intended to call attention to and reject as unwarranted this 'methodologism' and aspiration to disinterested impartiality – what David Linge terms 'the methodological alienation of the interpreter from his own historicity' – that Gadamer saw as the hallmark of this earlier hermeneutics. In the final analysis, we cannot do as Collingwood and earlier historicists had proposed doing: simply and straightforwardly come to an 'objective, neutral understanding' of the past by methodically reconstructing it as it was 'in and for itself'. Such a concept presupposes a subject or knower coming to know an independent object to which it is otherwise unrelated. Rather, following Heidegger's famous 'turn' away from this autonomous subjective knower of the world, Gadamer urges us to realise that, from our own cultural and historical vantage point, '*Understanding is to be thought of less as a subjective act than as participating in an event of tradition*, a process of transmission in which past and present are constantly mediated.'[10] True understanding is a mediation or translation of past meaning into the present 'through which the past (itself) already functions in and shapes the interpreter's present horizon'.[11] In *Truth and Method*, Gadamer writes,

Time is no longer a gulf to be bridged, because it separates, but it is actually the supportive ground of process in which the present is rooted. Hence, temporal distance is not something that must be overcome. This was, rather, the naïve assumption of historicism, namely that we must set ourselves within the spirit of the age, and think with its ideas and its thoughts, not with our own, and thus advance toward historical objectivity. In fact, the important thing is to recognise the distance in time as a positive and productive possibility of understanding. It is not a yawning abyss, but is *filled with the continuity of custom and tradition, in the light of which all that is handed down presents itself to us*.[12]

My own attempted explorations in this book of what is sometimes awkwardly termed the philosophy of the history of philosophy focuses on the nature of the relationship of philosophy to its own past, and the related question of what we learn about *the nature of philosophy itself* from an engagement with its history. In particular, like Gadamer, I have been interested in the philosophical uses of historical traditions, and in the role of custom and tradition – literally *traditio*, 'that which is handed down' – in the present practice of philosophy, 'in the light of which [in Gadamer's own words] all that is handed down presents itself to us'. Indeed, the purpose of this chapter is not so much to talk about Gadamer as to talk *about philosophy*: about what philosophy is and how it ought to be practised and about how its history figures essentially into that self-understanding.

The concern I have raised, however, despite this more general convergence of interests, is that Gadamer's own multiple influences from art and art history introduce problems into the otherwise antihistoricist understanding of hermeneutics. For example, Gadamer notes, a philosophic account of things is an unending process . . . realised not only [in] the conversation which each of us conducts with ourselves in thinking but also [in] the conversation in which we are all caught up together and never cease to be caught up.[13]

As Quentin Skinner drily observes, however, it is but a short step from this modest scepticism to the 'anarchistic conclusion that we ought not to think of interpretation as a method of attaining truths at all'.[14] That is to say: there is no core to this nested set of questions and interpretations, and hence there is no ground, no apparent ground rules, and certainly no clear terminus or resolution for the resultant conversation. It does only moderate good, in addressing the questions arising from Monet's paintings, to consult the numerous published works of art criticism that might offer informed perspectives on these issues, for the questions and opinions of their authors might stem from an interpretive context wholly alien to and incommensurable with my own. These works, while they might stimulate and edify, are not definitive or authoritative. Of the raising of interpretive questions there can be no end – as, once again, Gadamer has claimed. Philosophy, on this account, is the infinite circle of such interpretations.[15]

The comparison of philosophical questioning with the interpretation characteristic of critical enquiry in art, literature, and poetry leads to the cultural relativism that has become the hallmark of contemporary philosophical hermeneutics. In my illustration above, the facticity of the bridge itself plays little role in the narrative that the artist may choose to weave from it. And the artist's intentions, in turn, may be separable from the curator's in providing a telling display of what the curator takes to be the significance of the artworks. Although all of this *informs*, nothing of this *constrains*, the interpretive freedom of the gallery visitor. Each of us possesses a kind of poetic licence to construct the aesthetic world in our own image. If there is what Gadamer, in *Truth and Method*, terms a 'fusion of horizons'[16] here, it is largely coincidental. We are each 'fixed points' in the universe, and consequently each (like Brodsky's splayed piece of seaweed) homeless in that universe. Hermeneutics threatens to leave us with an incommensurable plurality of worlds – each world the creation of each one of us, as poet.[17]

Being versus Meaning in the Shapes of the Past

I believe, however, that this inference to infinity, and from aesthetic homelessness to metaphysical homelessness, is mistaken.

This mistaken inference stems from the neglect in philosophical hermeneutics of an important conceptual distinction between 'being' and 'meaning' – a distinction that Heidegger early on labels the 'ontological difference' but that I maintain is subsequently blurred in his bewitching analysis of the 'inexhaustibility of being'. By drawing its inspiration from areas of experience (such as art) in which this conceptual distinction is relatively unimportant, hermeneutics threatens to collapse this distinction altogether. This collapse or conflation of being and meaning would make it impossible, for example, to distinguish between history and fiction.

All of the emphasis in hermeneutics is upon interpretation and the interpreter – that is to say, on meaning, as if that is the only sense of being. In *Truth and Method*, for example, Gadamer observes that

> understanding is never a subjective relation to a given 'object' but [belongs] to the history of its effect [i.e., to the history of its influence]; in other words, *understanding belongs to the being of that which is understood*. . . .The true historical object is not an object at all, but the unity of the one and the other, a relationship that constitutes both the reality of history and the reality of historical understanding.[18]

In art, where the mundane details of the actual Waterloo Bridge are wholly sublated within a web of artistic and critical intentionality, it does indeed seem as if being and meaning are indistinguishable: here, at least, one might plausibly maintain a kind of Heideggerian conception of being according to which the 'being' of an aesthetic entity lies entirely in its ensemble of 'meanings', or in which (in Gadamer's own words) the understanding of the artistic object *belongs to* the being of that object. So it would seem, for example, in the Monet paintings discussed earlier.

But this identity of being and meaning does not follow so readily in other areas of human experience. George L. Kline, in his Presidential Address for the Metaphysical Society of America in 1986,[19] makes brief but instructive reference to the larger importance of the distinction between being and meaning in psychoanalysis, as this discipline encounters an individual patient's history. Because the technique of psychoanalysis as taught by Freud relied so heavily on the recovery, unweaving, and reweaving of personal narrative, Kline suggests, its practitioners tended uncritically to assume that the being of a patient's past lay entirely in the meaning or interpretation that the patient attached to it. The therapist's emphasis on encouraging a patient to weave a more functional personal narrative in psychotherapy in order to overcome neuroses often led, that is, to an unwarranted *philosophical* assumption among adherents of psychoanalysis that the *past itself* is *never* wholly fixed or unchanging.

But, Kline objects, it is false to assert that, in interpretive acts, the past itself is *remade*; rather, the past is always simply *reinterpreted*. Indeed, the very possibility of the desired therapeutic reinterpretation *presupposes* a conceptual distinction between the raw details, the brute facts of the patient's own past, and the dysfunctional interpretation or repression that the patient had attached to these details at the time or subsequently. If psychoanalysis is effective, it is precisely because there exists a set of forgotten details that can be recollected, and then (perhaps painfully) dissociated from their original dis-functional narrative context. Once this primordial disassociation is accomplished, the significance of these historical events may then be laboriously recalibrated, permitting these recollected details, in due course, to be rewoven into a more functional narrative interpretation.[20]

Being and meaning are *not* identical, and so they may not simply be conflated in this instance. Instead, in confronting the past, we have to do with *one* 'being' but *many* 'meanings'.

Law, History, and the Shapes of the Past

Apart from philosophy itself, another important case in which the distinction between being and meaning cannot be so easily collapsed is that of legal interpretation. Gadamer himself suggests the point I wish to make, although he apparently draws the opposite conclusions. Describing what he takes to be the central role of hermeneutics in juridical practice, he remarks,

> Mediating the universality of the law with the concrete material of the case before the court is an integral moment of all legal art and science. These difficulties become particularly heightened wherever the legal texts are no longer the authentic expression of our experience of the law, rooted in our actual life experience, and represent instead a historical inheritance taken over from a completely different social and historical situation. A legal order that has become obsolete and antiquated is a constant source of legal difficulties, for meaningful interpretation requires adaptation to the actual situation.[21]

This passage describes the possible dissonance between legal precept and changing cultural context. Gadamer has in mind as example the familiar historical conflict generated by the imposition and subsequent maintenance of Roman legal customs (reflecting the needs of a highly organised, culturally sophisticated empire) in later Europe (a loosely organised, culturally unsophisticated frontier–agrarian league). The Justinian Code had to be radically reinterpreted in the actual practice of jurisprudence to meet markedly different social needs in post-imperial Europe.

The experience of British colonial rule in Kenya or India, or of the French in Muslim North Africa, would provide a host of additional illustrations. Colonial administrators in all these cases were frequently confronted with situations that required dramatic and imaginative reinterpretation of legal statutes to apply to what, in effect, were culturally incommensurable situations. The alternative to adaptation would have been social chaos. Recent studies of these cultures under colonialism[22] suggest that colonial administrations are not simply imposed, despite the intentions of their perpetrators to do so. Rather than sullen compliance, locals infuse alien laws and practices with their own cultural content, and so creatively transform and even subvert their original meaning while retaining their shape or formal properties.

But such instances precisely underscore the *distinction*, rather than the conflation, of being and meaning. Especially in the instances of colonial rule, real persons confront the law as alien, as unintelligible. But the law is the law. The statutes stand as written, even though they are rooted in factual situations that no longer obtain, so that the statutes are made to confront factual situations to which they are literally not addressed. It is not the *being* of the law, but the *meaning* of the law applied in concrete situations that then changes, by means of interpretation and the establishing of legal precedent.

Were this not the case, we would have little need for recourse to courts and judges, who, in an ideal situation, are entrusted with the being of the law and charged with continually fixing its meaning under changing historical circumstances. This dialectic between being and meaning in legal interpretation is especially evident in American constitutional law: jurists are constantly confronted with the being of a document and its framers, onto which they must continuously graft new interpretations (meanings) through subsequent historical precedent established within specific cultural contexts. Indeed, the doctrine of original intent, by which more conservative jurists attempt to think themselves back into the *Sitz im Leben* of the framers, is an interesting attempt to collapse meaning into being (as though no subsequent interpretation were valid).

One of the most interesting examples of the importance of this distinction, however, is to be found in a situation where the law itself, as the very lifeblood and spiritual essence of a people, nevertheless confronts changing historical circumstances, forcing new interpretation to follow upon what are, in effect, alterations in fact. What I have in mind, once again, are the legal traditions of rabbinical Judaism.

The Torah consists of the core Mosaic code – simple, stark precepts well suited to the needs of desert nomads. From Exodus through Deuteronomy, this original code is encased in an elaborate, and culturally incommensurate, blanket of priestly precepts reflecting the adaptation of the Mosaic code to the needs of a settled agrarian population with a centralised, well-organised religious and military authority, empowered to issue edicts in the name of Yahweh. The resulting Torah is literally the speech of God: for the believer, it is not to be changed or merely obeyed, but loved, for, as the Psalmist says of the righteous man, 'his delight is in the Law of the Lord, and on this Law doth he meditate, day and night' (Ps. 1:2).

Well and good. But in the radically altered, postexilic context of the Babylonian diaspora, in the absence of priestly authority to petition for augmentation of the Law in the Temple of Yahweh, what had formerly been experienced as the living being of the law threatened to become static, inflexible, and irrelevant. Virtually every cultural situation and need to which this law had been originally addressed was transformed. Yet even in the context of the diaspora, the Torah is not simply (like colonial or imperial law) some sort of alien Other; rather, it is still, for the members of the covenant people, 'myself, my tradition, the narration of my significance as a member of the sacred community'. The maintenance of the Law was vital to the cultural integrity and identity of the Jewish exiles in strange lands, yet its precepts no longer governed or spoke to their radically altered historical conditions.

In such an extraordinary circumstance, what would normally follow is cultural assimilation and extinction. What the emergent tradition of rabbinical Judaism provided to prevent this, however, was a class of legal scholars who were lovers and sacred custodians of tradition, whose explicit mission was to safeguard and preserve this historical tradition. Torah, the Being of the Law, 'is what it is' and must remain unchanged. Their subsequent centuries of deliberation in The Talmud are not intended to replace the Torah; rather, these are applications of the law to concrete circumstances in the belief that the sacred Law, this 'speech of the Lord of the Universe', must be able, by definition, to call upon its own internal resources to address every new circumstance.

And so it is made, laboriously and lovingly, by generations of rabbis, to do. The enormousness of the task, and of its *chutzpah*, do not go unnoticed by its practitioners. The Talmud contains a wonderful and touching story of one of Israel's great rabbis, Akiva, that illustrates just how clearly adherents of that tradition are still able to distinguish between the being and the radical evolution of meanings of the past.

Rav Judah said in the name of Rav: When Moses ascended on high, he found the Holy One, praised be He, engaged in adding coronets to the letters of the Torah. Moses said, 'Lord of the universe! Does the Torah lack anything, that these additions are necessary?' He answered, 'after many generations, a man by the name of Akiva ben Joseph will arise, and he will expound heaps and heaps of laws based upon each jot and tittle'.

Moses, stunned at this possibility, asks God's leave to see this amazing man who will one day, in effect, reinterpret the Torah itself. His wish is granted, and he is instantly transported into the presence of Akiva and 'eight rows of his disciples'. Moses listens to Akiva's discourses on the Torah, but becomes 'ill at ease, for he was unable to follow their arguments'. Finally, one of Akiva's disciples interrupts the Master to ask how he knows that some particularly subtle and difficult point of Akiva's own interpretation of the Law is in fact valid. Akiva responds: 'Because it is a law given to Moses at Sinai!'[23]

Moses, in the audience, is amazed! What we who are witnesses to this gradual process of historical reflection observe, however, is a remarkable and wonderful paradox: a cultural tradition, so thoroughly endangered, is preserved intact, and in this preservation, it is nonetheless transformed. It becomes, once again, a living tradition.

There is a tragic postscript: Moses returns to the presence of God, marvelling at the brilliance, and the nerve, of this great teacher. 'What', he asks God, 'shall be his reward?' Moses is instructed to turn around, whereupon he (in the words of the Talmud) perceives Rabbi Akiva's flesh being weighed out in the marketplace. (Akiva was cruelly martyred during the Bar Kochba revolts, c.136–137 CE.) Moses is horrified: 'Lord of the Universe!' he exclaims, 'Such a wonderful Torah, and such a terrible reward?' But God is silent, and the implication for readers is clear: '*Become too much the clever artist with My Torah*, dare to take your meanings too far astray from the being of the Law, and *this* shall be your reward.'

Philosophy as Reflective Historical Engagement

Now let us turn finally to philosophy itself. Here, I suggest, 'interpretation' must likewise be understood in a sense quite different from that appropriate to art, literature, and poetry. The difference is precisely history, and, in particular, the philosophical uses of historical traditions. And here, to be sure, it is precisely upon history that Gadamer himself has encouraged us to focus.

Interpretation is our conversation with, and serial understanding of, the world in all its manifestations. In that sense, hermeneutics is not philosophy, but it is much more than philosophy. Philosophy, I maintain, is our conversation with our own intellectual history, with the record of our own previous thought as a culture. Philosophy is not itself *simply* intellectual history, however; intellectual history is the detailed record of what this or that individual or culture thought to be the case. Philosophy is, as Gadamer rightly surmises, our ongoing interrogation of and dialogue with that history. Thus, the sort of interpretation that belongs to philosophy is *historical* interrogation and reflective engagement, the provision of new meanings to the shape of the past.

From Socrates and Plato reflecting on Homeric myths of origin to Heidegger's return to the 'pre'-Socratics, philosophy is a reflective historical dialogue between interpreters and their historical legacy; philosophy is (to co-opt another famous saying of Gadamer) this historical 'conversation that we are'. Philosophy is, moreover, a peculiar kind of historical interpretation: as was the case with rabbinical Judaism, philosophy turns back upon itself and is the act of reflecting on, critiquing, and refining its own activity. It is 'thought . . . thinking . . . about thought; thought . . . thinking *itself*', as Aristotle and Hegel would have it.

Gadamer observes that 'the art of understanding [a] tradition, whether it deals with sacred books, legal texts, or exemplary masterworks, not only presupposes the recognition of these works but goes on further to shape their productive transmission'.[24] Philosophy *does*, in this sense, feed upon itself; its history is not an option for it but is the raw material for its own continuing activity. Its relationship to its history, however, is not that of the antiquarian, obsessed with minute detail simply for its own sake; nor is philosophy's relationship to its history that of the doxologist venerating tradition for its own sake merely as some sort of Homeric litany of sacred anecdotes and heroic accomplishments. Rather, philosophy's relationship to its history, to its own past, is like the relationship that obtained between the rabbis and Torah: both constitute a peculiar kind of *reflective engagement*, a self-absorption, a critique, and an ongoing argument that results in a transformation and reformulation of the narrative tradition that, in this instance, philosophy itself is.

I am suggesting that philosophy is, in effect, the secular counterpart of the rabbinical tradition. Philosophers are not poets, artists, or writers of fiction. They do not simply say or do whatever they please, nor do they simply create or narrate the world in their own image. Neither are their deliberations, any more than are legal deliberations, utterly unique or disconnected from their own past. Rather, the love of wisdom requires that philosophers be the lovers, interpreters, and stewards of their cultural tradition, of their predecessors' best and noblest attempts to understand themselves and their world. As in the case of rabbinical Judaism, moreover, the perpetual and ongoing conversation of the custodian with the tradition within the context of his or her own *Lebenswelt* provides, simultaneously and paradoxically, for the preservation of that tradition and for its transformation.

I began this chapter by considering the claim of hermeneutics to *be* philosophy. Although 'understanding' in the particular sense described by Gadamer is indeed central to philosophy, I concluded that hermeneutics is nonetheless both different from, and much broader than, philosophy. Philosophy is, rather, a particular kind of historical self-understanding, one that is most similar to rabbinical and perhaps legal reflection, and least similar to artistic and literary interpretation.

In linking philosophy to history in this rabbinical sense of reflective engagement, and in delinking it from art and literature, the quest for philosophic truth or wisdom is likewise distinguished in its ongoingness from the endlessness and often relativistic aimlessness that characterises the creativity and interpretive activity in the aesthetic fields. Although interpretation of the law is likewise ongoing and perhaps unending, it does not follow that individuals possess the licence to construct whatever legal interpretations they please. In that sense, I have suggested that philosophers are more like jurists and rabbis, and are much less like artists and poets, than is currently thought to be the case. The tale of Rabbi Akiva suggests that there is a Torah-anchor that grounds all rabbinical reflection and interpretation; I have likewise suggested that there is an anchor of historical tradition that grounds all philosophical reflection. The philosopher's ongoing dialogue *with this tradition* is what stands between the practice of philosophy and the unanchoredness or metaphysical homelessness of the poet or artist.

At the core of contemporary confusion over these points, I have charged that the bewitching and poetic language of Heidegger concerning the inexhaustibility of being has passed over into philosophical hermeneutics, resulting in a fatal and mistaken conflation of the important distinction between being and meaning. That confusion is further exacerbated by the reliance of hermeneutics on illustrations of interpretive understanding in art, literature, and poetry – precisely those areas of human experience in which being may well be reducible to its manifold meanings. But this does not justify the conflation; rather, this observation disallows, or at least drastically limits, the comparisons between aesthetic and philosophical hermeneutics. In particular, the rampant relativism in the former does not automatically apply to the latter. Merely from the fact that the last word has not been spoken in the reflective historical engagement that philosophy is, we are not entitled to conclude that any word whatsoever may be taken as edifying, let alone as intelligent, conversation.

The shape of the past from which meanings are to be drawn in philosophy is the presence within history of a tradition of reflective engagement. Philosophy, in this sense, is (unlike art) essentially historical. The resulting historical dialogue, the 'conversation which we are' and which philosophy itself is, is the conversation between ourselves and those who have gone before concerning what we might, together, become.[25]

Notes

1. Umberto Eco, *Foucault's Pendulum*, p. 237.
2. Joseph Brodsky, *Watermark*, p. 9.
3. Gadamer, *Reason in the Age of Science*, p. 106. In their introduction to Gadamer's work in *After Philosophy: End or Transformation*, editors Kenneth Baynes, James Bohman, and Thomas McCarthy correctly note in passing (p. 321) that Gadamer's 'question and answer' dialectical method is similar to that posed by R. G. Collingwood. I am grateful that someone has seen fit to provide such an overdue acknowledgement.

    In his *Essay on Metaphysics*, Part I, secs. IV–VI, Collingwood puts forth the proposition that 'every statement that anybody ever makes is made in answer to a question'; that such questions precede their answers both logically and temporally; that the questions, in turn, entail presuppositions (or nested sets of presuppositions); and that metaphysics is an historical science whose aim is to get hold of the absolute presuppositions (which are never answers to questions) that lie at the heart of individual and cultural worldviews [cf. pp. 23–5, 40–1, 47, 56–7 in the Regnery Gateway edition (Chicago, 1972)]. Absolute presuppositions are roughly analogous to Gadamer's 'horizons'. Like Gadamer, Collingwood views this historical task as open-ended and ongoing: 'The historian's work is never finished; every historical subject, like the course of historical events itself, is open at the end, and however hard you work at it the end always remains open' (p. 64). Whereas Gadamer comes to this insight via law and theology combined with his study of Bultmann and Heidegger, Collingwood tells us in his *Autobiography* (1939) that his method was first developed as an attempt to systematise archaeological studies in the 1920s.
4. Gadamer, *Reason in the Age of Science*, p. 19.
5. Gadamer, *Reason in the Age of Science*, p. 111.
6. Thus I intend to deny the comprehensiveness that Gadamer attaches to his reformulated concept of hermeneutics after Heidegger when he writes: 'Heidegger's temporal analytics of Dasein has, I think, shown convincingly that understanding is not just one of the various possible behaviors of the subject but the mode of being of Dasein itself. ... In this sense ... hermeneutics ... denotes the basic being-in-motion of Dasein that constitutes its finitude and historicity, and hence embraces the whole of its experience of the world.' See Gadamer's introduction to the second (revised) edition of *Truth and Method*, p. xxx.
7. Gadamer, 'Reflections on my Philosophical Journey' in *The Philosophy of Hans-Georg Gadamer*, p. 6.
8. As in the volume's title essay, at p. 284, and also at p. ix of the Preface to Martha Craven Nussbaum, *Love's Knowledge*. That the use of literature

and works of art are meant as a corrective to a certain rhetorical style of philosophising that is not always effective is nicely illustrated with reference to W. Newton-Smith's article, 'A Conceptual Investigation of Love', at p. 20, n. 33. I have taught this essay in introductory classes, and Professor Nussbaum certainly has a valid point!
9. It is important to differentiate this claim from any discussion of the ways artists appropriate the past more generally: e.g., a painter like Raphael depicting his impressions of Socratic dialogue in ancient Athens. Obviously, artists engage in interpretations of the past in all sorts of ways; it is the engagement with their own *artistic* past, however, that is the focus of the present discussion.
10. Gadamer, *Truth and Method* (1989), p. 290; emphasis in the original.
11. See David E. Linge's 'Introduction' to his translation of several selections from *Gadamer's Kleine Schriften*, pp. xiv, xvii. I have also been much instructed by Harald Johnsen and Bjornar Olsen's succinct historical summary of hermeneutics, included in their article 'Hermeneutics and Archaeology', pp. 419–36.
12. Hans-Georg Gadamer, *Truth and Method* (1975), pp. 264–5; my emphasis.
13. Gadamer, *Reason in the Age of Science*, p. 20.
14. See Quentin Skinner's 'Introduction' to *The Return of Grand Theory in the Human Sciences*, p. 7. This echoes Emilio Betti's charge that Gadamer's approach to hermeneutics abandons altogether, and without warrant, any pretext of or quest for objectivity in interpretation [*Die Hermeneutik als allgemeine Methode der Geisteswissenschaften* (Tübingen, 1962)]. More recently, Robert Neville has this normative critique in an unusual and forceful way, arguing for an older theory of interpretation in the critique of experience central to classical American philosophy, which preserves a notion of (in Peirce's terminology) 'one world, vaguely shared' as an objective measure of the adequacy of our interpretations. See Robert Cummings Neville, *Recovery of the Measure* and also *The Highroad Around Modernism*.
15. Cf. e.g., David Hoy, *The Critical Circle*. As Gadamer himself explains it: 'The very idea of a definitive interpretation seems to be intrinsically contradictory. Interpretation is always on the way. . . . Once we presuppose that there is no such thing as a fully transparent text or a completely exhaustive interest in the explaining and construing of texts, then all perspectives relative to the art and theory of interpretation are shifted. . . . The elaboration of the hermeneutic situation [which means becoming aware of the vague presuppositions and implications involved in a question that comes up], which is the key to methodical interpretation, has a unique element to it. The first guiding insight is to admit of the endlessness of this task. To imagine that one might ever attain full illumination as to his

motives or his interests in questions is to imagine something impossible.' See Gadamer, *Reason in the Age of Science*, pp. 105, 108.
16. For example, Gadamer, *Truth and Method* (1989), at pp. 305–7.
17. I am not quite content with this way of putting the matter. It would be more correct to focus on the cultural and historical background and horizon of the gallery visitors, in order to account for the 'fusing of horizons' within a common cultural context, notwithstanding individual idiosyncrasies. The 'plurality of worlds' of which I complain, then, would be seen as a plurality of cultures, rather than an infinity of individual interpretations. Poets grow in a common cultural soil; it is not individual numbers and differences, so much as the radical difference and incommensurability between Russian and Japanese poetry, or between English and Yoruba, with which we must contend. But I cannot explore this problem further here.
18. Gadamer, *Truth and Method* (1989), pp. xxxi, 299; my emphasis. It is only fair to recognise that the emphasis in this passage should be on 'belongs to'. Belonging refers to the transcendental relationship between being and truth; this is especially true of poetry and the 'poetic word', whose reality or understanding are detached from any 'subjective opinion and experience of the author'. See also pp. 469–70, 'Language as Horizon of a Hermeneutic Ontology'.
19. George L. Kline, '"Present", "Past", and "Future" as Categoreal Terms', pp. 219–25, esp. p. 221. This example is explained in somewhat greater detail, and the being–meaning distinction is first introduced and discussed, in Kline's 'Form, Concrescence, and Concretum' in *Explorations in Whitehead's Philosophy*, sec. IX (pp. 130–2).
20. I have expanded upon Kline's suggestive comments about psychotherapy; he is careful, for example, to distinguish the present *memories* of past events from the past 'objects' of those present memories. It is the *memories of* events, and not the events themselves, that are reconstructed. In addition, Kline cites numerous other intriguing examples, such as the historical births of subsequently famous figures like Dante and Einstein: the being of such events is fixed; but the meanings took some time to accrue and are still in process of development.
21. Gadamer, *Reason in the Age of Science*, p. 95.
22. For the experience of the French in Muslim Africa, see David Robinson, *The Holy War of Umar Tal* and 'French "Islamic" Policy and Practice in Late Nineteenth-Century Senegal'. For the English experience of governing in non-Muslim Africa, see Charles Ambler, 'The Renovation of Custom in Colonial Kenya' and *Kenyan Communities in the Age of Imperialism*.
23. *Menahot* 29b; in Arthur Hertzberg, *Judaism*, pp. 200–1.
24. Gadamer, *Reason and the Age of Science*, p. 97.

25. As Gadamer himself puts the matter, 'Every renewed encounter with an older tradition now is no longer a simple matter of appropriation that un-self-consciously adds what is proper to itself even as it assimilates what is old, but it has to cross the abyss of historical consciousness. ... The theory of fusion of horizons ... may provide a justification as to why I maintain that the situation of conversation is a fertile model even where a mute text is brought to speech first by the questions of the interpreter. ... We cannot change the fact that unacknowledged presuppositions are always at work in our understanding. Probably we should not want to change this at all, even if we could. It always harvests a broadened and deepened self-understanding.' See *Reason in the Age of Science*, p. 98.

6 A New Methodology for Philosophy

Decades ago, in one of my more optimistic periods, I sought to effect a *rapprochement* between contemporary analytic philosophers engaging in that species of metaphysics, and those followers of Yale philosopher Paul Weiss, who constituted members of the Metaphysical Society of America (of which, decades later, I would serve as president). I invited a friend and very eminent colleague from the University of Pittsburgh at the time, Professor Richard Gale, to give the keynote address on the annual MSA meeting topic, the metaphysics of time. Gale was, at that point, held to be one of the world's leading thinkers on this topic, and I for one was eager to hear what he would have to say.

Readers of all philosophical persuasions will not be surprised to learn, however, that my naïve experiment in ecumenism did not go well. The lecture itself focused on the different linguistic formulations used to address matters of space versus matters of time.[1] The philosophers present were interested in linguistic puzzles about time, but they were also curious about the nature of time itself, which it was no part of Gale's presentation to address. Afterwards, Professor Weiss, cane in hand, chased down and finally accosted the beleaguered guest, asking him brusquely, 'Whom do you *read*?'

That post-lecture question and Gale's answer revealed three interesting facts about Gale and, by extension, most of his community of like-minded enquirers during that time; namely: (1) that he had not read widely in the history of philosophy; (2) that he did not regard historical texts, figures, and traditions in philosophy as useful resources for his own work on the problem of time; and (3) as he himself explained it, the lecture we had just heard constituted a dialogue between himself as lecturer and his own earlier work on this topic, which he was now repudiating, or at least questioning. As a result, those who were not privy to this ongoing private discourse were shut out of the necessary interpretive context for understanding it. Many listeners, in addition, had the strange feeling of *déjà vu*: hadn't they heard some of this man's views before and perhaps elsewhere (e.g., in Augustine), and, if so, why then did this particular lecturer feel it necessary to reinvent the wheel on this topic?

Such lacunae and such attitudes towards history typified the practice of philosophy in Great Britain and America during most of the twentieth century. When it is not dismissed as a canon of sacred but irrelevant texts and a hagiography of famous but outmoded predecessors, the history of philosophy was often taken as a record of previous intellectual deficiencies and outright errors that had finally, by the mid-twentieth century, been discovered and rectified. The history of philosophy, for much of the twentieth century, that is to say, had about as much relevance for the *practice* of philosophy at that time as had the history of science for the then-current practice of physics or chemistry. To be sure: upon occasion a Thomas Kuhn or an Alasdair MacIntyre had risen to object that the histories of the sciences, too, *are* essentially and vitally related to the current practice of these disciplines. Notwithstanding such objections, however, practitioners of the natural sciences endeavour to this very day to behave as if their histories were merely antiquarian curiosities, while contemporary philosophers for the large part, still eager to cloak themselves in the mantle of authority of the sciences, have followed close behind.

Weiss, by contrast, throughout his long career (d. 2002) believed that philosophy depends upon a knowledge of and an ongoing dialogue with its history. What he found absent in the lecture described above was neither intelligence nor significance but philosophical depth and breadth of understanding – all of which would have been more in evidence had the lecturer's own reflections proceeded against the backdrop of a thorough grounding in past discussions of time by important predecessor philosophers.

As this book may have thus far made evident, I heartily agree with Weiss's basic position on the preeminent importance of the history of philosophy in the task of carrying out meaningful philosophical enquiry in the present. Such enquiry cannot start over from zero each time it is begun. Philosophical problems or puzzles of the sorts that Anglo-American analytic philosophers are wont to struggle over begin or arise out of somewhere, and that somewhere is an interpretive cultural context forged in the crucible of historical concerns.

The Roles of History in the Pursuit of Philosophy

The questions I wish to pursue in this chapter thus are: are there better and worse ways to approach that history? What *happens* to us – to our own philosophical convictions – when we study it? Finally, in what sense is the study of history supposed to give rise to contemporary philosophical reflection or participate in formulating contemporary philosophical problems?

There are several possible answers to these questions, and not all of them are entirely satisfactory. While the relationship of philosophy to its history may be essential, the relationship itself is nonetheless somewhat mysterious and imprecise. In particular, it seems to me that there are several possible relationships to history that are abusive and unproductive and that ought to be avoided. It is possible that the desire to avoid at least some of these abuses may serve to explain why so many contemporary or recent philosophers have been prone to ignore or downgrade the importance of the history of philosophy generally. Yet that tendency simply to ignore or downgrade the significance of history serves more to threaten the enterprise of philosophy itself than to solve the problem of 'bad historical consciousness' (to once again invoke Nietzsche's derogatory phrase).

One of Weiss's own recurrent metaphysical preoccupations had to do with what makes an actuality what it is, and what distinguishes one actuality from another. 'To be is to be incomplete', he writes in one of his earliest works.[2] A determinate entity is a complex mixture of conditional features, which define a given thing in relational contrast to other things, and essential features, which uniquely define the particular entity in question from its own perspective and which are shared with no one and nothing else. Essential features define privacy; conditional features are public.[3]

The problem with the analytic lecturer on time described above is that, cut off from the historical background discussion of the metaphysical question that concerns him, his own contribution to that question is entirely private and idiosyncratic. A dialogue with history provides, in Weiss's language, the 'conditional' features of one's own view that define it in relation to, and as distinct from, other views. Absent the historical or relational (conditional) components, the philosopher is bound to produce a purely private view framed in a private language, and hence inaccessible and unintelligible to others. Incompleteness, as Weiss notes, is a feature of existents that makes each dependent upon others. But our analytic lecturer's ahistorical view of philosophic discourse mistakenly attempts to generate philosophical positions that are completely *independent* of public discourse. Contrary to intention and expectation, however, the result of this discourse is not a novel insight but privacy and unintelligibility. Such philosophers speak only to themselves.

It is entirely appropriate for a poet or rhapsode to spin out or generate his or her own private world entirely as a product of imagination.

The philosopher, however, who is ostensibly engaged in a public quest for the *logos*, is *not* similarly licensed to say whatever he or she pleases. Philosophers are obliged to give reasons; Plato spoke of the quest for the 'causal *logismoi*', the narrative threads, that bind opinions together into coherent knowledge.

To be sure, philosophical reasons are not merely references to historical events as some sort of irrational appeal to authority. As Aristotle's mode of investigation illustrates, the grounds or reasons for reaching some philosophical conclusion or holding a given philosophical view are always couched in historical summaries and evaluations, and they result in historically generated narratives. Aristotle does not begin from nowhere to conduct an investigation of the Good or of *ousia*; rather, he begins always *in media res*, with an analysis of common opinions, of cultural orientations, of the views of previous authorities, and the like – all of which are *then* subjected to rational cross-examination. Plato's *dramatis personae* in each of the dialogues fulfil a similar function. In plain language, the philosophers (unlike the novelists) don't just 'make this stuff up'. Rather, they begin in the midst of historical conversations about historically generated questions or problems, and they proceed to give accounts or solutions to these, the intelligibility and plausibility of which are grounded in that same history.

Philosophers, as I suggested in Chapter 5,[4] are less like poets and litterateurs than like jurists and rabbis: their interpretive licence is anchored in some tradition of public discussion and dialogue within which they participate and in which their questions or philosophical problems are framed. Indeed, elaborating on this Aristotelian-historical model of appropriate philosophical method, MacIntyre suggests that the most substantive definition of 'truth' possible in science or in philosophy is an exhaustive narrative account of some issue that fully encompasses all prior and all rival positions on that issue, explaining in the process how reasonable persons could have held these rival views, what the views themselves explained, what they failed to explain, and why.[5] Jointly, these discussions of truth and of philosophical method suggest that history is not merely important, but paramount, in both philosophical and scientific explanation.

I do not dispute that there may be value in having some individual philosopher hammer out his or her own unique perspective on the world – some view that this individual is perhaps privileged to hold alone. There may be some comfort, and perhaps even some wisdom, for each individual who engages in such an enterprise. This activity, however, is not philosophy but poetry or mysticism: such activity, whatever it signifies and however creative it may be, is not enquiry directed towards a community and its common problems. If philosophy *were* the business of each individual forging his or her private and unique perspective on the world, then it is not clear what role discussion and criticism would play in this entirely aesthetic enterprise – nor, indeed, why one would bother to teach, promote, and publish one's views, since, by definition, there could be no conceivable audience for them. Again, as both Plato's and Aristotle's writings indicate, philosophical enquiry *begins* with this infinite multiplicity of private views; thus it would be quite odd to argue that such a multiplicity were its end or goal. One need not be committed to authoritarian or universalist notions of absolute truth to believe that philosophical enquiry is motivated by something more than the perpetuation of already-existing chaos, arbitrariness, and explanatory incoherence.

The history of philosophy provides the corrective for this creative excess towards infinite multiplicity. History is not simply memory and recollection; it is also the process of loss to oblivion and forgetting.[6] History itself winnows and selects, and it preserves for us not *everything* that *could* be said but only some of the most significant things that *have* been said. This is not to argue that such a Darwinian-like process of winnowing and selection is just and equitable, let alone infallible. Its very limitedness reminds us that there are voices in the margins of history that deserve to be heard, and perhaps also contributions lost to oblivion that should be recovered. But this, in turn, reminds us that such claims are public claims to address and to contribute to the *logos*. History does not celebrate privacy, but it records the legacy of public debate and discussion.

Discipleship: An Error from Which History might Spare Us

Discipleship is the surrender of one's self to the power of another. It is the antithesis of the 'privacy' that Weiss described as isolation and self-absorption, a kind of philosophical solipsism.

The disciple is not a self-absorbed solipsist but an uncritical advocate of another's views.[7] Such an attitude is appropriate in religion, where surrender and devotion or submission are required, but the disciple does not make the best philosopher.

It is often true that good philosophers, like charismatic religious leaders, attract disciples in addition to attracting the attention of a public audience. If philosophy is a kind of vital public discourse, then an audience is potentially a good thing – indeed, a prerequisite for doing philosophy itself. An audience to listen to and discuss one's views, however, is quite different from a disciple, who memorises and imitates them. The imitation is never equal to the original. Here I am led to think in unflattering ways of Husserlian phenomenologists, who treasure each scribble on scrap paper in the archives of the master, no matter how trivial, as a potential source of divine insight; or of the entire French tradition of the *homme de lettres*, as well as of that culture's fatal attraction to celebrity figures in philosophy. Indeed, in this instance I am obliged also to consider many of the self-styled students of Professor Weiss's own teacher, Alfred North Whitehead – disciples who pore over the texts of *Process and Reality* to the exclusion of every other source of philosophic insight, despite Whitehead's own frequent and urgent warnings that such scholasticism is not the avenue towards philosophical insight and truth.

Whitehead's aversion to discipleship as the antithesis of true philosophy is hardly original. It is, as he would have observed, merely a footnote to (or a gloss on) Plato, who on a number of occasions (e.g., in the *Phaedrus* and the *Meno*) has the person of Socrates gently but firmly contend with disciples and discount the substitution of memorisation and imitation for true knowledge. Thus Meno, the disciple of the famous sophist Gorgias, can do little else than recite what he was taught by his master, while Phaedrus, a young man infatuated with the celebrity Greek rhapsode Lyceus, desires to commit Lyceus's latest speech to memory. Against both, however, Socrates argues patiently and consistently that true learning and wisdom cannot be derived in such a fashion but can only come as the result of one's own independent enquiry.[8]

Dogmatic discipleship and the absorption with philosophical celebrities threatens to stifle true philosophical enquiry. The encounter with the history of philosophy, however, presents the would-be disciple with too many options to permit a surrender of his or her own critical independence. I have always found it significant that few of Whitehead's own students became his uncritical disciples; certainly no one would dare label Paul Weiss an uncritical disciple of Whitehead. Interestingly, the same holds true of Weiss's own best students, such as Robert Neville: few if any of these students could be accused of uncritical discipleship, despite their acknowledgement of their profound indebtedness to Weiss as their gifted teacher. It is the mark of a great teacher to produce not clones or slaves but creative individuals who are original thinkers in their own right. Both Whitehead and Weiss achieved this distinction.

In both instances, this independence of thought is nurtured in students and colleagues by forcing their continual encounter with the history of philosophy. Weiss's question to the ahistorical analytic thinker in the illustration above was not 'Have you read *my work* on time?' Rather, it was an admonition to the lecturer to immerse himself in philosophy's history. Both Whitehead and Weiss actively encouraged their students to undertake such an immersion, including careful study of past great philosophers whose views may have been contrary to their own. For both of these great teachers, the tradition itself promoted critical enquiry, originality, and independence, and it nurtured, rather than suppressed, what Derrida terms 'philosophy in the margins'. Surely Weiss himself represents a powerful philosophical voice from the cultural and economic margins of our society – a voice enhanced, rather than diminished, by encounter with the history of philosophy.[9]

Here I can identify a kind of dialectical tension and danger stemming from these first two abuses of philosophy that a study of its history seeks to avoid. Discipleship is a community activity and hence is an antidote to privacy. Likewise, privacy, though a form of existential incompleteness in Weiss's terms, is a celebration of individual creativity and independence, and hence it might emerge as a response to, or as an attempt to avoid, discipleship. Of these two abuses, it is my distinct impression that Weiss himself would find discipleship and the abandonment of one's own individuality to be far more loathsome than metaphysical privacy.

Weiss's students, in my opinion, tend to err in the direction of creative independence: by being encouraged to strike out on their own, by each being charged to forge for him-/herself a unique metaphysical vision, those students become prone to privacy and to metaphysical poetics in the name of individuality. While such creative expressions may be of value to each of the individuals who generates them, because they lack the conditional features of historicity and publicity, most of these idiosyncratic systems and worldviews lack value for the community.

Exegesis: An Abuse of History in Excess Devotion

One reason for the decided unpopularity of historical studies has been the characterisation of intellectual history as merely antiquarianism, pursued through textual exegesis. The creative philosopher wants to wrestle with problems, with issues, and not get bogged down in discussing who said what, said it when, or said it first. Weiss himself has shown a great impatience with supposed philosophic enquiry that reduces to mere textual exegesis of the sort that forms, for example, the cornerstone of German philosophical scholarship. Such studies, while learned and scholarly, are often lifeless and unenlightening, providing a bewildering welter of detail that masks the absence of an original and insightful interpretive framework. The problem with excessive reliance on exegesis, in short, is that the activity itself becomes the end in itself. The scholars pursuing such study are not motivated by substantive philosophical ideas. Accuracy, not wisdom, becomes the overarching goal.

Such scholarship, requiring a mastery of languages and of historical minutiae, certainly has its place in the service of philosophy, but it ought never to be mistaken *for* philosophy. In a sense, the exegetical tendency, characteristic of a good deal of European philosophy, is the handmaiden or fellow traveller to discipleship. The belief in the authority of a given text or author begets the willingness to attend to that text and its author with meticulous detail, abandoning, in the process, one's own creative distance and objectivity. Once again, this is an example of the bad historical consciousness of which Nietzsche spoke: each new philosopher's insight or contribution constitutes, at best, a footnote or annotation to the extant text or tradition, which thus becomes an intolerable burden on philosophical innovation.

The advocacy of the importance of history for philosophy should not be confused with this obvious abuse of history or with the scholasticism and pedantry it tends to foster. American philosophers, whether under the tutelage of Weiss or under the influence of positivism, tend to avoid the twin perils of discipleship and exegetical scholasticism, as noted – but, in the process, they become especially prone to philosophical privacy. European, and especially German philosophers, by contrast, labour under the burden of excessive discipleship and scholastic exegesis, both of which tend to suppress truly original scholarship even, paradoxically, while preserving intact a rich cultural heritage of philosophy. These mutual extremes and their shortcomings seem to constitute the twin ironies of possible cultural attitudes towards history among philosophers.

Hagiography: An Abuse of which Little Need be Said

Hagiography closely follows discipleship and exegesis and is the antithesis of the roles of history in the pursuit of philosophy. Richard Rorty refers to this tendency disparagingly as doxography,[10] the uncritical litany of 'great dead white European males' and their philosophical accomplishments. This is the sort of narrative characteristic of philosophy textbooks with an historical bent, perhaps prompting the kind of urge for independence that results in the excess of privacy. It is not the reverence for historical figures and the Western tradition that is at fault so much as the uncritical and uninspired celebration of these. The textbook doxology may have its place as the site of first acquaintance for many with the achievements of their ancestors. The truncated, excerpted, excised, caricatured CliffsNotes version of those achievements, however, is seldom the sort of recitative that inspires study and emulation of those accomplishments.

Caricature: The Sort of History One Does When One Doesn't 'Do' History

Among those who are impatient with history, and who see in the Germanic 'bad historical consciousness' an excess of discipleship, exegesis, and hagiography, there is a countertendency to caricature the history of philosophy as a series of mistakes and deficiencies and to take past philosophers in hand as though they were ignorant or recalcitrant schoolboys. Bertrand Russell's history of Western philosophy exemplified such a harsh, superficial attitude. Paul Weiss has not himself been immune from this cavalier treatment of history, and his Harvard graduate-school colleague Charles Hartshorne made a career of such rhetoric.[11]

The caricature of the history of philosophy as a series of problems and mistakes stems from seeing philosophy itself as inductive and empirical, but also deductive, rational, and logical, in analogy with the natural sciences. Philosophy, on this model, is primarily an argumentative and combative exercise. Accordingly, philosophy's history (on this same model) can be consistently portrayed as an ongoing competition between rival and mutually exclusive 'theories', each of which can be cast in propositional form. Such philosophical positions or 'theories' should be capable of falsification by appeal to evidence and to rational (i.e., deductive, syllogistic) argument – whence the history of philosophy can be portrayed as the refutation of rival positions and, ultimately, as the gradual triumph of truth over mistakes and deficiencies. The history of philosophy thus comes to occupy the position vacated by a similar (but now abandoned) view of the history of the natural sciences.

This background assumption about what philosophical activity is – namely, the discovery of truth through the successive refutation of false candidates for (or rival 'theories' of) truth – encourages caricature precisely through the reduction of complicated and delicately nuanced views to their most superficial propositional form. The matter is made all the worse if the historian's attempt to render a philosopher's position in terms of propositions yields (as it often does) propositions that the philosopher in question never actually held![12]

But, in truth, there is a kind of venerable tradition to this tendency to caricature: we find it first in Aristotle, who was often guilty of rendering what he took to be rival theories in false and even deliberately misleading propositional form, only to refute or 'correct' them himself. Let us also note that Aristotle's concept is grounded in an explicit appeal to history and is perhaps the first clear-cut example we have of a history of philosophy.[13]

Lest what I am about to say ends up providing merely another example of what I intend to condemn, let me hasten to qualify my remarks about Aristotle. We do not now know, for example, to what extent there may have been an ongoing collaboration or other sort of mutual influence of Plato and Aristotle upon each other in later years, a knowledge of which might serve to radically transform the general impression of mutual aversion, antagonism, and antipathy that has passed into history. Neither do we know what sort of once-complete texts, now lost to us, Aristotle himself may have possessed from the presocratics and upon which he may have based what would, in their light, turn out to be fairer evaluations than seem at present to be the case. Thus, what I am about to cite may itself be a vast misunderstanding and injustice, a case of a tradition of historical caricature in its own right.

What I refer to, then, may not be Aristotle's behaviour so much as the misimpression that historical transmission and loss have bequeathed to us. Nevertheless, regrettably, and perhaps unintentionally, it is Aristotle (or, at least, it is the implicit object lesson that many current philosophers derive from their limited reading of Aristotle) who gives rise to the notion that the literary and complex mythical views of presocratic philosophers can be cast into propositional form, boiled down, summarised, analysed, criticised, dismissed as inadequate, or 'corrected' after the manner of a stern missionary instructing ignorant savages.[14] It is Aristotle who bequeaths to Western civilisation the now-familiar and largely unquestioned proposition that Plato held a 'theory' of Forms that can be encapsulated in a few short sentences, despite the fact that Plato not only denies ever holding such a theory but also denies that such a theory could, in principle, ever be formulated.[15] It is Aristotle who seems, at least, to instruct by example, first how to caricature a predecessor or opponent by ignoring the historical or literary context of a philosophical discussion (such as the dialogic context of the discussion of the *eide* by Plato), and then how to demolish the resulting caricature under the guise of 'rational analysis'.

Thus through Aristotle, or else through an unfortunate partial and unflattering legacy from Aristotle, is born a now-venerable and longstanding tradition regarding the vocation of philosophy as a kind of warfare: a vicious debate between rival and mutually exclusive positions with more or less 'rational and evidential' warrant. Such an image of philosophy is utterly alien to the perspective of Plato, just cited above, in which one ascends to the realm of the true not by logical technique but by means of dialectic (which is never a source of certainty but rather of warranted belief) – and thus not to *episteme*, nor even to *theoria*, but to *sophia*.[16]

We find echoes of this presumed Aristotelian legacy throughout the history of philosophy. For example, R. G. Collingwood, in his *Autobiography*, bemoans the ascendency of the military style of philosophy as caricature and combat among the Oxford dons of his day.[17] It was apparently this view of philosophy as endless and pointless 'rational disputation' prevalent among late medieval Aristotelians that wearied Gassendi and may have impelled him (as Lynn Joy suggests) to seek alternative modes of philosophic investigation through his historical studies of the then largely forgotten works of Epicurus.[18] It was apparently also dissatisfaction with this argumentative and disputational style of philosophising that led Italian Renaissance scholars like Nicholas Cusanus and Vico to the radical view that philosophy consisted, after all, in rhetoric, and that (in Vico's famous phrase) 'the true is the made',[19] in which case the quest for irrefragable evidence or knock-down arguments is sophistry, and its pursuit is doomed to produce only foolishness and what David Hume, for similar reasons, termed 'false philosophy'.

It is this questionable Aristotelian legacy of rational combat that encouraged Rorty in his own lifetime (though perhaps there is a certain poetic justice in this) to offer frequently outrageous and historically naïve speculations on 'what an ideally reasonable and educable Aristotle could be brought to accept', or about the sort of 'premises' onto which Plato might be 'driven back' as adequate formulations of positions Plato himself never held, were he resurrected among us to participate in such thoroughly *un*edifying conversations about his philosophical views.[20] It bears further mention that this image of philosophy as 'warfare' has been assailed by feminist critics in recent years as the *arche* not of any presumed disinterested quest for wisdom or truth but merely of male violence and aggressiveness. Finally, I would venture to claim on the basis of personal experience that it is this mode of philosophising that has alienated philosophers from most of their academic colleagues in the modern university and in the process transformed philosophy as a vocation into an object of popular ridicule.

My point in airing all this dirty professional laundry is that this, the most infamous and now widely criticised and deplored method of doing philosophy, has deep historical roots in the Western tradition stretching back to Aristotle – and that, even there, this bellicose conception of the vocation of the philosopher is thoroughly grounded in, and depends vitally for its plausibility upon, a peculiar and still prevalent *abuse* of historical traditions that results in a caricature of philosophy and of the best philosophers.

Reflective Historical Engagement: A Better Way to Approach Philosophy and its History

I have thus far focused on some of the worst ways to approach history in the service of philosophy. I now wish to return to another important question. That question was: in what sense is the study of history supposed to give rise to contemporary philosophical reflection or contribute to the formulation and analysis of contemporary philosophical problems? Are there prescriptions for adequate uses of history in philosophy?

I have repeatedly invoked the image of Professor Weiss's own teacher, Alfred North Whitehead, during the course of the foregoing discussion. I make no secret of or apology for the fact that (as I document in greater detail in Chapter 7) I regard Whitehead as one of the twentieth century's most profound and original, and also misunderstood and underappreciated, philosophers.[21] Whitehead, I have argued, deserves a place in the canon of Western philosophy alongside the likes of those major figures whom he himself read with such inspiration: Plato, Locke, Descartes, and Hume. In the twentieth century, only Wittgenstein rivals Whitehead's originality and accomplishment.

I find it thus especially instructive to turn to the contrasting examples of Whitehead and of his own student and colleague, Bertrand Russell, regarding the manner in which both of these philosophers came to terms with the history of philosophy. Russell, as we know, wrote a best-selling history of Western philosophy and was renowned as an interpreter of Leibniz and Hume. Whitehead wrote no history, nor did he produce a book-length study of any of the major figures of Western thought. Yet when we examine the original work of each, it seems transparent to me that it was Whitehead, rather than Russell, who was actually reading, studying, and deriving inspiration through a kind of sustained dialogue with the history of Western thought.

Russell's 'history', for example, consisted largely of caricature and castigation of the errors and mistakes of past philosophers. He evidences no real knowledge of, let alone empathetic appreciation for, Kant, Hegel, or other more recent European philosophers. He was especially snide and dismissive of William James; yet, years later, Russell came to adopt as his own a metaphysical position quite akin to that which he had earlier repudiated, even going so far as to describe his own position as a kind of 'neutral monism', after James. Russell's distaste for Bergson and Bradley are, of course, legendary.[22]

Now contrast this with Whitehead: though he disagreed sharply with Bradley and cast himself as a critical realist in opposition to Bradley's monistic and mystical idealism, Whitehead studied Bradley carefully and incorporated a number of the latter's arguments and positions in the text of *Process and Reality*, acknowledging a deep indebtedness to this historical 'conversation' with Bradley's work.[23] To each of the other figures cited – Bergson, Hume, Leibniz, and James – Whitehead reacted with moderation, care, and historical sensitivity, carrying out a critical dialogue that resulted in the derivation of some important new insight from each of these historical figures for Whitehead's own, original philosophical position.

Indeed, when we survey Whitehead's magnum opus, *Process and Reality*, and his other great work, *Science and the Modern World*, we perceive that Whitehead did his best and most original work not in the form of private and idiosyncratic reflections of limited scope but in the form of a sustained, ongoing dialogue with the great figures of Western philosophical thought.

Science and the Modern World, for example, presents us with one of the first historical treatments of the rise of modern science in the demise of medieval and Renaissance thought. Indeed, almost half a century before Thomas Kuhn's great work, Whitehead argued on historical grounds that Newtonianism was an historical artefact whose nineteenth-century triumphs masked the inconsistencies and incoherence contained within its earlier synthesis of what had once been rival historical positions fraught with tension and debate. While demonstrating how historical consensus for a dominant scientific paradigm is gradually forged over time, Whitehead simultaneously exposed those hidden fractures and inconsistencies, suggesting precisely that new physical discoveries would threaten to blow apart this fragile consensus and bring about a revolutionary transformation in a culture's worldview.[24]

The original text of the 1927–8 Gifford Lectures, comprising the core of *Process and Reality*, continues this historical dialogue in broader compass. Whitehead's 'essay in cosmology' proposes, in fact, to discuss his own metaphysical system against the backdrop of what the history of philosophy 'discloses', according to Whitehead, as the 'two cosmologies which at different periods have dominated European thought, Plato's *Timaeus*, and the cosmology of the 17th century, whose chief authors were Galileo, Descartes, Newton [and] Locke'.[25] Part II of *Process and Reality*, the bulk of the Gifford text, introduces and 'derives' most of the main concepts of Whitehead's own event metaphysics as a product of his analysis of positions and arguments that he finds in Plato, Kant, Hume, Newton, Spinoza, and especially Locke.

The course of these arguments makes it clear that Whitehead was neither trained nor skilled as a textual exegete or intellectual historian. His reading of Locke, though detailed, enthusiastic, and appreciative, is quite idiosyncratic and selective. His interpretation of Kant is limited and highly suspect; his dismissive account of Hegel smacks of the worst excesses of Russell, and it certainly reflects the unlearned bias of the period. Whitehead's appreciative 'footnotes to Plato' consist much more in a series of footnotes to Aristotle, whom, according to R. G. Collingwood, Whitehead had not read extensively.[26] All these *desiderata* are treated in detail elsewhere.[27]

My point is thus certainly *not* to extol Whitehead as a consummate historian of philosophy. He was not.[28] Rather, Whitehead saw *philosophy itself* as irreducibly historical, as a kind of vast, ongoing conversation in which one must immerse oneself and to which one's own philosophic stance is constructed as a response. That method or approach – a critical reverence for the historical traditions of philosophy that I term 'reflective historical engagement' – constitutes Whitehead's greatest contribution, far beyond the specifics of his own cosmology.

Notes

1. Subsequently published as Gale, 'Disanalogies between Space and Time' in *Process and Analysis*, pp. 97–117.
2. Paul Weiss, *Reality*, p. 209.
3. Cf. Paul Weiss, *Privacy*; Robert C. Neville, commenting and elaborating upon this metaphysical definition of determinate being in *Recovery of the Measure*.
4. See also my 1993 APA invited symposium paper, 'Philosophy, Its History, and Hermeneutics' in *The Philosophy of Hans-Georg Gadamer*, pp. 173–89, with a response by Professor Gadamer. 'Library of Living Philosophers' series.
5. For example, in MacIntyre's *Three Rival Versions of Moral Enquiry*; cf. his more-recent essay, 'Narrativity and Truth', and my own analysis, 'Refutation, Narrative, and Engagement', both found in *Philosophical Imagination and Cultural Memory*.
6. I argue for this description of the history of philosophy in greater detail in 'Refutation, Narrative, and Engagement' in *Philosophic Imagination and Cultural Memory*.
7. On Collins's account, in *The Sociology of Philosophies*, discipleship is a necessary condition for philosophy descriptively to occur. But this may account for why so few philosophers have taken account of his book: if he is correct, it portrays philosophy as the antithesis of everything they claim to stand for.
8. Cf. Patricia J. Cook, 'Forgetting in the Dialogues of Plato'; also 'Recollection as Rhetoric: *Anamnesis* in the *Meno*' (unpublished).
9. In his own autobiographical remarks for his volume in the 'Library of Living Philosophers', Weiss himself provided ample illustrations of this point – none more charming than his experience as a young assistant professor and the first Jewish faculty member at Bryn Mawr College, to whom a female student remarked in wonder: 'You speak to us of Plato and Aristotle, but you sound like my tailor!'
10. 'The Historiography of Philosophy: Four Genres' in *Philosophy and its History*, pp. 61–7.
11. Cf. Lucas, 'Hartshorne and the Development of Process Philosophies' in *The Philosophy of Charles Hartshorne*, pp. 509–10.
12. Alasdair MacIntyre offers an instructive example of this process of caricature at work, attacking the impoverished and confused interpretation by R. M. Hare of *akrasia* as alleged 'moral backsliding' in Plato. In MacIntyre's account, Plato could not, with competence and plausibility, be made to hold the position that Hare attributes to him, and then proceeds to dismantle; cf. 'The Relation of Philosophy to its Past' in *Philosophy and its History*, pp. 35ff.

13. For example, in Aristotle's account of the developmental history of metaphysics in Book Alpha of *Metaphysics*, chapters 3 through 6; 983a24–988a32; and in *Physics* at several junctures: e.g., 187a11–187b6, 191a22–192b5, 196a17–196b10. Though he disagrees sharply with my attribution of this 'bad habit' to Aristotle, Alasdair MacIntyre also observes, against those who hold that Plato held positions and advanced arguments in the manner of a contemporary analytic philosopher: 'To call [a] context dialectical is to say that we misunderstand Socrates if we take him in these passages to be making *assertions* in the course of moving toward *conclusions*.... Socrates' philosophical activity... was a very different kind of activity from that in which most subsequent philosophers have engaged when they have asserted promises [*sic*; premises] and inferred conclusions, and the first subsequent philosopher to misunderstand him was Aristotle.' Cf. 'The Relation of Philosophy to its Past' in *Philosophy and its History*, p. 36.

14. So in *Physics*, I:8, for example, Aristotle discusses the 'difficulty of the early thinkers' who were 'misled in their search for truth and the nature of things by their inexperience' (191a22–25), offers a patronising account of their 'errors' (191b11), and asserts how, if only they had had the vision of truth now accorded to the author of the *Physics*, 'all their ignorance would have been dispelled' (191b43).

    In the famous passages from *Metaphysics*, I:3, Aristotle acknowledges the mythical origins of early Ionian views like those of Thales (983b29–984a5), but he does not perceive any philosophical or historical significance in this genetic account, other than to brand such views as early superstitious nonsense. Subsequently, he disparages the accounts of Hesiod and Empedocles concerning love and strife, suggesting that they grasped the significance of their own views 'vaguely, and with no clarity, but as untrained men behave in fights' (985a14); that, in general, the presocratics 'do not seem to know what they say' or were guilty of either inconsistency or, in the case of the atomists, 'lazy neglect' (985b19).

15. Aristotle discusses Plato's 'theory of forms' in the *Metaphysics* (Book Alpha, chapter 6) referring to the propositional summaries on this topic, which he attributes to Plato as a 'theory [which is] not a reasonable one'. (988a) The matter is complicated further, in that *theoria* does not carry the same connotations of 'foundational, propositional claim in falsifiable form' associated with the modern English term 'theory'. In addition, W. D. Ross (whose translations I am citing) frequently translates *eide* interchangeably as 'Ideas', 'Forms', 'universals', and 'essences' (cf., e.g., Ross's translation of 987b, l. 3, 14, 19; 988a, l. 9–11, etc.). See also Alasdair MacIntyre's comment on Aristotle in note 13 above.

Plato seems to deny the very possibility of a 'theory' of Forms, as well as to disavow his own formulation of such a theory, in his disputed 'VIIth Letter'. However, there is ample evidence for this position in canonical works. The Forms are certainly not to be described as logical or metaphysical essences or universals, as Aristotle (and many commentators since) sometimes seems to suggest. Rather, each *eidos* is, Socrates says, a *hypothetontas* (ὑποθέτοντας) [*Phaedo* 100b], a 'supposing', a provisional hypothesis. Indeed, Socrates describes dialectic in Book VI of the *Republic* (511b–c) as the procedure by which one ascends a ladder from opinion to truth – *logoi* passing through a series of *eide*, each described as 'assumptions *not* as absolute beginnings but literally as hypotheses, underpinnings, footings, and springboards so to speak, to enable it [reason] to rise to *that which requires no assumption* and is the *archai* of all' (Plato, *Republic*, trans. Richard Shorey, p. 115; my emphasis).

16. Indeed, Aristotle specifically rejects this Platonic conception of philosophy at *Metaphysics* 1004b25, describing dialectic as 'merely critical, whereas philosophy claims to know [episteme]'.
17. R. G. Collingwood, *Autobiography*, chapter VI 'The Decay of Realism'.
18. Cf. Lynn Sumida Joy's conjectures on this point in *Gassendi the Atomist*, pp. 37–8.
19. Cf. Donald Phillip Verene, 'The Canon of the Primal Scene in Speculative Philosophy', pp. 135–46, and *Vico's Science of Imagination*; cf. also Donald W. Livingston, *Hume's Conception of 'Common Life'*; Nicholas Capaldi, *David Hume*.
20. Rorty, 'The Historiography of Philosophy: Four Genres', pp. 51, 53.
21. Cf. Lucas, *The Rehabilitation of Whitehead, passim*.
22. I trace the evolution of Russell's thought in *The Rehabilitation of Whitehead*, chapter 7.
23. For example, *Process and Reality* (New York, 1929), pp. vii–ix. Cf. also Leemon McHenry, *Whitehead and Bradley*.
24. Indeed, it is worth considering Sidney Hook's comments to his history of philosophy class at New York University in 1950: '[Whitehead's *Science and the Modern World*] is one of the most intellectually exciting books of our time. I can still recall the stir and ferment it created when it was first published just 25 years ago. The opening sentence of John Dewey's enthusiastic review was "There is news in the realm of mind!" Across the sea, Bertrand Russell hailed it in what was for him an extravagant way. Literary critics, artists, educators – all responded eagerly to its position. Oddly enough it was only in the haunts of scientists that it failed to stir the [advocates/devotees?]. For they were busy making news in their own way.

    S&MW was not really about science but about human experience in a world whose most decisive cultural feature was the impact of science upon it. There was something for everybody in it. It was rich in ideas; even its apparent confusions were rich, suggestive of depths of meaning the reader had not yet fathomed. It breathed a certain gay spirit of speculative adventure and almost every page was lit up by a fresh perception which cast new light on many old problems. It was, and still is, a thoroughly unsettling book for those who [have/love?] a dogmatic, systematic philosophy even when they found, as I myself do, that Whitehead's own system is obscure, difficult, and unsatisfactory. But to the very end it remains stimulating, and except for some technical passages, written in a style that had verve and grace.' (Transcribed index card from Hook's class notes: Stanford University, Hoover Institution Archives, '*Hook, Sidney; Box 190, folder 33*'. Used by permission.)

25. Whitehead, *Process and Reality* (New York, 1929), p. ix.
26. That long-standing charge, incidentally, is something that has now been refuted decisively in the extensive notes from Whitehead's first lecture class in Emerson Hall, Harvard University (1924–5), wherein a very detailed knowledge of, and reliance on, Aristotelian philosophy is manifest. See *The Harvard Lectures of Alfred North Whitehead, 1924–1925: Philosophical Presuppositions of Science*, ed. Paul Bogaard and Jason Bell (Edinburgh: Edinburgh University Press, 2017).
27. I have simply given a quick summary here of arguments offered in great detail in my earlier work, *The Rehabilitation of Whitehead*. For further discussion of Whitehead's relation to Kant and Hegel, cf. my essays 'The Interpretation of Kant in Whitehead's Philosophy' and 'Eine Whiteheadische Auslegung der Naturphilosophie Hegels' in *Whitehead und der deutsche Idealismus*, pp. 13–32, 83–92.
28. For example, in *Process and Reality*, Whitehead argues that apart from actual entities and their adventures, 'all the rest is silence'. These words, which his disciples often quote and attribute to him, in fact represent Hamlet's final dying words in Act V. But here Whitehead misses a trick: if he were going to quote from *Hamlet* (*Process and Reality* is sprinkled with quotes from Shakespeare, including especially *Hamlet* and *A Midsummer Night's Dream*) he should have quoted Hamlet to Horatio earlier in Act V, Scene ii: 'Some god there is who shapes our ends, rough-hew them how we may.' The metaphysical doctrine of *Process and Reality* could be summed up by inverting the phrase: 'Some god there is who *rough-hews* our ends, shape them finally how we may.' History, its documents and traditions, needs to be carefully and thoroughly and thoughtfully used to make our case most effectively for us. Whitehead was, like most, something less than a master of this technique. But he was, unlike many, its conscious user and proponent.

7 The Critique of Enlightenment and the Question Concerning Metaphysics[1]

Within the British tradition of analytic philosophy, Bertrand Russell, G. E. Moore, and Alfred North Whitehead certainly rank as the foremost figures in the twentieth century. Together they represented the great trinity of British philosophy at Trinity College, Cambridge, early in the twentieth century, and their work largely defined English-language philosophy during a period just prior to World War I, when Wittgenstein first came to Cambridge to study philosophy with Whitehead's pupil and colleague, Russell. Without intending blasphemy, however, it is readily apparent in hindsight that Wittgenstein completely transcended this trinity, and he is now regarded by a vast majority of scholars as the most important figure in philosophy in any language and in any country during the twentieth century.[2]

In 1973, however, English-language readers were confronted with the possibility that Wittgenstein could no longer be understood adequately as a part of this British tradition in philosophy. In *Wittgenstein's Vienna*, Allan Janik and Stephen Toulmin argued that 'the preconceptions with which his English hearers approached [Wittgenstein] debarred them almost entirely from understanding the point of what he was saying'.[3] Their striking cultural observation in turn adds depth and documentation to earlier startling suggestions by one of my own professors, Eric Heller, in his essay on Wittgenstein in his magisterial work, *The Artist's Journey into the Interior*.[4] Heller there argued that the cultural antecedents of Wittgenstein's thought were to be found in the work of Austrian predecessors and contemporaries, specifically citing Otto Weininger, Adolf Loos, Karl Kraus, Franz Kafka, and Robert Musil, and Heller suggested that Wittgenstein himself exhibited far more intellectual affinity with Rilke, Pascal, and Nietzsche than with Frege, let alone any analytic British philosopher.

Heller notwithstanding, it remained the case that prior to the appearance of the Janik–Toulmin study, the so-called logical interpretation of Wittgenstein prevailed relatively unchallenged. This conventional interpretation portrays Wittgenstein as a bilingual genius who had refined the logical and analytical techniques of Russell and Frege to a degree unimagined by either of them. Janik and Toulmin argued, by contrast, for the primacy of the Viennese 'ethical' (one might also say, 'aesthetic') interpretation of Wittgenstein's work. They dramatically portray him as, first and foremost, an expatriate genius whose philosophical outlook was framed by the intellectual foment of *fin-de-siècle* Vienna and whose *Tractatus* owed as much to Hertz and Boltzmann as to Russell or Frege and was itself more comparable to Arnold Schoenberg's *Harmonielehre* than to Whitehead and Russell's *Principia Mathematica*.[5] So intellectually profound and engaging are the images they recollect of the cultural world inhabited by the likes of Bruckner, Mahler, Max Planck, and Sigmund Freud, that one begins to wonder whatever could have induced Wittgenstein to leave it!

Yet Wittgenstein did leave the complex and fascinating intellectual world of early twentieth-century Vienna, and he did decide to come to Cambridge; after a time, moreover, he returned; and finally he remained. To his friend David Pinsent he once described coming to Cambridge to study with Russell as 'my salvation'. Thus, in a spirit of broader understanding, rather than of narrow cultural patrimony, hegemony, or rivalry, we are rightly encouraged to take up, once again, the British context of Wittgenstein's thought. English-language philosophy, and Anglo-American analytic philosophers, have doubtless erred in stressing too one-sidedly and for too long the contributions of Wittgenstein as judged exclusively from the perspective of their own philosophical orientation, ignoring the deeper roots of Wittgenstein's own beliefs about the connection of logic and ethics – connections widely discussed among leading intellectuals in Vienna. A great deal of the personal anguish of Wittgenstein the man certainly stemmed from his having found himself divided between two radically incommensurable cultural worlds, at home in neither.[6] It may not really be possible to appreciate him apart from appreciating both of those worlds from which he was both alienated and attracted alike.

Whitehead's Place in Twentieth-Century Philosophy

Before drawing comparisons between Wittgenstein and Whitehead and other contemporaries in analytic philosophy, it is first necessary to say something about my own, decidedly unorthodox, reading of Whitehead himself. Of the various British analytic philosophers who were the contemporaries of Wittgenstein, Whitehead (alongside R. G. Collingwood) is perhaps the most difficult to categorise. Despite Whitehead's reputation for odd metaphysical views, several philosophers during the past decades have been drawn to study Whitehead on account of his scientific and mathematical interests and his desire to understand the implications for philosophy (broadly speaking) of the profound changes in the sciences wrought by revolutionary thinkers from Darwin, Maxwell, and Poincaré through Einstein, Planck, and Schrödinger. Whitehead was one of the earliest English-language philosophers to portray Newtonianism as a historical artefact and a modern, Western cultural ideology. He explicitly desired to understand the origins of Newtonianism in this fashion and also to suggest alternatives for what he took to be its necessary reconstruction in light of the work of these other major figures of science and philosophy past and present. Whitehead viewed Newtonianism and its alternatives in a sense quite similar to that in which Ernst Mach, another critic of Newtonianism, viewed scientific theories: that is, as complex assemblages of facts and interpretations that are intended to be descriptive of, rather than judgements on, experience (sensations).

Metaphysics as Whitehead practised it is surprisingly similar to Mach's approach to science; namely, both thought that theories should aim to save experience and should be routinely purged of abstract theoretical entities or constructs that were not grounded in or inferred from those experiences. Mach called such abstractions 'metaphysical'; Whitehead did not aim his criticism at metaphysics *per se*, but he condemned specific metaphysical entities in Newtonianism as examples of a fallacy of misplaced concreteness. Like Wittgenstein, Whitehead held that the business of philosophy was therapeutic: in Whitehead's case, this involved diagnosing cultural incoherence – the sense in which the conceptual underpinnings of Newtonianism were increasingly at odds with other cultural tendencies more closely tied to experience, and how Newtonianism was even at odds with ongoing scientific discoveries – leading to confusion and philosophical conundrums. The therapy lay in uncovering the artefacts of misplaced concreteness that resulted in the underlying incoherence of its worldview and in healing these anomalies by addressing and surgically removing the incoherencies in that predominant worldview. Philosophy would have succeeded in its task when these sources of confused incoherence – creating what Wittgenstein sometimes called 'bewitchment' – were set right, causing the anomalies and conundrums themselves simply to disappear. It certainly bears mention that Collingwood developed a similar, though much more detailed and sophisticated, conception of metaphysics as a therapeutic critique of tacit cultural presuppositions (what Collingwood termed 'absolute presuppositions'), which is one reason he found Whitehead's thought so congenial.[7]

Born the son of an Anglican minister at Ramsgate, England, in 1861, Alfred North Whitehead attended mathematics lectures at Cambridge. Along with Moore and the renowned idealist philosopher J. M. E. McTaggart, he was a member of the famous but secretive Cambridge Apostles club, which he credited for a good deal of his philosophical education.

Whitehead subsequently taught mathematics, mathematical physics, and logic, first as a Fellow at Trinity College (until 1910), and afterwards in University College and subsequently Imperial College at the University of London (1910–24). While at the University of London, he co-authored the monumental three-volume *Principia Mathematica* with his student and friend, Bertrand Russell. He published, in addition, a version of general relativity theory in 1922, which still stands as an alternative to Einstein's fundamental philosophical assumptions – one that nonetheless appears to yield both mathematically and empirically equivalent testable outcomes. Despite Einstein's own puzzled response to this challenge, and despite occasional examination, analysis, and discussion by a series of leading relativity theorists through the years, this alternative of Whitehead's has never been disproved or successfully dismissed as a legitimate challenge to Einstein.[8] During this period Whitehead also published several works that are considered classics in the foundations of algebra, geometry, and the philosophy of science, all of which earned for Whitehead the reputation as a leading figure in the early development of what came to be called Cambridge analytic philosophy.

Whitehead subsequently retired from the University of London and accepted an offer to come to the United States to serve as Professor of Philosophy at Harvard University. Apart from delivering the Gifford Lectures at Edinburgh during the academic year 1927–8, he did not return to his native land but remained in America as a naturalised citizen and active scholar until his death in 1947.

Whitehead was sixty-three when, in 1924, he assumed his position at Harvard with an inaugural series of lectures, revised and published early the next year under the title *Science and the Modern World*.[9] This, one cannot help but note, was the same age at which Kant published the first edition of his *Kritik der reinen Vernunft*. But this comparison with Kant, with whose influence on philosophy Whitehead had become so thoroughly disillusioned, must end at this point. For there is no dispute whatever among scholars about the importance of Kant's mature 'critical' work, beginning at the age of sixty-three. In marked contrast to Kant, Whitehead at this relatively advanced age in effect began a second career that, depending upon one's intellectual commitments, must be regarded either as the blossoming of broad and productive philosophical interests or else as a regrettable and inexplicable disaster.

What Whitehead did at this critical juncture was to turn his attention from an exclusive (some might say narrow) focus on logic and the technical problems in science and in the philosophy of science, to a wider preoccupation with the history of science – including the history of scientific revolutions and a historical approach to the logic of scientific discovery – as well as to philosophy of culture, philosophy of history, philosophy of religion, and, most characteristically, to problems in speculative metaphysics and cosmology. His grand work of this period, *Process and Reality*[10] (based upon the decidedly unsuccessful Gifford Lectures at Edinburgh),[11] represents an attempt to sketch a detailed cosmological foundation for twentieth-century physics intended to replace the cosmology of Newtonianism.

His wide and varied interests during this period earned a large audience in America, by no means limited to philosophers, and prompted comparisons of his work with that of grand systematic philosophers like Hegel, Leibniz, and Aristotle. It is true even today that Whitehead remains one of the most frequently quoted and cited authors in commencement addresses and other academic ceremonial occasions in the United States: he appears to be a useful resource whenever a university rector or president wishes to appear wise.[12] In Great Britain, by contrast, only R. G. Collingwood followed and approved of Whitehead's 'speculative turn', and for many decades Whitehead's work was almost unknown on the European continent.

As with Wittgenstein, it remains a matter of serious dispute how deep, in fact, is this alleged 'divide' between the early and the later Whitehead. At the time and since, and in the cultural context of Anglo-American analytic philosophy, Whitehead's later thought was regarded by non-disciples as an anomaly – as a throwback, in essence, to the worst unrestrained excesses of nineteenth-century speculative thought. It is said that the Harvard philosophy faculty had first hoped to persuade Bertrand Russell to join their department, and failing this, they turned to Whitehead as a suitable alternative. Although the department included at least one unreconstructed and unashamed metaphysician (William E. Hocking), the majority of the faculty held speculative metaphysics in low esteem, and so regarded Whitehead's surprising philosophical metamorphosis upon coming to America with profound dismay. While politely received and well thought of as a colleague, Whitehead found himself quietly isolated and largely without intellectual influence among his mainstream philosophical colleagues.[13] Ever since, philosophers from Reichenbach to Rorty have expressed profound disrespect and disaffection for this 'later Whitehead'.

It is possible, however, to portray Whitehead's interests during this period as a fairly consistent extension of earlier work and interests, enriched by reflection drawn from the extraphilosophical resources and influences – including his lifelong interest and immersion in literature, especially Romantic poetry, and history – that had constituted an essential part of his preparatory school training and intellectual background. Some scholars have also attributed these extraphilosophical interests to Alfred and Evelyn Whitehead's participation, for a time, in the Bloomsbury circle.[14] Whitehead's later thought surely seems characteristic of what we now recognise as a legitimate alternative style of philosophy to the analytic – namely, Continental or post-analytic philosophy. It remains to be seen whether this work by Whitehead was a throwback to outdated or inadequate modes of thought, or whether he will come to be seen as one of the earliest harbingers of a radically revised, broadly analytic philosophy, of which we have numerous more recent advocates today, ranging from Hilary Putnam and Richard Rorty to Whitehead's onetime pupil, Willard V. O. Quine.[15]

What is the evidence for this Continental interpretation of Whitehead? When we examine a work like *Process and Reality*, for example, we find that Whitehead – in a manner somewhat analogous to the approach of Heidegger, Gadamer, or Derrida – is engaged in a kind of dialogue or discussion with the great European philosophers of the past, and he is likewise engaged in an exegesis of many of the important philosophical texts of that European tradition. In addition to Plato's *Timaeus*, Whitehead discusses at great length in these Gifford Lectures many of the central works of Locke, Descartes, Spinoza, Hume, and Kant, and he engages in a thoughtful and critical reconstruction of the currents of thought giving rise to the modernist worldview. I shall return, towards the end of this chapter, to this critique of modernism that can be found in these works. For now I simply note that, like Jacques Derrida in particular, Whitehead is especially prone to offer interpretations of traditional texts and figures that strike many of his readers as unusual, unorthodox, and sometimes even unjustifiable. For example, Whitehead is quite fascinated by a brief comment of John Locke, that the passage of time is constituted by a 'perpetual perishing'.[16] Despite the fact that this text is hardly mentioned by other commentators, Whitehead uses this interesting and suggestive phrase of Locke's as the centrepiece of his own reinterpretation of the philosophy of being and of time.

It is principally this historical, etymological, exegetical, and even literary approach to a body of texts – what Heidegger liked to call 'the tradition' and Cambridge philosopher Michael Oakeshott termed 'the practical past' – that distinguishes European or Continental philosophical method from the largely nonhistorical, analytic, and empirical approach to specific problem-solving characteristic of American and British philosophy in the twentieth century. Russell wrote an interesting book on Leibniz as well as his infamous *History of Western Philosophy*. But he and Moore always regarded philosophical problems, like scientific problems, as entirely separable from the history of their discussion – most previous examples of which Russell thought to represent serious mistakes. Certainly the flowery, wide-ranging, and detailed literary and historical essays of Whitehead stand in sharp contrast to the largely ahistorical aphorisms of Wittgenstein, often taken as paradigmatic rhetorical expression for analytic philosophy. Despite his English and American roots, then, Whitehead seems to fit more comfortably within this Continental European tradition than he does within the logical–analytic tradition in which he began his career. There is this odd and somewhat ironic comparison with Wittgenstein; namely, that Whitehead perpetually seems strangely out of context, and so, I would maintain, subject to perennial misunderstanding and misinterpretation on that account. Whitehead and Collingwood somehow do not *belong* to their culture, while Wittgenstein found himself between cultures and hence a member of none.

A Sketch of Whitehead's Metaphysical Views

I mentioned the discussion of time and temporality in Whitehead's scientific and metaphysical writings, for which he is justifiably well known. These afford us an excellent brief illustration of his later metaphysical theories. Indeed, because of this emphasis on time, Whitehead is often associated with philosophers like Henri Bergson and non-analytic or pre-analytic British philosophers like Samuel Alexander, who (in Alexander's phrase) 'take time seriously' – either by placing primary emphasis on the subjective experience of flux and becoming or by defending the notion of 'pure becoming' and temporal passage as real rather than illusory.

These traditional associations are somewhat misleading. Like Einstein, and wholly unlike Bergson, Whitehead is first and foremost a philosopher of space rather than of time. He devotes a significant portion of *Process and Reality*, his most important work, to a complex discussion of the geometrical relations comprising what he termed the 'extensive continuum', the geometry of spacetime that he proposed as a linear and well-ordered alternative to the nonlinear spacetime of Einstein. This, in turn, continues a discussion of 'logical space' in the *Principia* and of the 'extensive continuum' and geometrisation of physical space that pervade other works of this early period.

Specifically, Whitehead does *not* (as Bergson and Alexander did) rhapsodise on time or portray time itself as something primordial, existing prior to and independent of discrete entities themselves. Neither, however, does Whitehead's focus on space and geometrical relations lead him to follow the example of those like Einstein and Reichenbach, who deny the reality of the apparent asymmetry in the present–past and present–future relationships and who accordingly attempt to reduce temporality and the experience of temporal passage and becoming merely to a set of spacelike relations. Both such familiar approaches represent, for Whitehead, the unjustifiable departure of metaphysical theorising from its ground in experience.

In *Process and Reality*, Whitehead frequently uses the aforementioned phrase borrowed from John Locke to describe time as a 'perpetual perishing'. Uniquely in Whitehead's thought, temporality, passage, and what the British astronomer Arthur Eddington famously described as the 'arrow of time' arise as a consequence of a more fundamental fact of nature: the becoming and the 'perishing' of episodic events or discrete occasions of experience. The genesis of, and the transition between, these quanta of experience define what Whitehead termed an 'epochal theory' (that is, a quantised theory) of time.

Borrowing traditional Latin terminology from Descartes, Whitehead labels these quantised episodes or events *res verae*, thereby indicating that these epochal events are the fundamental or foundational actualities from which all else derives. These *res verae*, or 'actual entities', are 'actual' in two possible senses. Each event is 'actual' in a primary sense of being *active* and actively self-relating, coming-to-be by constituting itself as a subject out of elements (or 'objective data') drawn from its past. Whitehead describes this primary activity as the '*concrescence* of an actual occasion'. Once fully constituted and determinate, an event 'perishes': that is, it *ceases* to be active or to experience its own subjective immediacy.

In contrast to the views of most of his interpreters and disciples, however, Whitehead did not hold that this fully constituted event then disappears or evaporates into oblivion. Rather, each no-longer-active 'actual entity' remains 'actual' in a secondary, but equally important, sense: that is, as *efficacious*. Each determinate entity now, in its turn, serves as an objective datum or element for inclusion within the self-constitution of *subsequent* (present) active occasions of experience.

This process of the becoming of actual entities, and of their subsequent 'perishing' (i.e., their transition from a state of active, subjective immediacy to one of fixed, passive, unchanging objective determinateness) defines a 'flux of becoming' and gives rise to the experience of temporal passage. Concresence defines the present, the event as subject. The perishing of subjectivity, the no-longer-active event serving as object, defines the past. Each actual entity, at different phases in its career, functions as both subject and object: constituting itself out of its own past and, in turn, serving as an objective datum in the past of subsequent (present) active occasions. This ongoing and perpetual transition from present subjectivity to past objectivity thus defines the 'arrow' or asymmetrical vector quality of temporal passage.[17]

This two-career doctrine of activity, in turn, comprises Whitehead's 'Reformed Subjectivist Principle'.[18] He defines this central principle of his own metaphysical position in direct contrast to what he termed the 'Subjectivist Principle' of Descartes, a principle that, Whitehead argued, characterises all of modern science and philosophy up until the beginning of the twentieth century. The Cartesian subjectivist principle distinguishes sharply between what is subject and what is object, between mental 'thinking substance' and material 'extended substance'. To this Whitehead contrasted his Spinozist doctrine of one substantial, underlying activity: epochalised, quantised, each 'quantum experience' of which functions at different phases in its career as 'subject' and as 'object'. This Reformed Subjectivist Principle is, quite obviously, a fundamental redefinition of objectivity and subjectivity in terms of temporal passage.[19]

A noted American philosopher and authority on Whitehead, George L. Kline, perceptively noted many years ago that Whitehead's concept may be helpfully illustrated in comparison with J. M. E. McTaggart's well-known analysis of time.[20] In Whitehead's case, the past objectified events literally serve as the material cause (in Aristotle's sense) of present activity. Hence his 'actual entities' can thus be ordered, in analogy with McTaggart's 'B-series', as 'earlier' and 'later': earlier entities are those that serve as objectified data in the constitution of the later. This causal relationship of past to present is further asymmetrical, in that the relations of present (or 'later') entities to their past (or 'earlier') antecedents are always *internal* (or constitutive), while the relations of past entities to subsequent (present) entities are always *external* to (i.e., nonconstitutive) and unaffected by their inclusion in the self-constitution of some later event.

This ontology of present (subjective) and past (objective) events gives rise, however, to a dramatic departure from McTaggart. In Whitehead's case there can be no such thing as a determinate 'future' event.

In contrast to 'the present' as locus of activity, and 'the past' as locus of determinate potentiality, 'the future', in Whitehead's account, is merely the locus of unrealised possibilities that may or may not come to be actualised in any of a variety of ways. A present moment is (to use an awkward phrase) as far forward into time as one can go, since there is nothing further on or beyond the present activity of the self-constitution or concrescence of actual occasions. In contrast to McTaggart, the Whiteheadian 'B-series', the asymmetrical causal relation of earlier to later events, thus does *not* entail that there are 'future events' of some determinate sort, moving steadily ever closer to and finally 'sliding into the shining present', and then moving out the 'other end' of the present and receding ever farther into the past.

There is nothing in Whitehead's account, then, analogous to McTaggart's 'A-series' of events, unrolling like fixed images on a spool of motion-picture film and giving rise to the illusion of future–present–past time as a 'moving image of eternity'. If one were to press this image in Whitehead's case: instead of 'unrolling' an already-produced picture film, the passage of time would be like the actual ongoing manufacturing of each successive frame of the not-yet-completed film. Each successive present moment would consist of composing yet another new 'frame' (episode or quantum of experience) as a unique synthesis of elements found in the preceding frames, and adding this new one on to the front of the ever-lengthening film strip.

No matter how incomplete the metaphors one employs, the important point to be borne in mind is that Whitehead's event ontology is intended to provide an account of time that squares with common experience without rendering that experience illusory or reducing it to something utterly unlike it, as Einstein and positivist philosophers like Hans Reichenbach, Adolf Grünbaum, or Richard Gale have proposed. Whitehead also avoids the troublesome proposals from Bergson and Alexander to elevate time itself to the status of some mysterious metaphysical abstraction 'within which' our temporal experiences somehow occur.

Whitehead and Wittgenstein: The Question of Metaphysics

The unorthodox dimension of my preceding account is that it portrays Whitehead as far more deeply embedded in the context and conversation of early twentieth-century British analytic philosophy than is customarily recognised. That said, however, certainly of the three members of the Cambridge trinity named above, Whitehead had the least influence on the formative education, let alone on the later substantive views, of Wittgenstein. Beyond a few polite invitations to dine with the Whiteheads while he was a young student at Cambridge, there is no historical evidence that Wittgenstein spent much time with, paid much attention to, or absorbed much influence from Whitehead while the latter was a teaching fellow at Cambridge. Whitehead is mentioned briefly in a few terse sections of the *Tractatus*,[21] where Wittgenstein modifies or challenges certain hidden or faulty presuppositions in the *Principia*. But it is Russell who dominates in this work. Wittgenstein never turns his attention to Whitehead in the manner in which he studied Moore, for example, in *On Certainty*. By the same token, there is no evidence that Whitehead read the *Tractatus*; in fact, by the time Wittgenstein returned to Cambridge for the second time in the 1930s, Whitehead had already long since departed for his appointment at Harvard and frankly was, by this time, too advanced both in years and in career to have taken much notice of the philosophy of the later Wittgenstein emanating by word of mouth from Cambridge, England, to Cambridge, Massachusetts, in the 1930s and 1940s.

Indeed, it is entirely in accord with convention to describe Whitehead as a philosopher stubbornly engaged during his Harvard years in continuing to try to do the very things that both the earlier and the later Wittgenstein said could not be done and should not be done. Though I mean to question this conventional wisdom, it is certainly apparent that Whitehead was, as we have noted, primarily interested in accounting for time, causality, unity, and plurality and in characterising 'Nature' as such and 'the World' as such, and even in assessing the nature of God and of the relationship of God and the World in his mature cosmology. Yet, Wittgenstein remarks famously[22] that 'the World' is the totality of facts, and so is not itself a fact; hence, phrases like 'the World' and 'Nature' name nothing of which there can be meaningful discourse.[23]

Later, in the *Philosophical Investigations*, Wittgenstein writes, 'What *we* do is to bring words back from their metaphysical to their everyday use.'[24] Whitehead, like Russell, however, mistrusted this 'everyday use' of words, and so he could be said to have been engaged in precisely the opposite task of taking words *from* their everyday use and refining them for metaphysical 'precision'. In Whitehead's case, this resulted in a technical vocabulary and categorial structure for metaphysics that is difficult, arcane, and frequently off-putting, quite apart from the decided disinterest that his later metaphysical themes themselves seem to arouse among a great many philosophers.

Whatever else he repudiated during his later period, Wittgenstein never abandoned the view that philosophy must tolerate *nothing* metaphysical, that the correct method in philosophy would be (as he concludes the *Tractatus*) that 'whenever someone wanted to say something metaphysical, to show him that he had given no meaning to certain signs in his sentences' (6.53). The later Wittgenstein describes the task of philosophy as clarification and description, not theorising, and never 'explanation'.[25] Metaphysics, in this view, as Joachim Schulte remarks, 'is a formal, systematic theory imitating natural science but (unlike natural science) necessarily mired in senselessness because of its language and theme'.[26] Once again, based upon the sample of Whitehead I have offered – his 'theory of time and temporality' – it must surely seem that Whitehead's later philosophy represents just such a systematic theory, imitating natural science. Just as surely, the elaborate cosmology of his great work, *Process and Reality*, setting forth an alternative cosmology to Newtonianism, describing the geometry of spacetime, and commenting upon the Primordial and Consequent natures of God, must seem like a grand, speculative metaphysical theory of the sort that Wittgenstein did not regard as the proper domain of philosophy and that many contemporary followers of Wittgenstein must still regard as the most alien and unintelligible form of *Sprachspiel*.[27] (Or what Wittgenstein himself might have labelled 'gassing'!)

We need not, of course, simply grant the young Wittgenstein without argument his exceedingly restrictive view of philosophy in the *Tractatus*, nor must we simply accept as apodictic his rather conventional (for the period) antimetaphysical rhetoric. If we set that aside and simply ask about the quality of the philosophy involved, I cannot escape the feeling (and it is only that) that Whitehead's account of time and temporality, and his elaborate description of the problem of causality (which I analyse in detail elsewhere)[28] present a fundamentally sound picture or working model of what is meant when we speak of time or of what is meant when we speak of causality in the natural world. When Wittgenstein himself writes,

We cannot compare a process with 'the passage of time' – there is no such thing – but only with another process (such as the working of a chronometer). Hence we can describe the lapse of time only by relying on some other process.[29]

It would not be the least bit misleading to describe Whitehead's work as providing a detailed gloss, and a fuller and more adequate commentary, on just what this terse comment might actually entail.

On the whole, the particulars of Whitehead's 'picture' seem to me more in keeping with what must finally be correct than do alternatives proposed that seem to me wholly intuitive, unverifiable, and often even wildly counterfactual. Many alternative accounts of time, moreover, are put forward by philosophers who in other respects hold themselves exemplars of exact, antimetaphysical philosophy, or by physicists who nevertheless rest their case on not one single shred of empirical detail either placed in evidence or conceivably so placed. The tendency to ungrounded speculation, it seems, runs deep in Western culture, and it is especially pronounced among modal logicians and theoretical physicists. Perhaps we should politely say that Whitehead is firmly rooted in a long-standing tradition of grand speculative metaphysics emanating from Cambridge University, spanning the period from Isaac Newton to Stephen Hawking.

But such remarks merely divert attention from what Heidegger calls 'the *question* concerning metaphysics'. My own approach has been to regard the elaborate categorial scheme put forth by Whitehead not as a literal account or as a 'theory of nature' in the usual realist sense but as a heuristic device designed to suggest – by implication, analogy, and the use of metaphorical language – aspects of the real that we must grasp. As such, an account of time or causality like Whitehead's is – like an account of the Bohr hydrogen atom, or a description of the tunnelling effect in quantum mechanics – not a *Vorstellung*, not a literal mental picture or representation – but rather a *bildliche Darstellung*, a public model or representation in the sense described by Wittgenstein's Viennese predecessors, Hertz and Boltzmann.[30] These are meant to be models that show publicly what is the best account we can give of experience, not to substitute as the literal truth of experience. And anyone who has had the interesting experience of trying to teach a first course on quantum theory to students thoroughly enmeshed in a Newtonian classical worldview knows full well that such models can only *show* what cannot be *said*.[31]

We need not rely on physics alone for examples of the kind of modelling I have in mind. The much-debated reliance on 'folk psychology' in cognitive science – including the description of human and animal actions in terms of levels of intentionality by Daniel Dennett[32] – provides further illustrations of a much-criticised, but apparently indispensable reliance on some form of modelling to develop economical accounts of what is the case. In all of these instances, the models, drawings, analogies, and diagrams invariably are meant to illustrate, to tease out aspects of the real, without attempting to provide the literal one-to-one correspondence between the logical structures of descriptions and of the facts themselves that the early Wittgenstein required of propositions. Instead, like the propositions of the *Tractatus* itself, such models – including Whitehead's models and metaphors of temporal passage and causality – aim to picture, portray, or *show* (but do not say) what must be the case.

In sharp distinction to most other process philosophers, I have long argued that Whitehead never meant his metaphysical categories to be taken literally. Rather, he seems to take for granted the modern physicist's belief that he is merely providing heuristic models – *bildlichen Darstellungen* – that would aid readers in the interpretation and understanding of experience itself.[33] If this is basically correct, then the disagreement with Wittgenstein is portrayed much differently.

The young Wittgenstein did not believe that such *Darstellungen* could be given for issues like values, ethics, or religious belief. One approaches these matters by defining the limits of descriptive discourse, distinguishing what can be said from what can merely be shown. Some of what Whitehead was interested in saying could, according to the early Wittgenstein, only be shown. Once the strict, univocal view of language and logic in the *Tractatus* is abandoned, however, it is no longer clear that Wittgenstein is entitled to draw so sharp a distinction between what can be shown or said, or indeed, regarding what might be 'shown' precisely by being (in a heuristic or metaphorical sense) 'said'. In any case, much of Whitehead's interest in physical cosmology, the major portion of his so-called metaphysics, is more of a piece with those accounts of objects and states of affairs that *can* be given, or else it consists of accounts of principles (like those of the *Tractatus* itself, or else like Hertz's underlying principles of physical economy, mathematical elegance, and least action) that are heuristic in the sense that they can be indicated through pseudo-propositions that, once understood, can be discarded.[34]

Whitehead, Wittgenstein, and the Critique of Enlightenment

Such considerations notwithstanding, however, there is simply no evidence that Whitehead, apart from his participation with Russell in the *Principia* project, ever exerted any meaningful influence on the development of Wittgenstein's thought; nor did Whitehead seem to take much notice of Wittgenstein in his own later philosophy. Surprisingly, however, there are a number of parallels. Some of these are merely interesting curiosities; others seem quite significant.

Straight away, for example, we notice that both philosophers were, for substantial portions of their productive lives, expatriates. I commented at the outset of this chapter on the obvious but routinely overlooked importance of this metaxalogical condition[35] – this cultural betweenness – for understanding Wittgenstein, who, though he did not wish to become (as he put it in a letter to John Maynard Keynes) an 'imitation Englishman',[36] felt compelled to accept British citizenship in lieu of German following the *Anschluss*. Much less is known about the impact of Whitehead's decision – made, to be sure, under considerably less duress – to leave London for Massachusetts. The change of intellectual climate certainly seems to have inspired a freedom of expression and a blossoming of interests unpursued in the British context.

Second, although I have contrasted Whitehead's later literary style with the terse and severely economical writing of Wittgenstein, still there are parallels. Whitehead's style of writing in his most technical work is difficult and web-like. He practises a kind of recurrence method – continuously cycling back through topics already introduced and considered at some length, adding additional information or insights with each pass.[37] The later Wittgenstein was similarly nonsystematic and recursive in his exposition. In the brief preface to the *Philosophical Investigations*, Wittgenstein describes his dilemma of being able only to provide 'sketches of landscapes' which he is compelled to 'criss-cross in every direction', yielding a book he characterises as his 'album' or as a kind of travelogue, compiled piecemeal 'in the course of these long and involved journeyings'.[38] Both writers, apparently, were attempting work of such complexity and intellectual demand, and were so inside their respective projects, that linear, systematic, topical exposition was apparently not possible. And in Whitehead's case, even though committed to providing an expository account of physical and metaphysical theories grounded, after the example of Mach, in experience, nevertheless he gravitated, as I argued earlier, increasingly towards the explicitly heuristic expression of the later Wittgenstein: in essence, we must 'ignore what I'm saying; grasp what I'm trying to show'.

Finally, it is interesting and worthy of note in its own right that both Whitehead and Wittgenstein received formal training principally in science and mathematics, while neither of these great philosophers received any substantial formal training in philosophy. Thus, in marked contrast to Moore, Russell, Collingwood, and many other contemporaries, neither Whitehead nor Wittgenstein was actually trained to pursue, nor did either apparently intend to pursue, the vocation for which they became most famous. Although it sounds shocking to say this, both were amateur philosophers. I do not mean, of course, that either was deficient in the practice of philosophy; rather, by 'amateur' I mean they were largely self-taught and self-directed, and they were informally educated as to what philosophy is and how it is done. This fact has the particular and important consequence that neither philosopher was ever forcibly indoctrinated through systematic study and apprenticeship into a community of discourse. Instead, each found his way into that community on his own. This led both to be perceived as mavericks and, I think, permitted both to be pathbreakers rather than contributors to philosophy practised simply as a 'normal science' industry (in Thomas Kuhn's sense).

Wittgenstein is, of course, rather famous for this. It is well known that he deplored 'professionalisation'.[39] Janik and Toulmin report[40] that Wittgenstein read comparatively little philosophy and saw himself as being none the worse for being a self-taught philosopher. Georg Henrik von Wright notes, in his famous biographical sketch of 1954, that

Wittgenstein 'had done no systematic reading in the classics of philosophy. He could read only what he could wholeheartedly assimilate.' Von Wright further notes that of the several philosophers Wittgenstein did read, and of the very few he could countenance, he (like Whitehead) apparently enjoyed Plato.[41]

Norman Malcolm, for his part, recalls that Wittgenstein once remarked to David Pinsent that Wittgenstein was 'extremely outraged', upon finally reading some of the philosophers whose historical reputations he had heretofore somewhat naïvely presumed was warranted, at discovering the 'stupid mistakes' they made.[42] Presumably among these stupid mistakes was Augustine's 'theory of language acquisition' as an ostensive 'naming game' that Wittgenstein found in the *Confessions*. What Wittgenstein scholars frequently describe as this 'Augustinian theory' of language, with which Wittgenstein opens the *Philosophical Investigations*, serves as an important symbolic and rhetorical device – a kind of foil – for the later Wittgenstein, against which his own view of 'language' as constituting an indefinite number of distinct and nonhierarchical 'language games', loosely grouped according to family resemblance, is developed as an alternative.

But historians of philosophy would quickly object that it is clearly not Augustine, or anything central to Augustine's own philosophy, that Wittgenstein is attacking. Rather, the 'Augustinian theory' in fact names the view of language found in the British and in the *Wienerkreis*-positivists' 'logical' reading of the *Tractatus* and presupposed in the *Principia*'s efforts to ground mathematics in logic as the preeminent foundational language. What is rejected as unpromising and infeasible is likewise not Augustine's own philosophy, with which Wittgenstein was presumably not concerned, but the later efforts of contemporaries like Otto Neurath or A. J. Ayer, inspired by the logical interpretation of the *Tractatus*, to develop an incorrigible language in which philosophical perplexities would not arise.

In this sense, Wittgenstein's infrequent, selective, and sometimes idiosyncratic appropriation of the history of philosophy is somewhat comparable to Whitehead's, as in the example of John Locke cited earlier. Whitehead, however, was less impatient with his predecessors than was Wittgenstein, tending to be instructed from them by inspiration, and willing for the most part to overlook their 'stupid mistakes'. Whitehead's sharpest barbs are aimed at Kant and at the so-called epistemological turn in philosophy after the Enlightenment. Whitehead portrays his own later philosophy as an attempt to recur to 'pre-Kantian' modes of thought, a revealing but nonetheless problematic assertion that has not aided in a sympathetic approach to his own thought, particularly in Europe.[43] Nonetheless, the later Whitehead found his way from ahistorical analysis back into the historical tradition of philosophy, within which constructive philosophical thought is conceived of as a dialogue with the positions of philosophers in the past. Wittgenstein apparently did not, in the end, find anything in that self-defined historical tradition worthy of detailed pursuit, and he remained, as did his colleagues in both British analytic and European logical empiricism, largely outside of it.

Both philosophers produced sharply divergent points of view in two distinct phases of a career. The degree of discontinuity between the earlier and later work of each philosopher is a much-disputed matter in the interpretation of both. There is, I believe, something quite remarkable about this Heideggerian *Verkehren*, this presumed radical conversion or transformation in the later orientation of both philosophers. This permits me to turn at last to my concluding observation concerning the enduring influence of both philosophers.

In his aforementioned biographical note on Wittgenstein, von Wright comments about this perceived *Verkehren* of Wittgenstein:

The young Wittgenstein had learned from Frege and Russell. His problems were in part theirs. The later Wittgenstein, in my view, has no ancestors in the history of thought. His work signals a radical departure from previously existing paths of philosophy.[44]

In a note to the second edition of this sketch, von Wright goes on to observe,

I have seen this statement, and the one preceding it, contested. But I think they are substantially correct and also important. The *Tractatus* belongs in a definite tradition in European philosophy, extending back beyond Frege and Russell at least to Leibniz. Wittgenstein's so-called 'later philosophy', as I see it, is quite different. Its *spirit* is unlike anything I know in Western thought and in many ways opposed to aims and methods in traditional philosophy.[45]

I do not now propose to quarrel directly with Professor von Wright, who was attempting to refute any suggestion of indebtedness or influence, during this later period of Wittgenstein's, to the work of G. E. Moore. The sharp differences from Moore's specific philosophy, upon which Von Wright quite rightly insists, are clearly apparent in Wittgenstein's detailed commentary upon Moore in *Über Gewissheit*,[46] in which Wittgenstein transforms Moore's epistemological and ultimately metaphysical claims regarding what we can know indubitably into a dramatically different, attitudinal account of the *language* of certitude.

I want to call attention to something else entirely. Although I have labelled this a 'critique of Enlightenment' according to prevailing philosophical fashion, in fact there is nothing so clear or precise in what

I now present. There is, I will argue, a strain of irony emerging from the rarefied philosophical air of Cambridge that, surprisingly, represents a rather severe distrust of, and even a reaction against, philosophy itself. While this reaction against the power of philosophical reason stops short of traditional scepticism, it does place a heavy emphasis upon fallibility. It would not be unfair to label it 'ironic' in the Socratic sense. Wittgenstein and the later Whitehead, I will argue, are representative of this tendency. Moore, in some respects at least, belongs to this reaction as well. Let me proceed to illustrate.

Russell and Frege, along with the Viennese positivists Schlick, Carnap, Reichenbach, and Neurath, all sought to provide an 'exact' scientific philosophy and logically precise language. Frege's work on sense and reference and Whitehead and Russell's *Principia Mathematica* were considered pioneering efforts towards this goal. All of them apparently took it for granted that the early Wittgenstein of the *Tractatus* both honoured this commitment to exactitude and promised its fulfilment.

The later Wittgenstein, by contrast, as we know, was extremely sceptical about the possibility of such 'exact' philosophy, always in regard to ethical propositions, and increasingly concerning metamathematical and metatheoretical conceptualisations in his later years. Merrill Hintikka and Jaakko Hintikka make this observation in the course of a brief discussion of Wittgenstein's 'finitistic, constructivistic . . . anti-platonist' philosophy of mathematics. Wittgenstein's later beliefs in language as a universal medium, in the ineffability of semantics, and in the consequent view that 'there cannot be any metatheoretical considerations about language' lead him consistently, they argue, to a 'descriptivistic and apparently resigned attitude to ordinary language' *and* to a concomitant 'highly critical attitude to mathematical, especially metamathematical, practice'.[47]

To a surprising degree, Whitehead, the early philosopher of mathematics and co-author of the *Principia*, developed, quite independently, a similar view of logic and of mathematical formalisation. One of the later Whitehead's most widely quoted, scandalous passages states: 'It is more important that a proposition be interesting than that it be true'; another is, 'In philosophical discussion, the merest hint of dogmatic certainty as to finality of statement is an exhibition of folly.'[48] Whitehead goes on to observe, 'the chief error in philosophy is overstatement . . . [which] consists [in part] in a false estimate of logical procedure in respect to certainty, and in respect to premises'.[49] And the co-author of *Principia Mathematica* then suggests that 'philosophy has been misled by the example of mathematics'.[50]

The later Wittgenstein and the later Whitehead represent a growing movement towards the position finally formalised in Kurt Gödel's

Incompleteness Theorem that the sort of exactitude sought by the likes of Russell and Frege was a massive deception and unattainable. Moore, as I read him in this context, at least to some extent shared in this ironic attitude towards philosophy itself. Permit me to explain.

Wittgenstein's original mentor, Russell, was intelligent, quick, sharp, and, above all, clever; he disdained ordinary language and common sense in particular. Moore, by contrast, often portrayed himself as slow and somewhat dull-witted, and this made him cautious. He was trained in the Cambridge classics stream, rather than the science curriculum; he distrusted mathematics; he essentially abandoned attempts to employ formal logic in his analysis of common sense. Indeed, it seems that he apparently distrusted 'clever' people. In contrast to Russell in particular, Moore had a high regard for the world as we find it and for the abilities of ordinary people to get along in this world. He spent his efforts as a philosopher focusing on the meanings of everyday language and propositions and, like Hume, invested his efforts towards putting clever 'false' philosophers and their fantastic theories about such language and ordinary knowledge to flight.

It seems to me that there is a rather stunning consensus on this ironic, antiphilosophical attitude that helps to pinpoint the origins of a historical dynamic that only now, in the ensuing century, are we in a position to appreciate fully. I would summarise it as follows.

In the Cambridge Trinity of Whitehead, Russell, and Moore, two radically different streams of the Western philosophical tradition are refracted. The first is thoroughly Enlightenment and modernist, stressing exactness and precision (which von Wright traces through Russell and the early Whitehead, back 'at least as far as Leibniz'). The second stream emerging from Cambridge, however, has a history even older and more venerable than the first stream as traced by von Wright. This second, alternative perspective on what philosophy is and how it is best pursued stretches back through Hume at least to Gassendi and to other Renaissance scientists and humanists who relied on history, custom, and textual evidence as well as on experiment and mathematical modelling in the quest for scientific truth and philosophical wisdom.

With the exception of Hume, none of the earlier representatives of this alternative Western tradition completely disavowed the power of science, nor did they shrink from the quest for verifiable knowledge. They were not, by and large, outright sceptics; nor were they early harbingers of the contemporary postmodernist attack on reason, rationality, and objectivity. Rather, in this alternative, long-standing philosophical tradition we perceive a fear of the growing hegemony, for example, of Galileo's exclusive reliance on mathematical method in the sciences. To critics like Gassendi and, later, Hume, such an approach offered a misleading promise of precision at the expense of engagement with the actual, just as the philosopher's Cartesian concomitant reliance on mathematical logic and logical method seemed to promise the possibility of (a false) precision in philosophy. Gassendi and his followers lost this quarrel, and they have been largely forgotten to history in comparison with Galileo and Descartes. And thus it became this triumphant modernist–Enlightenment faith in progress and perfectibility, based upon the power of human reason, that Hume was obliged to attack from the margins of the dominant culture.

Janik and Toulmin comment on the 'neo-Humean (and so pre-Kantian) empiricism of Moore, Russell and their colleagues',[51] but they do not follow up this cultural setting with anything like the attention they devote to the Viennese. For many historians (and I think this is a serious mistake), to be steeped in Hume, as Russell was, is to be steeped in the long-standing tradition of British empiricism. But, I would argue in contrast, to be steeped in Hume, the apostate from 'false philosophy', the author of the histories of England, and the advocate of tradition and a fuller understanding of British 'common life', is to be steeped in another attitude altogether – one that results either in outright philosophical scepticism or else in a tempering of the quest for exactness with an acute, ironic awareness of fallibility. Whitehead writes,

Metaphysical categories are not dogmatic statements of the obvious, they are tentative formulations of the ultimate generalities. . . . The useful function of philosophy is to promote the most general systematisation of civilised thought. There is a constant reaction between specialism and common sense. It is the part of the special sciences to modify common sense. Philosophy is the welding of imagination and common sense into a restraint upon specialists, and also into an enlargement of their imaginations. By providing the generic notions philosophy should make it easier to conceive the infinite variety of specific instances which rest unrealised in the womb of nature. . . . Error [by which Whitehead means here, logical imprecision, vagueness, ambiguity] is the price we pay for progress.[52]

The oft-noted feature of the early Wittgenstein is that his *Tractatus* came to embody the premier statement in the twentieth century of the tendency towards exactness and precision, and, in a sense, could be portrayed as the culmination of the Enlightenment–positivist project. Wittgenstein, as we know, was extremely uncomfortable with this reading of the *Tractatus* by Russell, Schlick, and others, though his reasons for this discomfort were never adequately conveyed to his puzzled followers – and, indeed, were all but unintelligible to them. Wittgenstein subsequently proposed explicitly to abandon the central role of logic derived from the earlier *Principia Mathematica* of Russell and Whitehead, relegating logic to the status, at best, of one of many descriptive 'languages' whose particular syntax and even semantics could be discerned only by entering into the varieties of human practices within which each originates. When this shift became evident, Russell commented bitterly,

> The later Wittgenstein . . . seems to have grown tired of serious thinking and to have invented a doctrine which would make such an activity unnecessary. . . . We are now told that it is not the world that we are to try to understand, but only sentences, and it is assumed that all sentences can count as true except those uttered by philosophers.[53]

I am now suggesting that the later Wittgenstein, by rejecting his earlier work and this Enlightenment–modernist reading of it, developed an utterly unique variation of a second stream of tradition present all along, but never named, at Cambridge: namely, this deep-seated *distrust* of exact philosophy and of those Hume had labelled 'false philosophers'. Precisely the measure of Wittgenstein's uniqueness and his greatness is that, once again, the *Philosophical Investigations* (and also the *Bemerkungen, On Certainty*, and other work from this later period) represent premier documents in this ironic reaction against the preeminent status of logic and philosophical rationalism.

An eminent European Wittgenstein scholar, Joachim Schulte, provides evidence for my interpretation in a discarded draft of Wittgenstein's foreword to the *Bemerkungen* of 1930. There Wittgenstein wrote,

> This book is written for those who can appreciate its spirit. This is a spirit different from that of the main current of the European and American civilisation of which we all are part . . . whose expression is the industry, architecture, music, fascism, and socialism of our time.[54]

And what is this 'main current' of European and American civilisation against which Wittgenstein sets himself? Presumably it is that attitude, that orientation, represented by the 'logical' rather than the 'ethical' reading of the *Tractatus*, that positivism with which Wittgenstein consistently refused to be associated and assimilated, that belief against which virtually all his later writing is set: the quest for totality and closure, the belief that logical precision and clarity in all human affairs are in the end an attainable goal of philosophical reflection, that all else is nonsense – in sum, that confidence in the final power of reason above all else that is the social legacy of the Enlightenment. (Indeed, we find Wittgenstein here coming dangerously close, like Collingwood, to accusing his academic colleagues of fascism.)

Like Moore and Whitehead, this later Wittgenstein is not an enemy of reason and does not discard the desire to know the truth. But all three exhibit a strong sense of Socratic irony: they are clearly distrustful of the arrogance of reason, suspicious of the promise of easy attainment of clarity, and most of all doubtful about the Enlightenment promise of progress towards perfectibility of human knowledge. Our Austrian engineer and logician, like Moore and like the later Whitehead, came to criticise the chief artefacts of social engineering and to see in these products the manifestation of a fundamental flaw in the dominant cultural worldview, or what Wittgenstein in this passage calls 'spirit', rather than a casual or unfortunate mistake in some specific detail or procedure. How else are we to understand the mature Wittgenstein's distrust of social engineering and of the overconfidence of social engineers like Russell,[55] his utter contempt for the high-flown moral theorising of professional philosophers like Schlick (whose work he regarded as 'twaddle'),[56] or his evident belief that the most important aspects of human existence, such as ethics and morality, could be shown or seen but could not be 'said'.

Galileo's project of 'reforming' science, the Cartesian project of 'reforming' philosophy, and the Enlightenment project of 'reforming' humanity itself are all expressions of this modernist confidence that Reason constitutes a wholly self-sufficient resource, capable of defining the Good in terms of practical, desirable human aims and goals and setting forth strategies for the eventual realisation of these goals. Russell in philosophy, logic, and mathematics, and the members of the Bloomsbury circle in aesthetics and literature, are typical representatives of these tendencies. It was beyond question to them, moreover, that the young Wittgenstein of the *Tractatus* and the young Whitehead of the *Principia* and *The Principles of Natural Knowledge* were to be numbered among them.

There developed at Cambridge, I am arguing, another, rival view – one that perceived the Good as indefinable, as that in terms of which all else is defined, as that towards which all things tend as a limit. Reason is not an expression of freedom or an instrument for engineering a certain path to perfection. Reason is employed not in the quest for certainty but in the quest for the Good, and it has the Good as its limit. That the Good is beyond definition, and that towards which all things tend, can be shown but cannot be said. This, of course, is precisely Moore's position in the *Principia Ethica*, and the famous 'naturalistic fallacy' described there is only a fallacy if this larger orientation is adopted. Despite Wittgenstein's distaste for that work of Moore's, this fundamental orientation is also his in the closing of the *Tractatus*, and ever afterward. In a conversation in 1929 he is reported to have said,

In ethics, people are forever trying to find a way of saying something which, in the nature of things, is not and can never be expressed. We know a priori: anything which one might give by way of a definition of the Good – it can never be anything but a misunderstanding.[57]

It is in this sense that we can speak of Wittgenstein's influence from Moore, and his commonality with Whitehead. All three reveal themselves in interesting ways as increasingly uncomfortable with the fundamental tenets and intellectual orientation of modernism. As a result, all three, each in his own way, developed a critique of the Enlightenment confidence in the power of Reason and its connection with freedom, progress, certainty, and perfectibility. That the later Wittgenstein ends up with Moore and with the later Whitehead arrayed *against* modernism is all the more remarkable when we recognise just how thoroughly both the younger Wittgenstein and the younger Whitehead began, or at least were taken without question by their contemporaries to be, on the side of the moderns. The rejection of the primacy of logic, the desire to recur to 'pre-Kantian modes of thought',[58] the distrust of certainty, the endorsement of common sense and the wisdom of common language and common life, the reconception of metaphysics as hypothetical, heuristic, and grounded in experience, and a belief in the ineffability of semantics and the indefinability of the Good, however, together link these three Cambridge philosophers in an ironic challenge to the worldview of their contemporaries and place them thoroughly on the side of the ancients against the moderns, as critics of the false promise of Enlightenment.[59]

Notes

1. Originally published in Jaakko Hintikka and Klaus Puhl, editors: *Ludwig Wittgenstein and the 20th Century British Tradition in Philosophy*. 'Proceedings of the 17th International Wittgenstein Congress' (Vienna: Verlag Hölder–Pichler–Tempsky, 1995), pp. 122–48; revised version published in *Process and Analysis*, ed. George W. Shields (Albany: State University of New York Press, 2003), pp. 67–93.
2. Justus Hartnack in the second edition of his seminal study, *Wittgenstein and Modern Philosophy*, prophesied in 1986: 'The intense interest in the philosophy of Wittgenstein probably has reached its peak, to decline in coming years' (p. xii). But about such matters, Whitehead had earlier observed: 'Philosophy *never* reverts to its old position after the shock of a great philosopher' (cf. *Process and Reality*, Corrected Edition, 1978, p. 11, a point to which Hartnack goes on to assent [p. xiii]).

    In 1992, I was delighted to have the honour of publishing in my philosophy series at the State University of New York Press an English translation of Joachim Schulte's 'Introduction' to Wittgenstein. Like Hartnack, I, too, supposed that the tremendous interest in Wittgenstein must by now have peaked, and so I was unprepared for the tremendous

interest this fine volume generated. It became, instantly, a book that outsold every other volume of philosophy published in that series, indicating that interest in Wittgenstein remains extremely high in the United States, as it does throughout the world.
3. Allan Janik and Stephen Toulmin, *Wittgenstein's Vienna*, p. 22.
4. New York: Random House, 1959.
5. Janik and Toulmin, *Wittgenstein's Vienna*, p. 107.
6. Norman Malcolm reports on the 'great distaste' that Wittgenstein had for English culture: cf. *Ludwig Wittgenstein: A Memoir*, p. 26.
7. Cf. Part I of Collingwood's *Essay on Metaphysics*. See also the discussions of 'tacit knowledge' in Michael Polanyi, *Personal Knowledge*.
8. For a more detailed account, see *The Rehabilitation of Whitehead*, chapter X. More recently, see physicist Ronald Desmet's analysis, 'An Aesthetic Comparison of Einstein's and Whitehead's Theory of Gravity', pp. 33–46.
9. New York: Macmillan, 1925.
10. New York: Macmillan, 1929. The 'Corrected Edition', as noted above, was reissued in 1978. All references in this essay are to that second edition.
11. Victor Lowe recounts the difficulties Whitehead encountered in delivering these lectures the year after Arthur Eddington, describing them as 'a fiasco'. Cf. Victor Lowe, *Alfred North Whitehead*, vol. 2, p. 250. See also his earlier, somewhat more detailed account: 'Whitehead's Gifford Lectures', pp. 329–38.
12. Lowe describes Whitehead as 'one of the most quoted philosophers of our century – and one of the least understood' (*Alfred North Whitehead*, vol. 1, p. 3.) I think this is fundamentally correct.
13. Cf. Lowe's chapter on 'The Migration to Harvard' in *Alfred North Whitehead*, vol. 2, esp. pp. 142ff.
14. Not much is actually known about Whitehead's participation in the Bloomsbury circle; Victor Lowe tends to discount this.
15. Such a transformation from analytic to 'Continental' figure is much discussed in the case of Richard Rorty; cf., for example, David Hall, *Richard Rorty*. Tracing a similar, more recent evolution of Hilary Putnam, Professor Edward Pols (in his 1987 Presidential Address for the Metaphysical Society of America) suggested that Putnam was on the road to becoming, by intention, 'the Compleat Continental Philosopher'; see Pols, 'On Knowing Directly', pp. 229–30.
16. Cf. John Locke, *An Essay Concerning Human Understanding*, Book II, chapter XIV, sec. 1; cf. Whitehead, *Process and Reality* (1929), pp. 222–3.
17. Cf. Alfred North Whitehead, *Adventures of Ideas*, Part III, chapter XI: 'Objects & Subjects'. This constitutes the main text of Whitehead's Presidential Address for the American Philosophical Association in 1931.
18. Cf. *Process and Reality*, Corrected Edition (1978), pp. 157–67.

19. I have not bothered to honour the distinction, so dear to Whitehead scholars, between the monistic theory of events in *Science and the Modern World* and the later Leibnizian and reductionistic account in *Process and Reality*, which I regard as a blind alley subsequently abandoned by Whitehead. For more on this, see my *The Rehabilitation of Whitehead*.
20. Cf. George L. Kline, 'Form, Concrescence, and Concretum' in *Explorations in Whitehead's Philosophy*, pp. 104–46. See also Kline, '"Present", "Past", and "Future" as Categoreal Terms', pp. 215–35.
21. Wittgenstein, *Tractatus Logico-Philosophicus*, e.g., at 5.252 and 5.452.
22. Wittgenstein, *Tractatus Logico-Philosophicus*, 1.1.
23. Cf. Hartnack, *Wittgenstein and Modern Philosophy*, p. 39.
24. Wittgenstein, *Philosophical Investigations*, Part I, sec. 116.
25. Cf. Wittgenstein, *Philosophical Investigations*, sec. 109.
26. Cf. Joachim Schulte, *Wittgenstein: An Introduction*, p. 43.
27. Although he speaks of death, God, and things beyond the world in the closing sections of the *Tractatus*, Wittgenstein denies that these can be elucidated meaningfully. In *Philosophical Investigations* he remarks (sec. 119): 'The results of philosophy are the uncovering of one or another piece of plain nonsense and of bumps that the understanding has got by running its head against the limits of language. These bumps make us see the value of the discovery.' It is hard to resist the inference that much of what Whitehead wrote would be classified as 'one or another piece of plain nonsense'.
28. Cf. Lucas, *The Rehabilitation of Whitehead*, pp. 87–91.
29. Wittgenstein, *Tractatus Logico-Philosophicus*, 6.3611.
30. See Janik and Toulmin's excellent account of this in relation to the *Tractatus* in *Wittgenstein's Vienna*, chapter 6, esp. pp. 139–40, 179–85.
31. I note in passing that this connection is mine; Whitehead mentions Hertz (referred to as Herz) twice in passing in *Science and the Modern World*, and not at all subsequently.
32. Cf. Dennett's essays, 'Intentional Systems' in *Brainstorms* and also 'Intentional Systems in Cognitive Ethology', pp. 343–90.
33. In comparison with Kant, whose Categories of Understanding sought to explain how all *knowledge* was possible, Donald Sherburne aptly suggests that Whitehead's categorial scheme aimed to define those more general conditions or constraints that make *experience itself* (of whatever sort, in whatever possible world) possible. Cf. Sherburne, *A Key to Whitehead's Process and Reality*, p. 41.
34. I read much of Whitehead's later metaphysical work as of this sort: once the basic principles are grasped, the detailed accounts can be discarded. I was much influenced by Wittgenstein's account of conceptual modelling in the *Tractatus* at 6.341 and 6.342. I confess that this interpretation

was not well understood or well received by those whose investment in literal metaphysics is greater than my own. Cf. George R. Lucas, *The Genesis of Modern Process Thought*, pp. 211–17.
35. I borrow this term from my colleague William Desmond. See his *Desire, Dialectic, and Otherness* and *Being and Between*.
36. 18 March 1938; quoted in Schulte, *Wittgenstein: An Introduction*, p. 11.
37. Lewis S. Ford, in his elaborate reconstruction of the phases of development of Whitehead's later metaphysical views, provides this account of his approach towards his written work: cf. *The Emergence of Whitehead's Metaphysics: 1925–1929*.
38. Wittgenstein, *Philosophical Investigations*, p. v. Cf. Hartnack, *Wittgenstein and Modern Philosophy*, pp. 100–1.
39. Cf. Malcolm, *Ludwig Wittgenstein: A Memoir*, p. 28.
40. Cf. Malcolm, *Ludwig Wittgenstein: A Memoir*, p. 176.
41. Cf. Malcolm, *Ludwig Wittgenstein: A Memoir*, pp. 18–19.
42. Here I cite Malcolm's account of Wittgenstein in the *Encyclopedia of Philosophy*, ed. Paul Edwards, vol. 8, p. 327.
43. I discuss Whitehead's treatment of Kant in explicit detail in my lecture for the Chair of Logic at Copernicus University in Torun, Poland: see 'The Interpretation of Kant in Whitehead's Philosophy', pp. 213–30.
44. Malcolm, *Ludwig Wittgenstein: A Memoir*, p. 14.
45. Malcolm, *Ludwig Wittgenstein: A Memoir*, p. 14, n. 17.
46. Wittgenstein, *On Certainty*; cf. *Philosophical Investigations*, Part II, sec. x on 'Moore's paradox', which Wittgenstein does take seriously and positively.
47. Merrill B. Hintikka and Jaakko Hintikka, *Investigating Wittgenstein*, pp. 25–7.
48. Whitehead, *Process and Reality* (New York, 1929), p. x.
49. Whitehead, *Process and Reality* (New York, 1929), p. 11.
50. Whitehead, *Process and Reality* (New York, 1929), p. 8.
51. Janik and Toulmin, *Wittgenstein's Vienna*, p. 22.
52. Whitehead, *Process and Reality* (New York, 1929), pp. 8, 17, 187.
53. Cf. Bertrand Russell, *My Philosophical Development*, p. 216ff.
54. Quoted in Schulte, *Wittgenstein: An Introduction*, p. 20.
55. Schulte reports that 'when Russell was on his way to give a speech at a congress dedicated to humanitarian goals and Wittgenstein showed his disapproval, Russell asked if he would prefer an organisation for war and slavery. Whereupon Wittgenstein answered, 'By far, by far!' (*Wittgenstein: An Introduction*, p. 23).
56. Cf. Janik and Toulmin, *Wittgenstein's Vienna*, p. 194.
57. Quoted in Toulmin and Janik, *Wittgenstein's Vienna*, p. 195.
58. Whitehead, *Process and Reality* (New York, 1929), p. xi.

59. Even more clearly and importantly, in giving credence to this profound divide in twentieth-century British thought, and positioning Wittgenstein centrally within it, we make a permanent place for him after all in the great dialectical sweep of Western thought, of which he is now so clearly a preeminent part. Of the many divisions that constitute this profound, deeply troubled, Picassovian figure – the early and the later, the British and the Austrian, the Cantabrigian and the Viennese – this final divide between Wittgenstein the modern versus Wittgenstein the *critic* of modernism may well prove to be the most illuminating and important of all.

8 Scientific Revolutions and the Search for Covariant Metaphysical Principles

From all that has been said to this point, it must perforce be obvious that Whitehead not only practised implicitly the method of reflective historical engagement that I am advocating. Even more, he himself is among those figures of recent modern philosophy who have been unjustly marginalised and worthy of recollection and rehabilitation. The case for this recovery can perhaps best be made by thinking anew about his most famous work, *Process and Reality*, and re-examining its significance for, and truly original contributions to, philosophy proper (as opposed to the various ways this technically demanding work has mysteriously served as inspiration to a wide range of popular interpreters who, quite frankly, are ill-equipped to have understood it).

Process and Reality, subtitled 'an essay in cosmology', was the title given by Whitehead to his Gifford Lectures, delivered at the University of Edinburgh in June of 1928 at the conclusion of the academic term. The text of this unusually technical and complex lecture series was subsequently revised and considerably expanded for publication by Cambridge University Press in England, while a slightly different edition was published in the United States by the Macmillan Publishing Company in 1929. Both editions suffered from a host of typographical errors and other textual anomalies that were resolved, insofar as possible, in a corrected edition of the text published in the United States in 1978, which serves as the standard reference edition of this classic work.[1]

Whitehead was a prolific and highly popular lecturer and author, especially during his later years in America. *Process and Reality* is his most famous, and arguably his most difficult, work of philosophy. It is rivalled only by the magisterial but ultimately failed attempt to provide an exact grounding for mathematics in logic in the *Principia Mathematica* (three volumes, co-authored with his pupil and colleague Bertrand Russell) and by the author's attempt to develop an alternative to Albert Einstein's theory of general relativity in *The Principle of Relativity* (1922), a work in which Whitehead sought to avoid some of the more problematic ontological features of Einstein's theory, such as the radical discontinuity of space, the paradox of simultaneity, and the reversibility of time.

Process and Reality was written at about the same time as Martin Heidegger's *Being and Time* (1927) and relatively soon after Ludwig Wittgenstein's *Tractatus Logico-Philosophicus* (composed towards the end of World War I and published in 1922). *Process and Reality*, however, is utterly unlike either of these other two classical works of early twentieth-century philosophy. *Process and Reality* is most often characterised as a work of systematic and speculative metaphysics in the grand tradition of Hegel, Spinoza, and Aristotle, and its author is considered to be the last in a long line of speculative thinkers in the Western philosophical tradition. Whitehead thus appears to exemplify habits of philosophy that both Heidegger and Wittgenstein decry. Whether this book, and Whitehead himself, represent a relic of philosophy's past or a harbinger of its future remains a matter of spirited debate.

This characterisation of his major work is surprising in light of the reputation and career of Whitehead himself. For much of that career, Whitehead stood in the mainstream of what has since come to be called Anglo-American analytic philosophy. Indeed, as we saw in Chapter 7, Whitehead, Russell, Wittgenstein, and their mutual friend and colleague G. E. Moore are among its principal architects at Cambridge University at the beginning of the twentieth century. Whitehead's earlier writings from the late 1890s well into the mid-1920s are primarily works on the philosophy of mathematics, logic, epistemology, and philosophy of science. It is standard convention to attribute his later metaphysical turn to his migration to Harvard upon retiring from the Imperial College of Science and Technology at the University of London in 1924. Much is made of his relatively advanced age, sixty-three, and of the new opportunities and relative intellectual freedom afforded by this second career in America.

In *The Concept of Nature* (1920), however, written while Whitehead was still allegedly in the grip of antimetaphysical and largely logical and empirical approaches to philosophy, he discusses for the first time the concept of an 'event' – a well-defined temporal activity or episode of finite duration, a quantum of experience – as an alternative fundamental notion to that of matter or substance at a single location in space and time. He likewise introduced the notion of a nontemporal 'form of definiteness' or 'enduring object' (examples include geometrical shapes or discrete shades of the colour blue) as among the components or constituents of events, the particular combination or 'togetherness' of which in a concrete episode of experience defines its novelty or uniqueness. The twin themes of permanence and change that dominate in Whitehead's later philosophical works – including attention to the 'flux of becoming', the radical temporality and transitory nature of discrete events, as set against the enduring, eternal backdrop of timeless, Platonic forms, everlastingly available as potential ingredients in finite, temporal experience – are thus quite evident in rudimentary form in this and other earlier works from Whitehead's analytic period. The deeper challenge, as once again illustrated in the discussion in the preceding chapter, is to understand why all four of the Cambridge philosophers associated with the heyday of analysis and logical empiricism in Britain each, in their own way, came to repudiate this early emphasis on logical precision, exactness, and rigour in favour either of broad and speculative metaphysical views (Whitehead, followed much later by Russell) or of the incorrigible ambiguities and indefiniteness of ordinary language and common life (Moore, followed by Wittgenstein).

Process and Reality is unquestioningly Whitehead's crowning achievement, but it can be viewed either as the culmination of an extraordinary burst of intellectual energy channelled into unconventional paths between 1925 and 1929 or else as the culmination of a much more sustained and long-standing attempt to develop a descriptive metaphysical system commensurate with early twentieth-century relativistic cosmology and quantum mechanics. In either case, Whitehead's thoroughgoing efforts to invert the traditional metaphysical priorities that historically (from Plato and Aristotle to Locke, Spinoza, and Newton) seem to give priority and pride of place to substance over process, being over becoming, permanence over change, and inert matter at a specific location over the pervasive interactivity of force and energy fields are what led to the choice of title for this work and to the subsequent tendency of scholars to identify Whitehead's thought with the label 'process philosophy'.

Process and Reality is a work that is virtually impossible to summarise in a simple and coherent fashion. It is replete with technical (some would say 'arcane') terminology, which Whitehead found necessary to invent for the sake of precision and clarity. In this he unfortunately follows Aristotle's lead in transforming ordinary and familiar but vague terminology into precise but less-transparent technical terminology, thereby unintentionally driving a wedge between the philosopher as steward of highly specialised and technical mysteries and the ordinary individual who cannot possibly be privy to them. It was likewise this elite 'guild' mentality that the later Wittgenstein joined Moore in eschewing. Following his exploration of the intricacies of process metaphysics in this work, Whitehead forever after abandoned the overly technical and formidable approach to philosophy that characterises this work, and he spent the remainder of his life and career expounding his views in clear and often elegant prose.

Process and Reality consists of five parts. The first provides an introductory overview or glossary of terminology and fundamental propositions informing the work, outlining what Whitehead terms his 'speculative scheme'. Part II, entitled 'Discussions and Applications', is thought by some scholars to contain the bulk of the material originally presented in the Gifford Lectures series.[2] It consists of a historical conversation in which Whitehead sets forth his 'philosophy of organism' as an alternative to a metaphysical synthesis that he identifies with classical modern thinkers from Descartes, Locke, and Newton to Leibniz, Spinoza, Hume, and Kant. This discussion is considered by many scholars largely as a further refinement and exemplification of views first set forth by the author in his 1925 Lowell Lectures, *Science and the Modern World*. There are, however, important differences that are introduced in this later material. Whitehead coined terms like 'organic mechanism' and 'philosophy of organism' in the mid-1920s to signal his challenge to the Newtonian metaphysical synthesis variously termed 'mechanism' or 'scientific materialism'. By the time of the Gifford Lectures, however, his initial conception of a process or ceaseless creative activity as a single, underlying, Spinoza-like substance whose 'modes' are the discrete objects of ordinary experience is replaced in *Process and Reality* by an atomistic, Leibnizian doctrine in which ordinary experience is held to be composed out of discrete episodes or quanta of process, termed 'actual occasions' or 'actual entities'.

Part III of *Process and Reality*, entitled 'Theory of Prehensions', seems intended to revise and reformulate many of the discussions and conclusions developed in Part II. Readers today in fact take the discussion there of positive 'prehensions' as 'feelings', together with the detailed distinction between what are termed physical, conceptual, and hybrid feelings, as evidence of Whitehead's conversion to idealism and a kind of mystical panpsychism. This tendency has been encouraged by a legion of process disciples, led by Charles Hartshorne and his students. In fact, Whitehead is in this section of his work dramatically recontextualising a once well-known discussion of feelings by the British idealist F. H. Bradley, arguing in effect, against Bradley, that the origin of consciousness and the so-called higher phases of experience in more complex organisms can be shown to be a continuous and natural outgrowth of more rudimentary processes, rather than proof of a radically distinct order of being or of the unreality of concrete, everyday experience.[3] It is an unfortunate irony that Whitehead, as a result of this treatment and of his profound respect (even in disagreement) with Bradley, thus is mistakenly thought to espouse mystical positions that he instead sought to explain and discard as vestiges of the metaphysical dualism he himself sought to overcome.

The two most pervasive terms employed in these first three portions of the book are 'actual entities' (or 'actual occasions') and 'eternal objects'. The first pair of terms actually represents a translation into English of Descartes's terminology in the *Meditations*, where the question is considered: 'What are the *res verae*' (that is, what are the *actual things* or *actual entities* that truly exist or that are real)? Whitehead invokes this Cartesian terminology to indicate that his enquiry, too, is aimed at discovering the true nature of being. The shift towards the term 'occasion' and away from 'entity' in turn suggests that those actualities are not entitative, substantive, or material in the traditional sense but are episodes or occasions of pure activity or 'process'. 'Actual occasions' designate the fundamental quanta, units, or building blocks ('monads') of which (according to Whitehead's Ontological Principle) all entities of whatever sort are composed. The Ontological Principle establishes the claim that at the core, change and becoming are the primary characteristics of 'true things', while being conceived as unchanging substance (Aristotle, Locke) or inert matter (Newton, Descartes) is either the product or the appearance of episodes or 'occasions' of creative, generative activity.

The discrete properties that occasions of experience possess, however, stem from two quite different sources. Each occasion or episode 'prehends' (that is, grasps or actively appropriates, either to incorporate as 'feelings' or to eliminate) elements or features achieved in past occasions of experience. This fundamental act of prehension distinguishes the present from the past: past occasions are themselves no longer active as prehending subjects, while the concrete results or outcomes of their brief episodic experience are available as determinate objects to be 'prehended' by subsequent subjective occasions of experience. Whitehead describes this account as the Reformed Subjectivist Principle (in contrast to what he characterises as Descartes's original 'subjectivist principle', stipulating extended and thinking 'substances'). A slightly different version of this point is stressed through Whitehead's Principle of Relativity; namely, that 'subject' and 'object', in contrast to Descartes, do not designate distinct categories of being. Nature is not divided into two quite distinct ontological categories; rather, these terms are *temporally relative*. Every actual occasion is at first an active subject, grasping and incorporating elements of its environment (its past) and synthesising these elements into a new and unique occasion of experience, after which this occasion, too, 'perishes' (loses its subjective immediacy) and persists thereafter indefinitely as an 'object' or datum for future experiences to take account of ('feel') or ignore.

There is, however, a second source of determinateness that contributes to the novelty and uniqueness of each experience. In *The Concept of Nature*, as noted, Whitehead had recognised that there are properties that not only are ingredients of specific occasions of experience but also seem to appear and reappear, or to be replicated, in precisely the same fashion in myriad different objects and states of affairs over time. Whitehead called these 'enduring objects' or 'forms of definiteness'. In *Process and Reality* he coins the term 'eternal objects' for these Platonic universals, to distinguish them from the characteristics of earlier, objectified occasions (which are themselves 'prehended' as data in each new occasion of experience, or 'concrescence'). These 'eternal objects' bear close comparison to the sense-data, sensibilia, universals, or (as psychologists prefer this terminology) *qualia* that permeated the epistemological theories of early twentieth-century analysis. Again, according to the Ontological Principle, such 'objects' are not 'actual', as they are not events or processes themselves but are components or ingredients in actual occasions.

The problem with which Whitehead is wrestling, somewhat in contrast to British and American sense-data theorists, is the origin of novelty (and the explanation, without resort to dualism, of differing degrees of novelty) in the process of becoming. He also felt compelled to address the question of how a 'process' ever issues in anything determinate. How is 'being' produced by 'becoming'?

Whitehead's metaphysical project subsumes the original 'sense-data' theorists' epistemological concern, since Whitehead must explain not only how a conscious subject (or even a sentient being) perceives and develops reliable knowledge of its surroundings, but how any entity of whatever sort interacts with its world, weaving elements of that world into its own self-constitution. The epistemological problem of perception and knowledge simply turns out to be a highly specialised variant of a much more generalised and pervasive activity, characteristic of all entities. In this manner, the problem of Cartesian dualism is avoided.

Likewise, what for Kant are categories of understanding and limitations or 'categoreal obligations' imposed upon Pure Reason become, for Whitehead, categories of experience generally, and categoreal obligations to which all experience, of whatever sort, must conform. Kant's twelve epistemological Categories of Understanding and the resulting categoreal limitations they impose on Pure Reason are replaced in Whitehead's architectonic by eight metaphysical 'Categories of Existence', which collectively impose twenty-seven limitations or 'categoreal obligations' on experience generally. Such views illustrate Whitehead's gradual migration away from the epistemological concerns of his British analytic colleagues and towards the uniquely American focus on a 'metaphysics of experience' as discerned in the thought of C. S. Peirce, William James, and John Dewey.

As noted earlier, the transition from past to present is achieved when a new occasion synthesises the objective data from its past. This process is termed 'perception in the mode of causal efficacy'. It characterises every experience of whatever grade of complexity. Much hangs on whether the replication is indeed precise or approximate. If approximate, then previous finite instantiations of particular qualities and properties might simply be inherited or transmitted from one occasion to the next, without recourse to the notion of 'eternal objects' at all. If *the same* colour or shape, however, is instantiated identically in occasions separated by substantial distance and time, then causal transmission and repetition do not fully account for the origins and multiple 'ingressions' (Whitehead's terminology) of these forms in concrete but discrete episodes of experience. Once again, this is a common problem in sense-data theory, and Russell, Moore, C. D. Broad, Ralph Barton Perry, and many others likewise struggled mightily with it.[4] Whitehead finds in favour of a modified Platonism, holding that the definiteness and timelessness of these forms as repeated in experience demonstrates that they 'exist independently' in some sense as objects.

But this claim itself presents quite a puzzle. Such objects are not themselves *res verae*, and if they 'exist' in some sense outside of the flux of ordinary occasions, they can only be characteristics of (or subsumed as properties within) some other kind of actual occasion. Whitehead postulates an everlasting actual occasion, 'God' or the 'Principle of Concretion', whose principal function seems to be a 'primordial envisagement' of the totality of eternal objects in an abstractive hierarchy that defines the most perfect possible arrangement of the possibilities collectively available for actualisation within each concrete episode of experience in the world. This proposal bears close comparison to Leibniz's preestablished harmony, except that the harmony here is relative, changing, and never fully established. Instead, an initial prehension of the prospects for actualisation represented in this divine primordial envisagement repeatedly constitutes the starting point for each new finite occasion of experience, with each occasion weaving 'feelings' of its past of various intensities more or less according to the pattern of possibilities offered by this 'initial subjective aim'.

It is possible to do without this elaborate account, however, if one abandons the notion of 'eternal objects' and, along with them, the view that forms are precisely and repeatedly instantiated in concrete occasions of experience. Causal efficacy, the power of the past, is sufficient to account for the repetition of form, while novelty is an outgrowth both of the inexactness of that replication and the uniqueness of the weaving of physical and conceptual feelings or prehensions of the past by present occasions of experience. There is no reliance of process upon a prior conceptual ordering or abstractive hierarchy of possibilities, and thus there is no need to postulate God, either as the locus of eternal objects or as the means by which their ideal ordering is mediated in concrete experience. The price to be paid for this is not only loss of the unusual theological dimensions of Whitehead's thought but also the notions of both an 'ideal order' and of 'harmony' themselves – the sorts of things that Bertrand Russell uncharitably dismissed as 'qualities which only governesses love'. Instead, such order and organisation, or achievements of value (or of disvalue) as are attained in the world are (in admittedly a more Wittgensteinian fashion) solely a function of the achievements and accidents of the finite and concrete occasions of experience that constitute the world as we find it.

Whitehead's discussion of 'prehension', perception, and causality lead to a surprisingly far-sighted evolutionary epistemology that anticipated much of the subsequent contemporary discussion of this topic. Causal efficacy is the underlying feature of connectedness between past and present, characteristic (as we have noted) of all entities. As a result of the comparatively sophisticated sentient experience possible for complex conscious and self-conscious organisms, however, such organisms are able to isolate and abstract certain precise features from the underlying flux of 'blooming, buzzing confusion' (William James) or 'thirdness' (C. S. Peirce), and attend to these features in detail. This, according to Whitehead, is what occurs in perception in the mode of 'presentational immediacy'. Early analytic philosophers had mistaken this kind of perception as the starting point for analysis, but in Whitehead's account, this 'primitive experience' is in fact a very complex mode of perception supervening upon the more fundamental experience of causal efficacy. Moore and his students (if Whitehead is correct) would have eventually discovered that the 'brown colour patch' and the oblong spheroid that they analysed as the typical primitive sense-data constituting their conference table were, in fact, the end result of a long process of selective abstraction from the concrete experience of transition, conceptual reversion, and isolation in presentational immediacy of the 'eternal objects' ingredient in the events that actually constitute the *appearance* of a solid, circular, brown table out of the ceaseless interaction of energy fields. Or so Whitehead would purport to address this common dilemma of the relation of sense-perception to veridical knowledge of the external world.

The remaining two parts of *Process and Reality* are, by comparison, quite brief, and they have had decidedly different historical impact.

Part IV, 'The Extensive Continuum', continues Whitehead's decades-long study of relativistic geometry, setting forth his views on the nature of the spacetime manifold, on measurement, and on the derivation of geometrical points and temporal 'point-instants' (which are abstractions) as a limit of overlapping finite volumes (which are concrete events). This material is seldom cited or studied in detail, and its important continuity with Whitehead's earlier work in general relativity theory accordingly is seldom acknowledged.[5] One set of very important distinctions between standard coordinate division and what Whitehead terms 'genetic' division is that an actual occasion may have parts or components that are logically and conceptually distinguishable, and even classifiable as occurring 'earlier' or 'later' than others in the overall process of concrescence, but that process of concrescence (the 'subjective immediacy' of an occasion) cannot be temporally subdivided into those parts. The occasion occurs, from an external standpoint, 'all at once' as a unified quantum and not as a sequence of stages.

The obscure fate of Part IV stands in marked contrast to the impact of the equally brief concluding Part V, Whitehead's 'final interpretation' devoted to the theme of 'God and the World'. The poetic remarks here were likely coined in compliance with the terms of the Gifford Lectures series, which require that the lecturer reflect on the implications of his work for natural theology. These twenty pages of modest and touching theological reflection have generated perhaps more commentary than the rest of the work combined, and they have given rise to an entire distinct field known as 'process theology', which has had enormous influence throughout the world since Whitehead's death. Here God is not only conceived as an actual occasion but also as unique in that this episode has as yet no determinate outcome. (Samuel Alexander's theory of the 'nisus' set forth in his earlier Gifford Lectures, *Space, Time and Deity* (1920), bears some resemblance to Whitehead's portrayal here of a fundamental incompleteness in God's nature.)

According to Whitehead, the 'subjective immediacy' of divine experience never 'perishes' but is everlasting; hence, God's nature is not fully determinate or complete. God not only provides abstract conceptual aims (hierarchical orderings of eternal objects) for the world that guide or 'lure' creativity towards its most optimal outcome (the 'Primordial Nature' of God) but also 'feels' the resultant experience of the world. The determinate outcome and achievements of the activity of discrete and finite actual occasions are thus ceaselessly 'causally objectified' in God's own being, in what Whitehead terms 'the Consequent Nature' of God. God is thus somewhat like Hegel's conception of 'absolute knowing' in *The Phenomenology of Spirit* (1807): a state of perfect recollection, in which all that is and has been is preserved and held together in an everlasting and perfect harmony as one. Hegel was, of course, no mathematician, and he was therefore perhaps less entitled to this elegant restatement of Pythagorianism than the mathematical and logical genius Whitehead. But it is significant that for both, as for Plato and Pythagoras before them, recollection is the key to immortality.

Epilogue

Whitehead enjoyed enormous influence during his lifetime, but the recognition of his philosophical significance eroded substantially after his death. This is in marked contrast to his reputation among intellectuals outside the discipline of philosophy, especially scholars in comparative religion and philosophical theology, and a great number of humanistically inclined and learned scientists, all of whom continue to hold Whitehead, and this monumental work, in high regard. Among Whitehead's most famous students were Willard Van Orman Quine, Gregory Vlastos, the Canadian philosopher Allison H. Johnson, and Paul Weiss. Their own diversity of interests and distinctive reputations is a tribute to Whitehead's influence as a teacher, rather than as a dispenser of doctrine or gatherer of disciples. Perhaps, as I averred at the beginning of this chapter, this demotion to 'footnote immortality' on Whitehead's part is not deserved. Instead, it would be appropriate to rescue some of his more perceptive philosophical positions (e.g., on sense-perception and what is now termed evolutionary epistemology) from oblivion.

Other distinguished thinkers have since made important critical contributions to our understanding of Whitehead or to the application of his philosophical views to new problems. These include Richard Rorty, Adolf Grünbaum, George L. Kline, James K. Feibleman, and Donald W. Sherburne. Robert C. Neville, the distinguished philosopher and theologian at Boston University, was profoundly influenced by both Whitehead and Weiss, eclipsing the reputation of earlier figures in the Boston personalist movement, like Edgar Sheffield Brightman, who were likewise indebted to Whitehead's thought. Whitehead is most often linked with Charles Hartshorne, who was and is still thought mistakenly by many to have been Whitehead's student at Harvard. Only towards the end of his long life did Professor Hartshorne clarify this mistake and move to minimise the relationship between his own lifelong interest in personal idealism and philosophical theology and Whitehead's markedly different and distinct philosophical interests.

Notes

1. These successive editions are as follows: *Process and Reality* (New York: Macmillan, 1929); *Process and Reality* (Cambridge: Cambridge University Press, 1929); and a paperback version of the Macmillan edition widely used for decades: *Process and Reality* (New York: The Free Press, 1969). The 'Corrected Edition' was issued by David Ray Griffin and Donald W. Sherburne, *Process and Reality: Corrected Edition* (New York: The Free Press, 1978).
2. For example, Lewis S. Ford, *The Emergence of Whitehead's Metaphysics: 1925–1929*. If so, however, it would be puzzling to see why (in contrast to the immensely successful public lectures in Cambridge in February 1925 that became *Science and the Modern World*) the Giffords were described by one of his later students, via the 'grapevine', as having been 'bound to be a fiasco'. See Victor Lowe, *Alfred North Whitehead*, vol. 2, pp. 221, 250. It bears mention that Volume 1 of *The Edinburgh Critical Edition of the Complete Works of Alfred North Whitehead* casts serious doubt upon the accuracy of Ford's reconstruction of the eventual book manuscript.
3. This issue is clarified by Leemon B. McHenry in his important and pathbreaking study, *Whitehead and Bradley*.
4. I discuss this central problem of realism in chapter 4 of *The Genesis of Modern Process Thought*.
5. But see the exceptionally clear account of the relationship and essential differences of Whitehead and Einstein on the geometry of spacetime as discussed in Joachim Stoltz, *Whitehead und Einstein*.

9 'People without a Name'

Prague, in Kafka's novels, is a city without memory. It has even forgotten its name. Nobody there remembers anything, nobody recalls anything. . . . Time [for Kafka] . . . is the time of a humanity that no longer knows anything nor remembers anything, that lives in nameless cities with nameless streets or streets with names different from the ones they had yesterday, *because a name means continuity with the past* and people without a past are people without a name. (Milan Kundera, *The Book of Laughter and Forgetting*)[1]

In 1993, at the relatively advanced age of seventy-six, a former Japanese army physician decided to break a long-standing code of silence and denial and speak out for the record concerning Japanese military atrocities during World War II. At issue were allegations, never acknowledged by the Japanese, that army doctors had conducted a variety of cruel and scientifically unwarranted experiments on Chinese and Korean prisoners of war. The physician, Dr Ken Yuasa, remarked, 'I must confess, with embarrassment for myself and the country, because I strongly believe everyone should know the truth. If I don't tell my story, what the Japanese military has done will be *erased from history*.'[2] But is such an erasure of history possible? What might this mean, and how might it occur?

It is the business of the historian to remember, but the tendency in history itself is to forget. In most instances the forgetting, the fading of immediacy, and the loss of intricate detail are inadvertent and seem unavoidable. After all, no narrative can be all-encompassing; even to attempt complete preservation of detail would result in a narrative that was hopelessly complex and unintelligible. But, as a consequence, the welter of immediate detail that cannot be woven meaningfully (and selectively) into a subsequent historian's narrative must either be accorded a cursory treatment or else be cast aside. This problem of perspectivalism in the hermeneutics of history is thoroughly familiar and seemingly inescapable.[3]

Forgetting, however, is not always simply unavoidable or inescapable; it is often intentional. The forgetting of history in many instances occurs as the end result of deliberate actions. We have considered at length a strategy of *suppression* of the work of a maverick philosopher in the nineteenth century. Dr Yuasa, by comparison, finally refuses to condone *repression*, a conspiracy of silence and denial concerning unsavoury medical and pseudo-scientific activities. Beneke's scholarly opponents, including Hegel, did not want him refuted so much as they wanted him not even to be heard, on the grounds presumably that his ideas were incompetent, unworthy, or dangerous. They sought to have him literally cast into historical oblivion, they wanted his thought *erased from history*. They very nearly succeeded. Some Japanese and German physicians and concentration camp kapos likewise would prefer that their misdeeds be forgotten, hoping that their own repression, combined with collective cultural amnesia, will ultimately lead to historical erasure altogether.

Attempts like these to force people to forget all about the historical record constitute the stock in trade of tyranny. Indeed, Czech author Milan Kundera maintains, in his *Book of Laughter and Forgetting*, that 'the only reason people want to be masters of the future is to change the past'.[4] Tyrants often see the need for this social or cultural amnesia, this need 'to change the past' (in Kundera's term), either to hide what they have done or to disguise or distort what they propose to do.

In this vein, soon after the collapse of the Berlin Wall, a retired Soviet army officer, Colonel Vladimir Malinin, related how he and his first wife, Yevgenia, first learned for themselves of how the Soviet state had dealt with political prisoners:

Yevgenia, an archivist for the state prison system, accidentally discovered a secret report written to Soviet leader Nikita Khrushchev by the director of the camps administration in the Far East. The report recited a litany of horrors that shocked the couple out of their previous unquestioning devotion to the Soviet state. According to Mr. Malinin, the report recounted that 17.5 million people had been imprisoned in a sprawling network of labor camps for political prisoners in the Kolyma River valley north of Magadan between 1933 and 1952. Of those, the report said, 16.3 million had died of exhaustion or illness and another 85,877 had been shot to death. Having stumbled upon such forbidden knowledge, Mr. Malinin said, he agonized over it for months, then finally shared his secret and sought advice from a friend named Ivan Chistiakov, who held a high position in the Magadan regional administration. 'He told me, "It's better you forget all about it",' Mr. Malinin said.[5]

The attempt to have us 'forget all about it' may come in the form of a suggestion from a friend, offered in the interests of one's own safety or well-being, as in the case of Col. Malinin. Or it may come in the form of a campaign of intimidation, terror, and misinformation, as Kundera relates in the aftermath of the brutal Soviet suppression of Alexander

Dubček's experiment with 'socialist humanism' during the Prague Spring in Czechoslovakia in 1968.

In response, Kundera proclaimed in his novels that 'the struggle of man against power is the struggle of memory against forgetting'.[6] The fruits of victory in this struggle are the preservation, intact, of the lives and the experiences of ordinary people – or rather, of the events out of which those lives and precious individual identities are constituted. Eyewitnesses, even participants in historical events, may decide after decades of silence and denial to speak out, as did Dr Yuasa, committing their testimony to some sort of enduring record. Guilt by the perpetrators or by compliant witnesses, or anger and desire for vengeance on behalf of victims, provoke individuals to commit themselves to the cause of recollection. And through it all, the principal insurrectionists, the chief guerrilla warriors in this struggle against forgetting, are historians.

Towards the end of the Cold War (in the West, at least), a debate raged in the academic field of twentieth-century Russian history between what was characterised as an older generation of conservative political historians, led by Robert Conquest of Stanford University, and a newer generation of social historians, led by J. Arch Getty of the University of California and Sheila Fitzpatrick of the University of Chicago. The lengthy and acrimonious debate between these two factions over 'methodology' in fact concealed a larger conflict between memory and forgetting.[7]

The social historians accused the older political historians of having developed an overly dramatic and personalised view of Russian history. This view, based upon what the social historians characterised as 'subjective and anecdotal' testimony of dissidents and victims, tended to focus on and demonise the role of Stalin and his henchmen in carrying out the terrible purges in Russia during the 1930s and downplay or ignore the role of other factors that might have contributed to the magnitude of the widespread party purges that culminated in the Great Terror (c. 1936–8).

The revisionist social historians, by contrast, were suspicious of the narrative that anecdotal 'eyewitness' accounts yielded, and they argued that this ought to be corroborated and supplemented by the more 'objective and impartial' data derived from official records and archival sources. The political historians responded that the official records of tyrants could hardly be regarded as impartial and reliable; that often, such 'records' were Orwellian[8] instruments of forgetting – airbrushed, sanitised, and falsified in order to hide the truth.

This bitter debate on historical methodology suddenly sputtered to a moot halt shortly after the collapse of the Berlin Wall, however, when the social historians were finally able to obtain full access to the sorts of hitherto restricted archival materials to which Col. Malinin also refers, following the collapse of the Soviet Union itself. Bureaucrats are nothing if not meticulous in their attention to detail, beyond, it seems, even the power of the tyrant to corrupt. In the then-newly opened 'Center for the Preservation and Study of Documents of Contemporary History' (formerly the Central Party Archives of the Communist Party) in Moscow, Professor Getty himself discovered neatly typed records like those Col. Malinin had accidentally encountered earlier – chilling, impersonal, 'objective' government records providing unmistakable documentation of atrocities of a magnitude at least as great as Professor Conquest's numerous witnesses and scholarly allies had envisioned.[9] Airbrushed photographs, official silences, campaigns of disinformation, and surreptitious warnings 'to forget all about it' could not, in the end, obscure or cast into the oblivion of forgetfulness the sheer historical massiveness of the Stalinist purges, the Ukrainian famines, or the terror of the Gulags.

Japanese medical atrocities, the European Jewish Holocaust, Stalinist Gulags, and the Ukrainian famines are, however, all world-historical events of massive proportions involving millions of people. These events generated widespread anguish, pain, suffering, and anger. It would be a monumental task to attempt to erase such events from history – perhaps, owing to their dimensions, therefore impossible in practice. There is always someone left, someone willing to speak out.

In the quite ordinary, unimportant, and decidedly non-world-historical case of Herr Dr Beneke, however, no one (certainly no eyewitnesses or participants) spoke out on behalf of Beneke to any recognisable degree. Rather, in Beneke's case, forgetting seems to be inhibited solely by the presence of a modest physical legacy. Beneke wrote a number of books, which still exist (though they are perhaps largely ignored) on library shelves; these are referred to in other books. Beneke did succeed in influencing a few pupils who made reference to their teacher and carried on some of his ideas. There is enough of this physical legacy of the scholar, Friedrich Beneke, that subsequent historians, so to speak, bump up against it and have to take some account of its stubborn presence. A historian of philosophy is then invited to write a brief encyclopaedia article accounting for this physical presence, while other historians are required, in effect, to justify their decisions to set this material aside, to fail to weave it in a more central way into their various narratives of this period of German history. History, the history of philosophy, and every library's groaning shelves are replete with such instances of partial forgetting.

Such ongoing forgetting is arrested in some instances by the interposition of the occasional historian who recollects the neglected physical evidence and reweaves previous historical narratives to find a more central place for it, assuming that historian finds the physical record sufficiently interesting. The revisions and reinterpretations may be especially pronounced, as in Beneke's case, when carried out by social historians informed by a hermeneutics of suspicion that casts doubt on the hagiography of earlier, self-conscious narratives.

Analogous to the Conquest–Getty debate referred to above, here, too, the contemporary historian might argue that more can be learned by correlating and corroborating written texts, eyewitness accounts, and 'received' official narratives of a period with other things that lie beneath their surface. Thus our social historian might discern during Beneke's lifetime the influence of political trends in the aftermath of the French Revolution – such as the conservative antirevolutionary disposition of the waning aristocracy that empowered orthodox, 'right-wing' Hegelians in the early nineteenth century and sought to suppress their opponents in part to protect positions of privilege and power in the state. Or the historian might fasten on the influence of demographic and economic trends and their impact on higher education – such as the mass exodus of students from philosophy curricula in the 1840s and 1850s in Germany in favour of careers in medicine, physics, and law (where, unlike Beneke, one could make a successful career out of the pursuit of truth for its own sake without incurring the wrath of the political establishment).

Only in such instances, it would seem, is the rescue from oblivion carried out. Otherwise, even the physical record is a historical artefact with a finite lifetime: students die and are themselves forgotten; the books, and other books citing these books, and even the encyclopaedias recording the unimportance of it all, likewise fade and crumble with a temporal measure only somewhat longer than that of their authors. This casting aside, this loss to oblivion, seems to constitute the larger process and the wider backdrop of history against which the historian's memorial task forms a modest, or even an insignificant, foreground.

The tragic case and the rescue from oblivion, perhaps only temporarily, of Friedrich Beneke leads us to wonder whether there might have been circumstances in which such a rescue would have been impossible in principle. Are there Orwellian-like scenarios in which Beneke's scholarly enemies might have succeeded, for their purposes, in effecting a complete erasure from history?

In Beneke's case, we claim that the physical brute presence of a written legacy grounds the recovery, recollection, and rescue of his name from eventual oblivion. But this in itself is not especially reassuring – for, in recognition of this, his enemies might have found it possible to erase this record, to obliterate it completely, so that their deliberate strategy of forgetting would succeed.

Let us try a thought experiment. Suppose, hypothetically, that the unfortunate Beneke did not fall into the Berlin canal on account of poor health, or throw himself in, driven to suicide by the understandable despair over his failed career. Suppose he was in fact pushed by a well-meaning disciple of theological idealism and the divine right of kings. Suppose further that this hypothetical intellectual terrorist realises that his strategy would be even more effective if the body were weighted down so that, instead of being found and perhaps inspiring the curious sympathy of some later encyclopaedist, Herr Dr Beneke himself would simply disappear, only the crayfish at the bottom of the canal the wiser and the happier for it. His books could be located and burned. His few students could also be found and either forcibly intimidated into silence or terminated like their teacher.

Suppose that, by such a radical, Orwellian procedure, every trace of the physical legacy of this unfortunate scholar were thus thoroughly and efficiently expunged from the historical record. Would Beneke *himself* then pass into utter oblivion, as though he had never been? Would he cease *to have* existed at all?

The last question is put in a deliberately puzzling, counterfactual form to illustrate the intractable conceptual confusion – I would term it an ontological confusion – inherent in the hypothetical strategy pursued by Beneke's scholarly enemies in this instance, as well as by all who seek, for their own purposes, to effect such 'erasures' from the historical record. The forgetting that is the warp and woof of history, it seems, is always a subsequent matter. Forgetting is not simply the failure to remember; it is not merely an omission. Forgetting is the cessation, or the active prevention, of an act of transmission of memorial data from preceding to subsequent *moments of consciousness*. What the intellectual terrorist *may* be able to achieve (if entirely successful) is totally impeding transmission of even the slightest trace of a given moment, or sequence of moments, to the next – a termination or discontinuation of a series of events.

But such a cessation or active discontinuation of the transmission of the legacy of a thing, or of a related series of things, is rather obviously not the same as a *retroactive obliteration* of the *thing itself*. Our intellectual terrorist will have succeeded only in preventing or preempting the possibility of memory or later recollection. Contrary to science-fiction accounts, he would not thereby also have been able to work backwards in time and unmake the original existent, the very being of the thing thus forgotten.

By imagining certain slight variations on the actual details of a minor historical episode, we discover that forgetting as the essence of history is confined entirely to *subsequent* history. Forgetting affects the transmission of the past, which in turn grounds our conscious assignment of meaning to the past, but it does not thereby affect the being *of the past itself*. In the case of *suppression*, we note that a human being born in 1798, and upon whom was conferred a doctoral degree in 1820, does not cease to have been born or to have been once thus honoured, simply because his enemies later destroy his body, burn his books, and intimidate his family, friends, and students in 1854. Likewise, in the case of *repression and amnesia*, our failing to pay attention to records and memories of past medical atrocities in 1993 does not mean that those events themselves somehow failed to occur as they did occur in 1937 or in 1941 – let alone does it mean that such past events are themselves 'reversible' or 'unmakeable'.

All that forgetting can accomplish, either inadvertently or deliberately, is that what once was, or what was once achieved, is subsequently unrecollected by consciousness in subsequent moments. Past events do not cease to *be*; rather, they can only cease to be *consciously remembered*. This result holds true for the commonplace as well as for larger, world-historical events; as we shall see, the conclusion is thus not a matter of magnitude but of fundamental metaphysical principle.

The Ontological Status of Past Events

What sorts of entities are past events themselves?[10] Temporal passage from the present to the past is usually understood to involve the cessation or completion of (present) concretising activity, once this activity has resulted in the achievement of determinateness or closure. But does the attainment of determinateness also necessarily entail that the completed and determinate event and its objective achievements thereupon literally disappear into oblivion? If not, then where do past events 'go'? What becomes of them? In particular, does the subsequent existence or being of such past events depend solely thereafter upon their *being remembered*? Virtually every instance of forgetting discussed above – and in particular, the strategies of forgetting pursued by the tyrant – presuppose that so far as the past is concerned, to be is nothing more or less than to be remembered. Thus it is possible in principle, as Dr Yuasa fears, for events to be *erased from history* by bringing about a complete failure of collective memory.

But can it be true that the very existence of events in the past ceases to be, or that past events somehow lose the ontological determinateness they once possessed, when they are totally forgotten? And if so, by what means are they recollected – as dead, gone, and 'forgotten' events sometimes seem to be?

These questions represent more than merely idle philosophical curiosity. Something about our commonly held views of the past makes it conceivable to the tyrant that a forgetting of history is possible, that the past can be undone and cast into oblivion. Kundera suggests, in fact, that actual loss of the past is possible partly because of the sheer welter of detail, the relentless and oppressive weight of subsequent events crowding out the prior ones, perhaps aided by weariness, complacency, or despair. He writes,

> The bloody massacre in Bangladesh quickly covered over the memory of the Russian invasion of Czechoslovakia, the assassination of [Chilean Marxist President Salvadore] Allende drowned out the groans of Bangladesh, the war in the Sinai Desert made people forget Allende, the Cambodian massacre made people forget Sinai, and so on and so forth *until ultimately everyone lets everything be forgotten.*[11]

Something about historical recollection, however, calls this common presupposition into question: the past is not *merely* memory and interpretation, nor does the being or actuality of past events depend solely upon their being remembered. Rather, the past *itself* may comprise something else, something external to conscious acts of memory, as well as something beyond the kin of deliberate or unconscious acts of forgetting. The past, in and for itself, consists of a set of what Alfred North Whitehead called 'stubborn, irreducible facts' – determinate, fixed episodes of experience-that-was, each of which is itself *unaltered* by inclusion or omission in subsequent episodes of experience. In that ontological sense, every past event possesses an internal integrity, a 'being' that is beyond any subsequent act of forgetting – be it loss of memory, suppression, or distortion – to erase. In that case, we would be forced to conclude that this ontological past must itself reside 'somewhere', so as to be capable of being recollected. The moral rectification of the tragic effects of tyranny, cited above, seems to necessitate or legitimate this odd metaphysical view of the ongoing existence of an unalterable past as a kind of meta-archival record of events 'as-they-were-in-and-for-themselves', as a kind of Kantian *Ding-an-sich*, providing an objective ground or warrant for our knowledge and our memories.

This important distinction between the *meaning* or interpretation of an historical event and its *being*, though reminiscent of the 'ontological difference' of Heidegger, was first clearly set forth in two essays by George L. Kline.[12] Drawing upon Whitehead's analysis of the structure of events or 'actual occasions' of experience, Kline suggested that the being of the past – what past events were in and for themselves – is fixed, determinate, and unaffected by inclusion or exclusion in subsequent events. By contrast, Kline argued, the meaning of the past – that is, the myriad ways a past event can be included (or excluded) in a subsequent event – is never fixed, never finished, and always, in principle, open to subsequent reinterpretation. Meaning is always (in Heidegger's phrase) 'on the way'. Illustrating the complexity and importance of this subtle distinction in one of the aforementioned two essays, Kline wrote,

> I do not deny that there are cases – especially those which bear significantly on the history of human culture – in which the relation between the being and the meaning of past events is complex and even opaque. For example, a day, a year, or even half-a-dozen years after the births – on particular days in 1265, 1756, and 1879 – of Dante, Mozart, and Albert Einstein, respectively, it would *not* have been possible to state that the author of the *Divine Comedy* (or even 'a great poet', or even 'a poet'), or the composer of *The Magic Flute*, or the formulator of the Special Theory of Relativity had been born on those particular days. The *being* of these recently past or 'ex-' events did not yet have the meaning which they later came to have. One could say only that male infants of a certain description had been born in such-and-such places, of such-and-such parents, etc.[13]

The *meaning* of all such cultural events is cumulative and slow to emerge, requiring decades in ordinary cases and centuries in extraordinary ones. In a sense, it is never completed: there is no end to the valuing 'up' and the valuing 'down' of the contributions to human civilisation even of such geniuses as the three just named. But the *being* of ex-events such as these three births, I insist, is not affected by accretions, erosions, or other changes in their *meaning* (evaluation, interpretation).[14]

This philosophical *aporia* regarding the ontological status of the past thus presents us with two clearly distinct alternatives.

1. The past is ontologically grounded, as symbolised but not limited to the examples of archives and artefacts that persist independent of conscious acts and are available and amenable to subsequent recollections and reinterpretations. 'The past' consists of determinate and fixed 'events-that-once-were', each of which has its being, its *facticity an und für sich*, regardless of our subsequent conscious memories of it. Our interpretations of the past affect *us*, but they are utterly powerless to affect *it*. We cannot go back in time and unmake, or remake, what once was and ever shall be, world without end.
2. In decided contrast, 'the past' consists of nothing more or less than our collective memories in the present of earlier events. Those events themselves, in Whitehead's technical metaphysical terminology, 'perish;'[15] they live, then die, and once dead are themselves gone forever, except as their determinate outcome is included as a datum in some subsequent act of memory and recollection. The past thus exists only as memory. When recollection fades or ceases, then past events pass utterly into oblivion and are forgotten forever.

If the first alternative is correct, then the tyrant's strategy of forgetfulness is conceptually flawed in principle and rests upon a mistake. Memory can be managed, but the past is always available independently 'somewhere' for recollection. The past persists, 'somehow, somewhere', awaiting full disclosure.

If, by contrast, the second alternative is correct, then the tyrant's ploy is foiled only by contingent circumstances: by a failure of effort, a lack of thoroughness, or perhaps just plain bad luck. But the tyrant's ploy is *not* flawed in principle; indeed, it is always in danger of succeeding. We are thus perpetually haunted by the ever-present danger of becoming, in Kundera's phrase, 'a people without a name'.

The Hiding Places of Memories

Towards the end of his novel, Kundera has the heroine, Tamina, taken by a friend into the countryside, many miles from Prague. There, a walk on a muddy hillside, in almost Proustian fashion, awakens lost memories of a similar walk taken with her husband, whose death she now grieves.

Yes! Yes! Now she understood. Finally! We will never remember anything by sitting in one place waiting for the memories to come back to us of their own accord! Memories are scattered all over the world. We must travel if we want to find them *and flush them out from their hiding places*![16]

Where *do* memories hide? From its very beginnings, philosophy has concerned itself centrally with this question. The ancient Pythagoreans engaged in daily rituals of recollection, believing that by developing a perfect capacity to hold everything in mind all at once, they would thereby attain immortality. The 'Myth of Er' in Plato's *Republic* describes forgetting or a sense of forgetfulness as endemic to the human condition. The philosopher is one who responds to that absence, recognising and lamenting this perceived loss, and willing to spend a lifetime in the quest to recover those lost, primordial memories. Heidegger described the whole of Western culture as *Seinsvergessenheit*, the forgetfulness of Being, and set himself the task of recollecting, behind centuries of tradition, custom, and linguistic practice, the unmediated acquaintance with Being that humankind once possessed but has now lost. For Augustine and for Whitehead, perfect recollection and the overcoming of forgetfulness – and, for Whitehead, the final achievement of the Pythagorean's 'objective immortality' – are finally attained in an ongoing act of divine recollection.[17]

Hegel figures prominently in this Western philosophical preoccupation with the problem of memory and forgetting. Like Plato, Hegel suggests in *The Phenomenology of Spirit* that it is *forgetting*, rather than memory, that is the true engine of history: consciousness forgets what it has learned, and it is forced to retrace painful steps on the road to the recovery of the forgotten truth. The loss, the absence, and the sense of 'something missing' or incomplete impels consciousness on its historical journey – on what Hegel, in the Preface to this great work, dramatically terms 'its highway of despair'.[18]

The cessation of suffering, the metaphorical end of consciousness's journey on this historical highway, the rectification of injustice, and the antidote to tyranny – all, by contrast, lie in recollection. At the conclusion of the *Phenomenology* – on its final page, in fact – Hegel suggests that philosophical wisdom lies less in the attainment of some new, undiscovered truth than in the recollection and full retention of all that consciousness has already learned – like the ancient Pythagoreans, holding the Whole all together simultaneously. This full internalisation of what Hegel terms philosophical or 'comprehended' history is characterised, in an interesting and poignant metaphor, as 'the Calvary of absolute Spirit' – an image of an end that is also a beginning, of suffering that is also triumph through suffering.[19]

The later confessions and acknowledgements of Japanese war crimes, delving the depths of Stalinist terror in the archives of the former Soviet Union, as well as memorial events like the opening of the United States Holocaust Museum in Washington, DC, all likewise signify that historical recollection – recovering, retaining, and reweaving what was forgotten, suppressed, and distorted by the tyrant into a full and complete narrative of the present – alone can bring us to closure, to reconciliation, and to some measure of peace with ourselves. All of these memorial events are instances of moral closure, of ends that are simultaneously beginnings, of narrations of suffering, the final and full narration of which is simultaneously a *triumph over* suffering. Our earlier awareness of absence, of loss, of incompleteness, even in the absence of a full knowledge of the forgotten details, is what prompts and prods historical consciousness, in these instances, not to rest, not to remain content with indifference and forgetting, but to press on along the highway of despair towards a full understanding of what actually occurred and why.

The very sense of absence that partial forgetting engenders – that gap or space in the airbrushed image of our collective experience – seems to guarantee the final triumph of recollection over forgetting, awaking that discomfort and what Plato characterised as *eros*, the desire to know, to recover that which was lost. It is almost as if a society or culture functions like a vast analogue of a Freudian personality in such instances: its memories of trauma and tragedy having been forcibly suppressed or repressed, the society itself suffers the kind of widespread malaise, the psychological disorientation and disorder that Kundera so masterfully narrates in his native Czech Republic. Like an individual patient in psychoanalysis, moreover, the social malaise can only be set right by a full and therapeutic recollection of, and by a coming to terms with, the original tragedy or trauma. The loss of memory amounts to a loss of self, and these lost or partial selves, like Kundera's Tamina or Plato's philosopher, wander the Earth in search of the hiding places of memory.

Of the two alternative accounts of the ontological status of the past that I outlined above, common opinion seems implicitly to favour the second. Considered in full detail, the first alternative represents a commitment to a form of historical realism that is problematic and implausible, if not fantastic. The specific instances that might seem to give credence to the notion of an ontologically independent past – a meta-archival, objective record independent from memory – turn out to be cases, like several of these we have considered, that are almost clichéd in their very magnitude. The enormity, the monstrosity, the sheer extensiveness of the crimes committed in the German Jewish Holocaust, in the Stalinist Great Terror, in 'the deportation of a million Lithuanians, the murder of hundreds of thousands of Poles, the liquidation of the Crimean Tatars' (not to mention the butchering of nearly a million Rwandans, or the massacre of hundreds of thousands of Syrians) ensures somehow that these events 'will remain in our memory' even when no photographs or records any longer exist, and even though the state subsequently proclaims the events themselves 'a fabrication'.[20] Here the tyrant's ploy fails in circumstance (though not in principle) because the massiveness of the events, and the psychological weight of their memory, are simply too vast and extensive to obliterate.

But what, then, are we to make of instances like the much more modest resurrection of Dr Beneke and the rectification of the historical record in the name of justice effected by Professor Köhnke? If nothing else, that story from Chapter 2 served as recognition that the physical or material rooting or grounding of life experiences in some sort of permanent historical record was not merely a matter of size and magnitude but of fundamental metaphysical principle. It is recollection of the ordinary and of the limited – and likewise, the failure of forgetting even in these instances where it should practically succeed – that might seem to give credence, after all, to the first alternative of an ontologically grounded past, independent of memory and interpretation.

The sceptic might still enquire of what use is such an admittedly fantastic metaphysical principle? And indeed, what good does it do to claim that past events possess an ontological integrity that is beyond the power of subsequent tyrants, terrorists, or even the ravages of time to obliterate – if, in the end, the 'being' of this allegedly immutable past gradually becomes lost and inaccessible to us in conscious memory?

In history, after all, we have to do primarily *not* with raw, brute, uninterpreted 'facts' or 'data' (whatever that might mean) but with recollection, narrative, and interpretation. If it *is* possible to impede the recollection of certain events, so that historical interpretation is ever thereafter impoverished by their absence, then does not forgetting triumph in any case, and have not the tyrants succeeded in their desire, as Kundera characterises it, to be 'masters of the future in order to change the past'?

The historical sceptic can, however, be answered. We *can* give a straightforward account of the existence of an ontologically distinct past, immune from the mutability of Orwellian tyrants and postmodern historical–hermeneutical constructivists and preserve intact the complete meta-archive of our collective experience, including the ordinary and the mundane as well as the world-historical. Moreover, such an account need not rely on implausible claims regarding other possible worlds, such as a realm of the Forms or a distinct repository of the past; neither do I rely in this account on the *deus ex machina* of an Augustinian divine mind or Whiteheadian Consequent Nature of God as perfect knowers. If one desires to fasten upon analogues and antecedents of the view I shall adumbrate, I would suggest – in addition to Hegel and Whitehead, already cited – the 'holy and despised' Spinoza, or perhaps the Bergson of *Matter and Memory*.

The key to our dilemma is to recognise not merely that past events never cease to exist but that they never cease to be with us as *material ingredients* in the present. In memory, there is *the act* of remembering, and *the thing* remembered, as in perception there is an act of perception and the object or content of that perception, the thing perceived. Neither 'thing' ceases to be, simply because of a subsequent failure to include it in a memory or perception.

Against an earlier generation of 'scientific, methodological' hermeneuticists who thought of the past as something incredibly distant and alien that we had to demythologise and think our way back into, Hans-Georg Gadamer objected that the past is not to be thought of as something distant, alien, separated by a vast gulf of time and incommensurability. Rather, in language reminiscent of Whitehead's account of repetition and prehension of every aspect of the past in each element of the present, Gadamer maintained that 'the past' is what is 'handed down' to us, it is literally *in* the present, with us now.[21] This, in turn, is an interesting restatement of R. G. Collingwood's principle of the 'incapsulation' of the past in the present.[22] The past, according to these thinkers, is the material ground, and its 'ex-events' are the ingredients, of present experience.

Our problem of forgetfulness in the present is thus not an utter loss to oblivion of what once was, but rather it is an *inability to recognise and to decipher or interpret the past in our midst.*

Physicists now routinely remind us that each one of us contains within our own bodies quite a large number of atoms and elementary particles – stardust, if you will – left over from the primordial cosmic Big Bang. The effects of this primordial Event are evident in the present in many other ways – in, for example, the universal background radiation at a temperature of 3 Kelvins that pervades the known universe. Radio astronomers eventually mapped this radiation, creating what they described as a pattern of 'ripples' in the spacetime fabric left over from that primordial generative event billions of years ago.[23] The cosmos itself is thus literally a vast memory of the details of the event of its own genesis. The very physical details of this cosmic history are woven indelibly into the present fabric of the universe.

There is, for the physicist and the astronomer, no vexed metaphysical or ontological question concerning the whereabouts of this determinate past. That past is present; it is *in* the present, and it constitutes the present as the material cause of the present. Our cosmic past has always been with us, and indeed, it has always been us: presumably, Socrates and Phaedrus gazed out wonderingly at the same heavens with the same background radiation as do we now, and their bodies were likewise presumably composed of the same percentage of stardust as are ours. We have, however, only comparatively recently recognised the *presence* of this 'past within us', and even more recently we have begun to learn how to 'read' and to decipher these 'texts'. Bergson, in *Matter and Memory*, was after all fundamentally on the right track: matter is in truth a kind of vast hologram, enfolding the details of its own past; the very physical stuff that we are and that surrounds us is nothing more or less than a record of its – and of our – past.[24]

The 'being' of our determinate physical past, the narration of our origins, is thus now, and always has been, present, determinate, and ready to hand. That presence has, until comparatively recently, gone unrecognised. Once that presence of that past is recognised, moreover, the *meaning* of that past is still unclear. What is clear is that the physicist and the astronomer are, in this case, *historians*, working to uncover and to provide interpretations, narrations, of that cosmic past.

It is likewise with our biological and cultural past. We do not for a moment doubt that we had human ancestors long before the dawn of written records. Indeed, quest for greater knowledge of ancient peoples – of their lives, of the rise and fall of their civilisations – constitutes the principal focus of research in physical anthropology and Palaeolithic archaeology. The memory of their names, if they had names, and the details of their lives, are largely lost to us, forgotten to consciousness. Yet we do not doubt that these 'people without a name' once existed, nor can we reasonably doubt that their lives and experiences had as much determinateness and authenticity for them as do our own for us. They live in our present consciousness more in imagination than in conscious memory. But that does not imply that they themselves were fictitious or that their former being is in any way altered by our inability to recollect and to interpret their lives.

In fact, we have discovered only recently that these people without a name dwell in our midst in the present more readily than any of us might have imagined possible only decades ago. Genetic biologists inform us that, alongside the physicist's stardust, we carry the living biological material, the genetic inheritance, of these ancient peoples and their civilisations. Anthropologists remind us, in addition, that our gait and gestures – raised eyebrows, smiles, salutes, and handshakes – enfold millennia of cultural history stretching back into prehistoric antiquity. The past is biologically and culturally, as well as physically, present in our midst.

In the most literal sense imaginable, we ourselves are constituted out of the *legible texts* of those nameless ancestors. Those temporally distant events and those ancient peoples are within each one of us; we are literally as well as metaphorically constituted (or, more accurately, reconstituted) out of their previous lives and experiences. As we are, each one of us, physically constituted out of the first galactic stars, so each of us carries within us a genetic code that is a complete historical text describing in minute detail every previous connection of ourselves to one another and to those who have gone before us, down to the distant beginnings of time itself. Once more, this physical fact about what we are did not begin to be the case yesterday; rather, persons (and objects and states of affairs) in the world have always been thus constituted. The new development is that we have begun to recognise the presence of the being of the past in our midst only during the last few decades. And, once again, we are far from knowing how to read these 'texts' fully and accurately in their entirety. But were we able – and indeed, insofar as we are becoming increasingly able – to read them, we could recover the details of those ancient prehistoric lives as reliably as we now infer the details of more recent cultures and peoples from the written texts and material cultural artefacts they have bequeathed to us. In the case of primordial prehistory, the genetic biologist, the physical anthropologist, and the archaeologist must serve as our historians, attempting to recollect and interpret what has always been in us and present among us, unrecognised, unnamed, and unknown.

The past has its being in the present; it is not 'located' in some mysterious elsewhere, or solely in the Mind or in the Consequent Nature of God. Rather, the past is with us, and *is* us, in the present. We cannot say and as yet we do not know what other artefacts from the past are present among us – Beings from the past that are ready to hand, whose presence we do not yet recognise, and whose historical texts we do not yet begin to comprehend.

Here, then, is the rectification of Anaximander's 'injustice' and the redemption of what is otherwise seemingly lost to oblivion in the Order of Time. Our history, it turns out, is much more than simply a legacy, one prized possession among many belongings. Rather, *the past is all we have, and it is literally what we are* in the present.

Notes

1. Milan Kundera, *The Book of Laughter and Forgetting*, p. 157; my emphasis.
2. Dr Yuasa, imprisoned for three years as a war criminal at the conclusion of World War II, as quoted in an Associated Press article on Japanese war crimes: *The Baltimore Sun*, Tuesday, 7 September 1993, p. 7A; my emphasis.
3. According to Karl Popper, who first coined the term 'perspectivalism' for this problem now central to the hermeneutics of history [cf. *The Open Society and its Enemies*]: there is not, nor can there be, any one, single, Archimedean, observer-invariant account of past events. Rather, the most one can strive for in historical narrative is 'perspectivalism': 'objectivity' in this case refers only to the attempt to offer an unbiased and impartial or disinterested narrative account from the standpoint of some clearly delineated and reasonably well understood (cultural) perspective; i.e., 'objectivity relative to a certain point of view'.
4. Kundera, *The Book of Laughter and Forgetting*, p. 22.
5. *Newsday* article on Soviet prison camps, reprinted in *The Baltimore Sun*, 'Photo helps ex-Soviet officer recall U.S. prisoner', Monday, 20 September 1993, p. 3A.
6. Kundera, *The Book of Laughter and Forgetting*, p. 3.
7. Robert Conquest's magisterial study of Stalinism, *The Great Terror*, was first published by Oxford University Press in 1968, and it has since been revised, enlarged, and translated into a number of languages (including Russian). His study of forced collectivisation and the Great Ukrainian famine under Stalin, *The Harvest of Sorrow*, was published by Oxford in 1986.

    J. Arch Getty's doctoral dissertation at Boston College in 1979 represented the first venture of social historians into this period and these topics, heretofore the exclusive domain of political commentators, political scientists, and economists. Getty attacks the reliance of Conquest, in particular, on what he defines as 'the totalitarian model' of history and accuses him of 'demonising' Stalin: cf. J. Arch Getty, *Origins of the Great Purges*.

Conquest and Getty were among the participants in a symposium devoted to the 'revisionist history' of Stalinist Russia in *The Russian Review*, vol. 46, no. 4 (October 1987). That symposium, in turn, was prompted by extremely sharp and negative reactions to the lead paper in a previous year's issue of the same journal by Sheila Fitzpatrick: 'New Perspectives on Stalinism', *The Russian Review*, 45, no. 4 (October 1986), pp. 357–74. In addition to these lengthy exchanges, two issues of *The Slavic Review* (Spring 1983 and Summer 1986) also featured discussions of revisionist social history and Stalinism.

8. In his acclaimed novel *1984*, British author George Orwell vividly described the manufacture of 'memory holes', in which the historical record – newspapers, etc. – are systematically rewritten on a daily basis. Archival documents that cannot be rewritten are 'vaporised'.

9. Getty discovered, for example, a report prepared by the Ministry of Internal Affairs in December 1953, documenting the numbers of persons repressed by state security from 1921 to 1953, prepared using KGB archives housed at TsGAOR archive. The charts for each year provided orderly records of the number of persons arrested, the reason for sentences, the numbers executed, and by whom they were sentenced. These documents are included in the 'Annals of Communism' series, some thirty-one volumes published by Yale University Press. See particularly J. Arch Getty and Oleg V. Naumov, *The Road to Terror*.

10. Those knowledgeable about the history of metaphysics in Western philosophy will recognise that this issue constitutes a central motif in the 'process' or event metaphysics of Alfred North Whitehead, described in detail in Chapter 8. Though the problem is not exclusively treated in his thought alone, the problem of the ontological status of past events is treated with a great deal of sophistication there, and, by contrast, largely ignored in most other philosophical discussions since Kant. Not even Hegel, to my knowledge, bothered to thematise or give an account of the 'somewhere' or accessibility of the past – although such an account could be derived by more fully developing certain tacit features of his thought. It is, as Henry Kissinger might say, a symbol of what has happened to philosophy that neither philosophers of history, historiographers, nor historians themselves bother with this question. This is, I suspect, largely because they presuppose one of the two possible positions I discuss: namely, that the past persists only in the form of memory and its artefacts. I attempt to discuss this issue here without delving into the intricacies of Whitehead's systematic thought. But

those interested in a more technical discussion will find the matter treated in somewhat more detail in my *The Rehabilitation of Whitehead*, chapter IX, esp. pp. 161–73.
11. Kundera, *The Book of Laughter and Forgetting*, p. 7; my emphasis.
12. George L. Kline, 'Form, Concrescence, and Concretum' in *Explorations in Whitehead's Philosophy*, pp. 104–46; and '"Present", "Past", and "Future" as Categoreal Terms', pp. 215–35. Kline's obituaries in 2015 in the *Slavic Review* and the *Proceedings of the American Philosophical Association* offer testimony to his considerable contributions to recollecting the lives and work of scholars and literary figures whose work, careers, and even lives were destroyed and suppressed during this dark period of Russian history. Kline is especially credited with having discovered, translated, and subsequently aided in the emigration of Russia's greatest twentieth-century poet, the Nobel laureate Joseph Brodsky.
13. Kline, 'Form, Concrescence, and Concretum' in *Explorations in Whitehead's Philosophy*, p. 131.
14. Kline, 'Form, Concrescence, and Concretum' in *Explorations in Whitehead's Philosophy*, p. 131. This discussion does not appear in an earlier version of this essay, published in the *Southern Journal of Philosophy*, 7 (1969–70), pp. 351–60. In the subsequent paper, the text of Kline's Presidential Address to the Metaphysical Society of America in 1986, Isaac Newton, Jane Austen, and Igor Stravinsky are substituted for Dante, Mozart, and Einstein in the present quote. There Kline concludes: 'Clearly, the meaning of past existents within the history of human civilisation is cumulative and slow to emerge, requiring decades in ordinary cases and centuries in extraordinary ones. Strictly speaking, it is *never* completed; the reinterpretation and reassessment, the *Verwertung* and *Entwertung*, of the contributions to human civilisation of even such geniuses as the three here named is a continuing and unending process. Still, the *being* of such past existents as those three births, at given times and places, is *not* modified by changes in their *meanings*'. [Cf. Kline, '"Present", "Past", and "Future" as Categoreal Terms', p. 223.]
15. Whitehead adopted a phrase from John Locke to describe time itself as 'a perpetual perishing'. The flux of experience that gives rise to temporal passage is quantised, according to Whitehead, into discrete episodes or distinct occasions of experience. Each such active episode or occasion eventuates in its own determinate result or outcome, after which its own internal, self-constituting activity ceases.

In one interpretation of his Lockean variation, these 'ex-events' or finished episodes then 'perish' – that is, they pass out of existence altogether, into oblivion – except and unless they are 'positively prehended' and included as data in the self-actualising activity of some subsequent occasion of experience. Their ultimate loss to oblivion is also prevented by their being caught up as an element in the ongoing divine experience – what Whitehead terms 'the Consequent Nature' of God.

In another interpretation, held by Professor Kline and myself, the 'perishing' of these past or 'ex-events' (Kline, in 'Form, Concrescence, and Concretum', defines these as 'concreta') does not entail their utter loss to oblivion. Rather, their objectified determinateness or 'being' persists indefinitely as potential data for subsequent ('future') acts of becoming. This latter interpretation offers, to my mind, a more satisfactory account of Whitehead's central notion of causality and 'causal efficacy' as the ground of experience, avoids the reliance on a *deus ex machina* to account for the persistence of the past, and yields a more nuanced meaning to Whitehead's oft-quoted Principle of Process, that 'being is *constituted by* becoming' [*Process and Reality*, Corrected Edition (1978), p. 23].

The revised and enlarged version of Professor Kline's article, 'Form, Concrescence, and Concretum' in *Explorations in Whitehead's Philosophy* provides, in my opinion, the best commentary on this problem. Readers may also wish to consult my *The Rehabilitation of Whitehead*, pp. 167–74 and pp. 87–91.

16. Kundera, *The Book of Laughter and Forgetting*, p. 167; my emphasis.
17. Whitehead writes movingly: 'God is the poet of the world . . . sav[ing] the world as it passes into the immediacy of his own life [as] the judgement of a tenderness which loses nothing that can be saved' (*Process and Reality*, Corrected Edition (1978), p. 346).
18. At several key junctures in the *The Phenomenology of Spirit*, in fact, one finds Hegel asserting that *acts of forgetting* are what bring about the flux of historical events – that is, generate time and the historical process itself. For example, he writes: 'The dialectic of [consciousness] is nothing else but the simple history of its movement or of its experience, and [consciousness] itself is nothing else but just this history. . . . Consciousness . . . is always reaching [its] result, learning from experience what is true in it; but equally, it is always *forgetting* it and starting the movement all over again. . . . The consciousness which is this truth has this path behind it [but] has *forgotten* it. . . . It merely asserts that it is all reality but does not itself comprehend this; for it is along that *forgotten path* that [each] immediately expressed assertion is comprehended.' See Hegel's *The Phenomenology of Spirit*, pp. 64, 141.
19. Cf. Hegel's *The Phenomenology of Spirit*, pp. 492–3. See also Donald Phillip Verene, *Hegel's Recollection*, pp. 111–14.
20. The phrases in quotation are from Milan Kundera, *The Unbearable Lightness of Being*, p. 67.

21. Gadamer refers to this feature of the past and of our interpretation of it as 'phenomenological immanence'. See the Foreword to the second edition of his *Truth and Method* (1993), p. xxxvi; see also pp. 264–5.
22. Collingwood, *The Idea of History*; see also *Autobiography*.
23. The chief astronomer of that project, interviewed subsequently in the *Chronicle of Higher Education* in 1992, described this computer-generated 'photograph' of these spacetime ripples, with a touching sense of wonderment, as 'gazing upon the face of God'.
24. Cf. Henri Bergson, *Matter and Memory*, chapter IV. Matter and mind, Bergson observes, are both forms of duration. Matter is in fact wavelike, he opines, consisting of pulses of energy of extreme brevity, bound together by a thread of memory. This view corresponds quite closely to Whitehead's notion of an 'enduring object', constituted of serial societies of actual entities, each inheriting from its predecessors a common element of subjective form. This theory of 'serial inheritance' by Whitehead corresponds, conversely, both to what Bergson seems to describe and also to what is meant in the present essay, by 'physical' memory.

Bibliography

Allen, George, *The Importances of the Past* (Albany: State University of New York Press, 1986).

Ambler, Charles, *Kenyan Communities in the Age of Imperialism* (New Haven: Yale University Press, 1988).

Ambler, Charles, 'The Renovation of Custom in Colonial Kenya', *Journal of African History*, vol. 30, no. 1 (1989), pp. 139–56.

Arendt, Hannah, *Eichmann in Jerusalem: A Report on the Banality of Evil*, 13th edn (New York: Viking Press, 1973).

Arendt, Hannah, *The Human Condition* (Chicago: University of Chicago Press, 1958).

Aristotle, *Metaphysics*, trans. W. D. Ross (Oxford: Clarendon Press, 1924).

Aristotle, *Physics*, trans. W. D. Ross (Oxford: Oxford University Press, 1936).

Barnes, Jonathan, 'Aristotle's Theory of Demonstration', in *Articles on Aristotle*, ed. Jonathan Barnes, Malcolm Schofield, Richard Sorabji (London: Duckworth, 1975).

Baynes, Kenneth, James Bohman, Thomas McCarthy, eds, *After Philosophy: End or Transformation?* (Cambridge, MA: The MIT Press, 1987).

Bergson, Henri, *Matter and Memory*, trans. N. Paul and W. S. Palmer (New York: Macmillan, 1911).

Bogaard, Paul, 'Introduction', in *The Harvard Lectures of Alfred North Whitehead, 1924–1925: Philosophical Presuppositions of Science*, ed. Paul Bogaard and Jason Bell (Edinburgh: Edinburgh University Press, 2017).

Brann, Eva, *The Logos of Heraclitus* (Philadelphia: Paul Dry Books, 2011).

Brann, Eva, 'Presocratics, or First Philosophers?' *Review of Metaphysics*, vol. 70, no. 3 (2017), pp. 435–51.

Brodsky, Joseph, *Watermark* (New York: Farrar, Straus & Giroux, 1992).

Capaldi, Nicholas, *David Hume* (New York: Peter Lang, 1990).

Collingwood, R. G., *Autobiography* (Oxford: Clarendon Press, 1939).

Collingwood, R. G., *Essay on Metaphysics* (Oxford: Oxford University Press, 1940).

Collingwood, R. G., *The Idea of History* (Oxford: Oxford University Press, 1946).

Collins, Randall, *The Sociology of Philosophies: A Global Theory of Intellectual Change* (Cambridge, MA: Harvard/Belknap Press, 1999).

Conquest, Robert, *The Great Terror* (Oxford: Oxford University Press, 1968).

Conquest, Robert, *The Harvest of Sorrow* (Oxford: Oxford University Press, 1986).

Cook, Patricia J., 'Forgetting in the Dialogues of Plato' (Diss. Emory University, 1992).

Cook, Patricia J., 'Recollection as Rhetoric: *Anamnesis* in the *Meno*' (unpublished).

Dahlstrom, Daniel, 'Negation and Being', *Review of Metaphysics*, vol. 64, no. 2 (2010), pp. 247–71.

Danto, Arthur C., *Connections to the World* (New York: Harper & Row, 1989).

Danto, Arthur C., *Encounters and Reflections: Art in the Historical Present* (Berkeley: University of California Press, 1990).

Danto, Arthur C., *The Philosophical Disenfranchisement of Art* (New York: Columbia University Press, 1986).

Dennett, Daniel C., 'Intentional Systems', in *Brainstorms* (Cambridge, MA: The MIT Press, 1981), pp. 3–24.

Dennett, Daniel C., 'Intentional Systems in Cognitive Ethology: The "Panglossian Paradigm" Defended', *Behavioral and Brain Sciences*, vol. 6, no. 3 (1983), pp. 343–90.

Derrida, Jacques, *Margins of Philosophy* (Chicago: University of Chicago Press, 1982).

Desmet, Ronald, 'An Aesthetic Comparison of Einstein's and Whitehead's Theory of Gravity', *Process Studies*, vol. 45, no. 1 (2016), pp. 33–46.

Desmond, William, *Being and Between: Metaphysics and Transcendence* (Albany: State University of New York Press, 1995).

Desmond, William, *Desire, Dialectic, and Otherness* (New Haven, CT: Yale University Press, 1987).

Desmond, William, 'Flux-gibberish: For and Against Heraclitus', *Review of Metaphysics*, vol. 70, no. 3, (2017), pp. 473–506.

Diels-Kranz, Hermann, *Die Fragmente der Vorsokratiker* (Berlin: Weidmannsche Buchhandlung, 1906).

Eco, Umberto, *Foucault's Pendulum* (New York: Harcourt Brace Jovanovich, 1989).

Feyerabend, Paul, *Against Method: Outline of an Anarchistic Theory of Knowledge* (Atlantic Heights, NJ: Humanities Press, 1975).

Feyerabend, Paul, *Science in a Free Society* (London: NLB, 1978).

Fitzpatrick, Sheila, 'New Perspectives on Stalinism', *The Russian Review*, vol. 45, no. 4 (October 1986), pp. 357–74.

Ford, Lewis S., *The Emergence of Whitehead's Metaphysics: 1925–1929* (Albany: State University of New York Press, 1984).

Foucault, Michel, 'Questions of Method', in *After Philosophy: End or Transformation?* ed. Kenneth Baynes, James Bohman, Thomas McCarthy (Cambridge, MA: The MIT Press, 1987), pp. 100–17.

Gadamer, Hans-Georg, *Reason in the Age of Science*, trans. Frederick G. Lawrence (Cambridge, MA: The MIT Press, 1981).

Gadamer, Hans-Georg, 'Reflections on my Philosophical Journey', in *The Philosophy of Hans-Georg Gadamer*, ed. Lewis E. Hahn (LaSalle: Open Court, 1997).

Gadamer, Hans-Georg, 'Reply to George R. Lucas, Jr', in *The Philosophy of Hans-Georg Gadamer*, ed. Lewis E. Hahn (Chicago: Open Court Press, 1997), pp. 190–1.

Gadamer, Hans-Georg, *Truth and Method* (New York: Seabury Press, 1975).

Gadamer, Hans-Georg, *Truth and Method*, 2nd (revised) edn (New York: Crossroads Publishers, 1989).

Gadamer, Hans-Georg, *Truth and Method*, trans. and ed. J. Weinsheimer and D. G. Marshall (New York: Continuum, 1993).

Gale, Richard, 'Disanalogies between Space and Time', in *Process and Analysis*, ed. George W. Shields (Albany: State University of New York Press, 2003), pp. 97–117.

Garber, Daniel, 'What's Philosophical about the History of Philosophy?' in *Analytic Philosophy and History of Philosophy*, ed. Tom Sorell and G. A. J. Rogers (Oxford: Clarendon Press, 2005), pp. 129–46.

Getty, J. Arch, *Origins of the Great Purges: The Soviet Communist Party Reconsidered, 1933–38* (Cambridge: Cambridge University Press, 1985).

Getty, J. Arch and Oleg V. Naumov, *The Road to Terror: Stalin and the Self-Destruction of the Bolsheviks, 1932–1939* (New Haven, CT: Yale University Press, 2010).

Gracia, Jorge E., *Philosophy and its History: Issues in Philosophical Historiography* (Albany: State University of New York Press, 1992).

Gracia, Jorge E., *The Sociology of Philosophies: A Global Theory of Intellectual Change* (Cambridge, MA: Harvard/Belknap Press, 1999).

Grünbaum, Adolf, *The Foundations of Psychoanalysis: A Philosophical Critique* (Berkeley: University of California Press, 1984).

Guthrie, W. K. C., *A History of Greek Philosophy, Vol. I: The Earlier Presocratics and Pythagoreans* (Cambridge: Cambridge University Press, 1962).

Hacking, Ian, 'Five Parables', in *Philosophy in History*, ed. Richard Rorty, Jerome Schneewind, Quentin Skinner (Cambridge: Cambridge University Press, 1984).

Hall, David, *Richard Rorty: Prophet and Poet of the New Pragmatism* (Albany: State University of New York Press, 1994).

Hartnack, Justus, *Wittgenstein and Modern Philosophy*, 2nd edn (Notre Dame: University of Notre Dame Press, 1986).

Hegel, G. W. F., *The Phenomenology of Spirit*, trans. A. V. Miller (Oxford: Clarendon Press, 1977).

Heidegger, Martin, *What is Called-Thinking?* (1951), trans. J. Glenn Gray (New York: Harper & Row, 1976).

Heller, Eric, *The Artist's Journey into the Interior* (New York: Random House, 1959).

Hertzberg, Arthur, ed., *Judaism* (New York: George Braziller, 1962).

Hintikka, Merrill B. and Jaakko Hintikka, *Investigating Wittgenstein* (Oxford: Basil Blackwell, 1986).

Hook, Sidney, Class notes, Stanford University, 1950. Sidney Hook Papers, Box 190, Folder 33, Hoover Institution Archives, Stanford University, Stanford, California.

Hoy, David, *The Critical Circle: Literature and History in Contemporary Hermeneutics* (Berkeley: University of California Press, 1978).

Janik, Allan and Stephen Toulmin, *Wittgenstein's Vienna* (New York: Simon & Schuster, 1973).

Johnsen, Harald and Bjornar Olsen, 'Hermeneutics and Archaeology: On the Philosophy of Contextual Archaeology', *American Antiquity*, vol. 57, no. 3 (1992), pp. 419–36.

Joy, Lynn Sumida, *Gassendi the Atomist: Advocate of History in an Age of Science* (Cambridge: Cambridge University Press, 1987).

Joyce, James, *Finnegans Wake* (London: Faber and Faber, 1939).

Joyce, James, *Portrait of the Artist as a Young Man* (New York: B. W. Huebsch, 1916).

Kelly, Sean and Hubert Dreyfus, *All Things Shining: Reading the Western Classics to Find Meaning in the Secular Age* (New York: Free Press, 2011).

Kimball, Bruce A., *Orators and Philosophers: A History of the Idea of Liberal Education*, expanded edn (New York: College Board, 1995).

Kirk, G. S., J. E. Raven, and M. Schofield, *The Presocratic Philosophers*, 2nd edn (Cambridge: Cambridge University Press, 2007).

Kline, George L., 'Form, Concrescence, and Concretum', *Southern Journal of Philosophy*, vol. 7, no. 4 (1969–70), pp. 351–60.

Kline, George L., 'Form, Concrescence, and Concretum', in *Explorations in Whitehead's Philosophy*, ed. Lewis S. Ford and George L. Kline (New York: Fordham University Press, 1983), pp. 104–46.

Kline, George L., '"Present", "Past", and "Future" as Categoreal Terms, and the "Fallacy of the Actual Future"', *Review of Metaphysics*, vol. 40, no. 2 (December 1986), pp. 215–35.

Köhnke, Klaus Christian, *The Rise of Neo-Kantianism: German Academic Philosophy between Idealism and Positivism*, trans. R. J. Hollingdale (Cambridge: Cambridge University Press, 1991).

Kuhn, Thomas, *The Structure of Scientific Revolutions* (1960), revised edn (Chicago: University of Chicago Press, 1972).

Kundera, Milan, *The Book of Laughter and Forgetting*, trans. Michael Henry Heim (London: Penguin Books, 1983).

Kundera, Milan, *The Unbearable Lightness of Being*, trans. Michael Henry Heim (London: Faber & Faber, 1984).

Linge, David E., 'Introduction', in *Gadamer's Kleine Schriften: Philosophical Hermeneutics* (Berkeley: University of California Press, 1977).

Livingston, Donald W., *Hume's Conception of 'Common Life'* (Chicago: University of Chicago Press, 1984).

Locke, John, *An Essay Concerning Human Understanding* (London: Thomas Basset, 1690).

Lowe, Victor, *Alfred North Whitehead: The Man and His Work* (Baltimore: Johns Hopkins University Press, vol. 1 1985; vol. 2 1990).

Lowe, Victor, 'Whitehead's Gifford Lectures', *Southern Journal of Philosophy*, vol. 7, no. 4 (Winter 1969–70), pp. 329–38.

Lucas, Jr, George R., 'Eine Whiteheadische Auslegung der Naturphilosophie Hegels', in *Whitehead und der deutsche Idealismus*, ed. George R. Lucas, Jr, and Antoon Braeckman (Frankfurt & Bern: Peter Lang, 1990).

Lucas, Jr, George R., *The Genesis of Modern Process Thought: An Historical Outline with Bibliography* (Metuchen, NJ: Scarecrow Press, 1983).

Lucas, Jr, George R., 'Hartshorne and the Development of Process Philosophies', in *The Philosophy of Charles Hartshorne*, ed. Lewis E. Hahn. The Library of Living Philosophers, vol. 20 (LaSalle: Open Court Press, 1991).

Lucas, Jr, George R., 'The Interpretation of Kant in Whitehead's Philosophy', *Ruch Filozoficzny Kwartalnik*, vol. 47, no. 3/4 (1990), pp. 213–30.

Lucas, Jr, George R., 'The Interpretation of Kant in Whitehead's Philosophy', in *Whitehead und der deutsche Idealismus*, ed. George R. Lucas, Jr and Antoon Braeckman (Frankfurt and Bern: Peter Lang, 1990).

Lucas, Jr, George R., 'Philosophy, its History, and Hermeneutics', in *The Philosophy of Hans-Georg Gadamer*, ed. Louis E. Hahn (LaSalle: Open Court Press, 1996), pp. 173–89.

Lucas, Jr, George R., 'Refutation, Narrative, and Engagement: Three Philosophies of the History of Philosophy', in *Philosophical Imagination and Cultural Memory*, ed. Patricia J. Cook (Durham, NC: Duke University Press, 1993), pp. 104–23.

Lucas, Jr, George R., *The Rehabilitation of Whitehead: An Analytic and Historical Assessment of Process Philosophy* (Albany: State University of New York Press, 1989).

Lucas, Jr, George R., 'The Seventh Seal: On the Fate of Whitehead's Proposed Rehabilitation', *Process Studies*, vol. 25 (1996): 104–16.

McHenry, Leemon B., *Whitehead and Bradley: A Comparative Analysis* (New York: State University of New York Press, 1992).
MacIntyre, Alasdair, *After Virtue* (Notre Dame: University of Notre Dame Press, 1981).
MacIntyre, Alasdair, 'Epistemological Crises, Dramatic Narrative, and the Philosophy of Science', *The Monist*, vol. 60, no. 4 (October 1977), pp. 453–72.
MacIntyre, Alasdair, *First Principles, Final Ends, and Contemporary Philosophical Issues* (Milwaukee: Marquette University Press, 1990).
MacIntyre, Alasdair, 'Narrativity and Truth', in *Philosophical Imagination and Cultural Memory: The Philosophical Uses of Historical Traditions*, ed. Patricia Cook (Durham, NC: Duke University Press, 1993).
MacIntyre, Alasdair, 'The Relationship of Philosophy to its Past', in *Philosophy in History*, ed. Richard Rorty, Jerome Schneewind, Quentin Skinner (Cambridge: Cambridge University Press, 1984).
MacIntyre, Alasdair, *Three Rival Versions of Moral Enquiry* (Notre Dame: University of Notre Dame Press, 1990).
MacIntyre, Alasdair, *Whose Justice? Which Rationality?* (Notre Dame: University of Notre Dame Press, 1988).
Magill, Frank N., ed., *Dictionary of World Biography* (Oxford: Routledge, 2003).
Malcolm, Norman, *Ludwig Wittgenstein: A Memoir* (Oxford: Oxford University Press, 1958/1984).
Malcolm, Norman, 'Wittgenstein, Ludwig Josef Johann', in *The Encyclopedia of Philosophy*, ed. Paul Edwards (New York: The Free Press, 1967), vol. 8, p. 327.
Nadler, Stephen, 'The History of Philosophy: What is it Good For?' *Proceedings & Addresses of the American Philosophical Association* (2014), pp. 39–48. Available online at www.apaonline.org/default.asp?page=presidents (accessed 15 December 2019).
Neville, Robert C., *The Highroad Around Modernism* (Albany: State University of New York Press, 1992).
Neville, Robert C., ed., *New Essays in Metaphysics* (Albany: State University of New York Press, 1986).
Neville, Robert C., *Recovery of the Measure* (Albany: State University of New York Press, 1989).
Nietzsche, Friedrich, *On the Advantages and Disadvantages of History for Life* (1874), trans. Peter Preuss (Indianapolis: Hackett Publishers, 1980).
Nussbaum, Martha C., *Cultivating Humanity: A Classical Defense of Reform in Liberal Education* (Cambridge, MA: Harvard University Press, 1998).
Nussbaum, Martha C., *Love's Knowledge: Essays on Philosophy and Literature* (New York: Oxford University Press, 1990).
Nussbaum, Martha C., 'Recoiling from Reason', *New York Review of Books*, 7 December 1989, pp. 36–41.

Orwell, George, *1984* (London: Secker & Warburg, 1949).
Pinkard, Terry, *Hegel* (New York: Cambridge University Press, 2000).
Plato, *The Collected Dialogues*, trans. R. Hackforth, ed. Edith Hamilton and Huntington Cairns (Princeton: Princeton University Press, 1961).
Plato, *Republic*, trans. Richard Shorey (Cambridge, MA: Harvard University Press, 1946).
Polanyi, Michael, *Personal Knowledge* (Chicago: University of Chicago Press, 1974).
Pols, Edward, 'On Knowing Directly: The Actualization of First Philosophy', *Review of Metaphysics*, vol. 41, no. 2 (1987), pp. 229–30.
Pols, Edward, *Radical Realism: Direct Knowing in Science and Philosophy* (Ithaca: Cornell University Press, 1992).
Pols, Edward, 'Realism vs Antirealism: The Venue of the Linguistic Consensus', *Review of Metaphysics*, vol. 43, no. 4 (June 1990), pp. 717–49.
Popper, Karl, *The Open Society and its Enemies* (London: Routledge, 1945).
Price, H. H., 'Appearing and Appearances', *American Philosophical Quarterly*, vol. 1, no. 1 (1964), pp. 3–19.
Quine, Willard V. O., 'Mr. Strawson on Logical Theory', *Mind*, vol. 62, no. 248 (1953), pp. 433–51.
Quine, Willard V. O., *Pursuit of Truth* (Cambridge, MA: Harvard University Press, 1990).
Rajchman, John and Cornel West, eds, *Post-Analytic Philosophy* (New York: Columbia University Press, 1985).
Reichenbach, Hans, *The Rise of Scientific Philosophy* (Berkeley: University of California Press, 1951).
Ricoeur, Paul, *The Philosophy of Paul Ricoeur: An Anthology of His Work*, ed. C. Reagan and D. Stewart (Boston, MA: Beacon Press, 1978).
Robinson, David, 'French "Islamic" Policy and Practice in Late Nineteenth-Century Senegal', *Journal of African History*, vol. 29, no. 3 (1988), pp. 415–35.
Robinson, David, *The Holy War of Umar Tal. The Western Sudan in the Mid-Nineteenth Century* (Oxford: Oxford University Press, 1985).
Rorty, Richard, *The Consequences of Pragmatism* (Minneapolis: University of Minnesota Press, 1982).
Rorty, Richard, 'The Historiography of Philosophy: Four Genres', in *Philosophy in History*, ed. Richard Rorty, Jerome Schneewind, Quentin Skinner (Cambridge: Cambridge University Press, 1984).
Rorty, Richard, *History of Western Philosophy* (London: George Allen & Unwin, 1946).
Rosen, Stanley, *The Ancients and the Moderns* (New Haven, CT: Yale University Press, 1989).
Rosen, Stanley, *Hermeneutics as Politics* (London: Oxford University Press, 1987).

Rosen, Stanley, *Nihilism: A Philosophical Essay* (New Haven, CT: Yale University Press, 1969).
Russell, Bertrand, *My Philosophical Development* (London: George Allen & Unwin, 1959).
Schneewind, Jerome B., *Essays on the History of Moral Philosophy* (New York: Oxford University Press, 2009).
Schneewind, Jerome B., *The Invention of Autonomy* (New York: Cambridge University Press, 1998).
Schneewind, Jerome B., *Moral Philosophy from Montaigne to Kant* (Cambridge: Cambridge University Press, 1990).
Schulte, Joachim, *Wittgenstein: An Introduction*, trans. William H. Brenner and John F. Holley (Albany: State University of New York Press, 1992).
Sherburne, Donald, *A Key to Whitehead's Process and Reality* (New York: Macmillan, 1966; reprinted by University of Chicago Press, 1986).
Skinner, Quentin, 'Introduction: The Return of Grand Theory', in *The Return of Grand Theory in the Human Sciences*, ed. Quentin Skinner (Cambridge: Cambridge University Press, 1985).
Stoltz, Joachim, *Whitehead und Einstein* (Frankfurt am Main: Peter Lang, 1995).
Sullivan, David, 'Hermann Lotze', *The Stanford Encyclopedia of Philosophy* (Winter 2014 edition), ed. Edward N. Zalta. Available online at plato.stanford.edu/archives/win2014/entries/hermann-lotze
Taylor, Charles, 'Philosophy and its History', in *Philosophy in History*, ed. Richard Rorty, Jerome Schneewind, Quentin Skinner (Cambridge: Cambridge University Press, 1984).
Thomas, Dylan, 'Do not go gentle into that good night', *The Poems of Dylan Thomas* (New York: New Directions, 1952).
Verene, Donald Phillip, 'The Canon of the Primal Scene in Speculative Philosophy', *Journal of Speculative Philosophy* New Series, vol. 1, no. 2 (1987), pp. 135–46.
Verene, Donald Phillip, *Hegel's Recollection* (Albany: State University of New York Press, 1985).
Verene, Donald Phillip, *The History of Philosophy: A Reader's Guide* (Evanston: Northwestern University Press, 2008).
Verene, Donald Phillip, *Philosophy and the Return to Self-Knowledge* (New Haven, CT: Yale University Press, 1997).
Verene, Donald Phillip, *Vico and Joyce* (Albany: State University of New York Press, 1987).
Verene, Donald Phillip, *Vico's Science of Imagination* (Ithaca: Cornell University Press, 1981).
Weiss, Paul, *Privacy* (Carbondale: Southern Illinois University Press, 1983).
Weiss, Paul, *Reality* (New York: Peter Smith, 1939).

Wheelwright, Philip, *The Presocratics* (New York: Pearson, 1966).

Whitehead, Alfred North, *Adventures of Ideas* (New York: Macmillan, 1933).

Whitehead, Alfred North, *The Edinburgh Critical Edition of the Complete Works of Alfred North Whitehead*, Volumes 1–6, series eds Brian G. Henning, George Lucas, Joseph Petek (Edinburgh: Edinburgh University Press, 2016).

Whitehead, Alfred North, *Process and Reality* (New York: Macmillan, 1929).

Whitehead, Alfred North, *Process and Reality* (Cambridge: Cambridge University Press, 1929).

Whitehead, Alfred North, *Process and Reality* (New York: The Free Press, 1969).

Whitehead, Alfred North, *Process and Reality*, Corrected Edition, ed. David Ray Griffin and Donald W. Sherburne (New York: Free Press, 1978).

Whitehead, Alfred North, *Science and the Modern World* (New York: Macmillan, 1925).

Wilshire, Bruce, *The Moral Collapse of the University* (Albany: State University of New York Press, 1989).

Wittgenstein, Ludwig, *On Certainty*, trans. Denis Paul and G. E. M. Anscombe, ed. G. E. M. Anscombe and G. H. von Wright (London: Basil Blackwell, 1969).

Wittgenstein, Ludwig, *Philosophical Investigations*, 3rd edn, trans. G. E. M. Anscombe (New York: Macmillan, 1968).

Wittgenstein, Ludwig, *Tractatus Logico-Philosophicus* (London: Kegan Paul, 1922).

Zweig, Arnulf, 'Beneke, Friedrich Eduard', in *The Encyclopedia of Philosophy*, ed. Paul Edwards (New York: Macmillan, 1967).

Index

absolute knowing, 16, 17, 133
Absolute Spirit, 17, 136
academia
   politics of, 24–5, 26, 34, 118
   revolution in, 34, 37, 43
   see also university
academic disciplines
   interdependence of, 38–9
   personal preferences in, 40
   separation of, 24, 25, 26, 30–2, 39, 55
   subjective versus objective, 39
   in university culture, 41
   see also university
actual, definition of, 105
actual entities (res verae), 105, 128, 129
   ordering of, 106
   see also actual occasion; event
actual occasion, 105, 128, 129
   definition of, 129
   and eternal object, 130
   everlasting, 131
   God as, 133
   parts in, 133
   perishing of, 105–6
   and process, 129
   properties in, 131
   subsequent, 105
   see also actual entities
actuality
   and being, 64, 143
   and memory, 143
   versus representation, 64
   and Weiss, 83
adaptation, and context, 71, 72
aesthetic homelessness, 69
aesthetic interpretation, 62–6
   versus philosophical interpretation, 65–9
After Virtue (MacIntyre) (1981), 36, 37, 47
Akiva ben Joseph, 73–4, 76
Alexander, Samuel, 104, 133
   and time, 107
American Philosophical Association, 37
Amos (prophet), 16
analytic philosophy *see* philosophy, analytic
Anaxagoras, 14
Anaximander, 151
   and anger, 5, 16
   and experience, 14–15, 16
   and historical process, 17
   and injustice of history, 13–17
   and justice, 15–16
   and movements in philosophy, 2
   and ordering of time, 13–17, 25–6
   and process, 15
   and role of philosophy, 17
   and task of philosophical thinking, 13–17
   and unmediated experience, 8
Anaximenes, 14
Ancients and the Moderns (Rosen) (1989), 53
anger
   and Anaximander, 5, 16
   and fairness, 15–16
   and Hebrew prophets, 16
   and marginalisation, 16
answer
   interpretation as, 65
   statement as, 64–5
Aperion, 14, 15
Aquinas, Thomas, 30
   marginalisation of, 33
   and progress in philosophy, 49
   renewed interest in, 37, 43
Arendt, Hannah, 9, 18n5
Aristotle, 57
   caricature by, 89
   and history of philosophy, 89
   master narrative in, 51
   method of, 4, 51, 59, 84, 85, 90–1
   morality in, 35–6
   and passionate engagement, 55
   and progress in philosophy, 49
   relationship of, with Plato, 89–90
   renewed interest in, 37, 43
arrow of time, 105–6
art
   and hermeneutics, 68–9
   interpretation of, 64–5, 69, 70, 74
   movements in, 48
   narrative in, 37
   passionate engagement in, 55
   and philosophy, 65–6
   as philosophy, 65
   progress versus history in, 39–41
   successive movements in, 48
   transitions in, 55
art, history of, 39–41
   and hermeneutics, 68–9
   importance of, 66-7
   versus history of philosophy, 48
artist
   creation of worlds by, 67, 75, 76
   intentions of, 69
   interpretation by, 78n9

Artist's Journey into the Interior (Heller) (1965), 98
Augustine, 50
  language theory of, 113
  and recollection, 145
Austen, Jane, 37
Autobiography (Collingwood) (1939), 90
Ayer, A. J., 113

Bacon, Francis, 4
bad historical consciousness, 6, 6n6, 38, 83, 88
becoming
  and being, 127, 129, 130, 153–4n15
  experience of, 104
  and flux, 104
  flux of, defined, 105
  of occasions, 105
being
  and actuality, 64
  and becoming, 127, 129, 130, 153–4n15
  categories of, 129
  disclosure of, 19–20n16
  forgetfulness of, 145
  incompleteness of, 83
  inexhaustibility of, 64, 70, 76
  and justice, 15
  and meaning, 153n14
  as meaning, in Heidegger, 70
  versus nonbeing, 13
  openness to, 11, 12
  in philosophical activity, 9
  and process, 130
  recollection of, 145
  of thing in itself, 64
  and thinking, 9
  and understanding, 70
  and value, 15
  see also ontology
being, versus meaning, 76, 79n20, 143
  distinction between, 69–70
  in history, 69–71
  in law, 71–4
  in psychoanalysis, 70
Being and Time (Heidegger) (1927), 126
Beneke, Friedrich Eduard, 21–7
  and academic disciplines, 25
  biographical sketch of, 22–3
  career of, 22, 23
  death of, 23, 28n6, 141
  denunciation of, 23
  and Hegel, 23, 137
  influence of, 23, 24
  marginalisation of, 23, 137, 140, 141–2
  memory of, 147
  and Mill, 21–2
  persecution of, 23
  philosophy of, 22–3
  and philosophy as science, 25
  physical legacy of, 139
  recollection of, 140–1
  suppression of, 25, 28n6, 137, 140–1
Berger, Peter L., 36
Bergson, Henri, 104, 148, 149
  marginalisation of, 33
  matter and mind in, 155n24
  and memory, 149
  and Russell, 92
  and time, 107
  and Whitehead, 92
Berkeley, George, 36
Big Bang, residue of, in present, 149
biology, as subdiscipline of philosophy, 32

blooming, buzzing confusion, 12, 132
Bloomsbury circle, 103, 119
Boltzmann, Ludwig
  influence of, on Wittgenstein, 99
  and model of time, 110
Book of Laughter and Forgetting (Kundera) (1979), 136, 137, 145
Bradley, F. H., 9, 36, 128
  dualism of, 36
  and Russell, 92
  and Whitehead, 92
Brann, Eva T. H., 9, 11
Brightman, Edgar Sheffield, 134
British colonial rule, 71–2
Broad, C. D., and sense-data theory, 131
Brodsky, Joseph, 66
Bruckner, Anton, 99

called-thinking, 18n5
  for Arendt, 18n5
  definition of, 9, 18n4
  and history of philosophy, 9–10
  and unmediated experience, 11
Cambridge, University of, philosophy in, 115, 119, 126
Cambridge Apostles, 101
Cambridge trinity, 98, 107, 116
caricature
  by Aristotle, 89, 94n12
  and British philosophy, 90
  and Collingwood, 90
  and Cusanus, 90–1
  effects of, on collegiality, 91
  as error of interpretation, 88–91
  as false philosophy, 91
  and Gassendi, 90
  by Hartshorne, 89
  in history of philosophy, 88–91
  and Hume, 91
  in philosophy, 36, 89, 90–1, 92, 94n12
  of Plato, 94n12
  and Rorty, 91
  and Russell, 89, 92
  as sophistry, 91
  and Vico, 90–1
  by Weiss, 89
Carnap, Rudolf
  and history of philosophy, 30, 49, 54
  and scientific philosophy, 43, 115
Carnot, Marie François Sadi, 63
categoreal obligations, 130
Categories of Existence, 130
Categories of Understanding, 130
causal efficacy, 131–2
causality, 108, 109, 110, 132
Cervantes, Miguel de, 3, 37
change, versus permanence, 127
Cicero, 3
Collingwood, R. G., 100
  and caricature, 90
  cultural context of, 104
  and history of philosophy, 30, 33, 44
  and history of science, 41
  marginalisation of, 26, 33
  and past, in present, 148
  and philosophy as science, 43
  and politics of academia, 34
  renewed interest in, 43
  and role of philosophy, 100–1
  and statement as answer to question, 77n3
  and Whitehead, 102

Index 167

common sense
    and Moore, 116, 120
    and philosophy, 117
    and Russell, 116
    and science, 117
    and Whitehead, 117, 120, 127
    and Wittgenstein, 120
Comte, Auguste, 22
Concept of Nature (Whitehead) (1920)
    enduring objects in, 130
    event in, 126
Connections to the World (Danto) (1989), 48–9
Conquest, Robert, 138–9
consciousness
    bad historical, 6, 6n6, 38, 83, 88
    and experience, 21
    and forgetting, 141, 142
    origin of, 128
    and remembering, 142
consensus, 25, 27
    in the arts, 40
    decline in, 35–6, 44
    desire for, 42–3
    divergence from, 26
    eschatology of, 42–3, 54
    rejection of, 42–3
    in science, 93
    in scientific philosophy, 32, 35
Consequent Nature of God, 17, 148, 153–4n15
conversation
    in Gadamer, 68–9
    with history, 19n14, 80n25, 83, 128
    with history of philosophy, 103
    interpretation as, 65, 74
    participation in, 56
    philosophy as , 2, 4, 36–7, 44, 50, 54, 57, 69, 74–5, 76, 84, 92, 93, 107, 114
    with tradition, 57
conversation which we are, 44, 54, 75, 76
cosmology
    and philosophy, 93
    of Whitehead, 109, 111, 125
    and Wittgenstein, 109
Critique of Pure Reason (Kant) (1781), 32, 101
Cusanus, Nicholas, 90–1

Dante Alighieri, 3, 37
Danto, Arthur, 27, 36, 44, 47, 48–9, 54
Darwin, Charles, 100
definiteness, 126, 130, 155n24
Dennett, Daniel, 110
Derrida, Jacques, 103
    and decline of philosophy, 37
    and deconstruction, 55–6
    and history of philosophy, 103
    and philosophy in the margins, 87
Descartes, Réné, 3–4, 42, 93, 103
    and history of philosophy, 49
    method of, 4
    and preference for science, 38–9
    and reform of philosophy, 119
    res verae of, 105, 129
    Subjectivist Principle of, 106
    and Whitehead, 128
Desmond, William, 13
determinate entity *see* entity, determinate
determinateness, 105, 130, 142, 150
Dewey, John, 33, 37, 52, 131

dialogue *see* conversation
dike, definition of, 14–15
Dilthey, Wilhelm, 24, 56
    hermeneutics of, 67
Diogenes Laertius, 29
direct realism, 11
disciple(s)
    of Husserl, 85–6
    Meno as, 86
    Phaedrus as, 86
    in philosophy, 85–6
    in religion, 85
    of Whitehead, 86
discipleship
    definition of, 85
    as error of interpretation, 85–7
    and exegesis, 87–8
    and history of philosophy, 85–7
    and privacy, 85
discourse *see* conversation
divine mind, 148
doxography, 29, 55, 58n9, 88
Dreyfus, Alfred, 63
Dubček, Alexander, 137–8

Eco, Umberto, 62, 66
economics
    history in, 41
    as science, 41
    as subdiscipline of philosophy, 32
Eddington, Arthur, 105
Eichmann, Adolf, 9
eide (Forms), 90, 95–6n15, 127, 148
Einstein, Albert, 100
    and space, 104
    theory of general relativity of, 101
    and time, 105, 107
Empedocles, and unmediated experience, 14
Enlightenment
    critique of, 111–20
    and Moore, 120
    and perfectibility, 119
    and progress, 119
    rejection of, 120
    and Whitehead, 120
    and Wittgenstein, 120
Enquiry Concerning the Principles of Natural Knowledge (Whitehead) (1919), 119
entity, actual, 105, 128
entity, determinate, 83
epistemology
    grounded in experience, 23
    history of, relevance of, 30
    and history of philosophy, 36
    repudiation of, 55
    return to, 23–4
    and unmediated experience, 12–13
    and Whitehead, 126
epochē, 11, 12
Erkenntnislehre, as proper philosophy, 25
Erkenntnislehre nach dem Bewusstsein der reinen Vernunft (Beneke) (1820), 22–3
Erkenntnistheorie, 23
eternal object *see* object, eternal
ethics
    history of, relevance of, 30
    models for, 111
    renewed interest in, 37
    rise of, 27
    as scientific philosophy, 115
    in Wittgenstein, 99, 119

event
  definition of, 126
  discrete, temporality of, 127
  objective, 106
  perishing of, 105
  subjective, 106
  in Whitehead, 126
event, past
  being of, 143, 153–4n15
  existence of, 148
  location of, 142
  and oblivion, 142
  ontological status of, 142–5
  prehension of, 153–4n15
exegesis
  and discipleship, 87–8
  as error of interpretation, 87–8
  errors in, 89
  function of, 87–8
  by Whitehead, 103
existence
  categories of, 130
  and injustice, 15
  and justice, 15
  and memory, 142
  potential, 15
  and recollection, 149–50
experience
  and Anaximander, 8, 14–15, 16
  of becoming, 104, 104
  categories of, 130
  and causal efficacy, 131
  concrete, abstraction from, 132
  and consciousness, 21
  and determinateness, 130
  and eternal object, 131–2
  flux of, 153–4n15
  historical, 8
  in Joyce, 19n12
  and justice, 14–15, 16
  limitations on, 130
  and metaphysics, 11–12, 105, 112, 130–1
  and myth, 11, 13, 14
  occasions of, 105, 129, 130
  and order, 132
  ordering of, 11–12, 13, 14
  origin of, 128
  and philosophy, 8
  potential, 15
  primordial *see* experience, unmediated
  quantum, 106, 107, 126
  and science, 100
  of temporal passage, 105–6
  and theory, 100
  and time, 109
  veridicality of, 13
experience, unmediated (primordial), 132
  concept of, 10
  definitions of, 12
  and epistemology, 12–13
  exemplars of, 12
  and Heraclitus, 13
  and Husserl, 12
  and James, 12
  and knowledge, 12–13, 14
  and myth, 14
  openness to, 11
  ordering of, 11–12, 14
  and Peirce, 12
  and phenomenology, 12
  philosophy of, 11–12

  and pragmatism, 12
  and presocratics, 10–14
  principles of, 13–14
  quest for, 8, 10–13
  and time, 14
  in Verene, 11
  in Vico, 11
explanation versus understanding, 56, 61n31, 86
extensive continuum, 104, 133

fairness, 15–16
fallacy of misplaced concreteness, 100
feelings, 129
  and occasions, 131
  in *Process and Reality*, 128
Feibleman, James K., 134
Feuerbach, Ludwig Andreas, 21
Feyerabend, Paul, 53
Finnegans Wake (Joyce) (1939), 11
firstness (Peirce), 11, 12, 14
Fiske, John, 52
Fitzpatrick, Sheila, 138
flux
  and becoming, 13, 104
  of becoming, 105, 127
  experience of, 8, 19n12, 104
  of experience, 153–4n15
  of historical events, 154n18
  in Joyce, 19n12
  of ordinary occasion, 131
  primordial, experience of, 14
  of sense-impressions, 12
flux-gibberish, 13, 18n14
forgetting
  and consciousness, 141, 142
  definition of, 141
  and existence, 142
  failure of, 147
  and flux of historical events, 154n18
  and history, 85, 136, 145–6
  history of philosophy as, 16–17
  intentional, 136–7, 140–1, 143
  and interpretation of past, 148–9
  and Kundera, 146–7
  and memory, 138
  and 'Myth of Er', 145
  partial, 146
  past, 136, 137
  and recollection, 138, 146
  and research method, 138–9
  resistance to, 138
  see also memory; recollection; remembering
Forms, 90, 95–6n15, 127, 148
Foucault, Michel, 33, 37, 55
Foucault's Pendulum (Eco) (1988), 62
Fragility of Goodness (Nussbaum) (1986), 48
France, unrest in, 63–4
Frege
  and mathematics, 116
  and scientific philosophy, 115, 116
  and Wittgenstein, 98, 99, 114
French colonial rule, 71–2
Freud, Sigmund, 99
Freudian repression, as analogy for cultural amnesia, 146–7
future
  in McTaggart, 106–7
  and present, asymmetry of, 105
  in Whitehead, 106–7

Index

Gadamer, Hans-Georg, 56
    and conversation, 68–9
    and conversation with history, 74
    fusion of horizons in, 69
    and history of philosophy, 33, 67, 103
    and interpretation, 65–6
    and law in social context, 71
    marginalisation of, 33
    and past, 148
    statements and questions in, 64–5
    and task of philosophy, 57
    and understanding, 68, 70
Gale, Richard, 81
    and history, 86
    private philosophy of, 81, 83, 84–5
    rejection of history by, 81, 83
    and time, 107
Galileo, 42, 93
    and mathematics, 116
    and preference for science, 38–9
    and reform of science, 119
Gassendi, Pierre, 3, 42
    and caricature, 90
    and false precision, 116–17
    and history, 116
    humanism versus science in, 38
    and mathematics, 116
    and science, 116
Gassendi the Atomist (Joy) (1987), 27, 38
Geistesgeschichte, 50, 54, 58n9
general relativity *see* relativity, general
geometry, relativistic, in *Process and Reality*, 133
Geschichte des Materialismus (Lange) (1866), 22
Getty, J. Arch, 138–9
Gifford Lectures, 103
    MacIntyre's, 59
    Whitehead's, 93, 101, 102, 125, 128, 133
God
    as actual occasion, 131, 133
    and eternal objects, 132
    nature of, 109, 133–4
    in *Process and Reality*, 133
    in process theology, 133
    and recollection, 133–4
    and Whitehead, 108, 109
    and Wittgenstein, 122n27
Gödel, Kurt, 115–16
Good
    and Moore, 120
    and reason, 119
    and Whitehead, 120
    and Wittgenstein, 119, 120
Great Terror (Soviet Union) (1936–8), 138–9, 147
Grünbaum, Adolf, 10, 134
Guthrie, W. K. C., 8

Habermas, Jürgen, 56
Hacking, Ian
    and history of philosophy, 44, 47
    and history of science, 41, 42
hagiography, as error of interpretation, 88
Hamilton, William, 52
Harmonielehre (Schoenberg) (1922), 99
harmony, 132
    preestablished, 131
Hartshorne, Charles, 134
    caricature by, 89
    and history of philosophy, 89
    interpretation of Whitehead by, 128
Hawking, Stephen, 110

Hegel, Georg Wilhelm Friedrich, 30
    absolute knowing in, 133–4
    and Beneke, 23, 137
    and cultural shifts in philosophy, 26
    and forgetting, 145–6
    and history of philosophy, 44
    idealism of, 36
    marginalisation of, 16, 33
    and philosophical insight, 16
    and progress in philosophy, 49
    marginalisation of, 16
    master narrative of, 5, 16, 17
    renewed interest in, 37, 43
Hegel (Taylor) (1975), 47
Hegelian idealism, dominance of, 21
Heidegger, 34, 110
    and being, 64, 70
    and decline of philosophy, 37
    definition of philosophy by, 9
    and forgetting, 145
    and history of philosophy, 44, 103
    and presocratics, 75
    renewed interest in, 37
    and unmediated experience, 10, 11
Heller, Eric, 98
Helmholtz, Wilhelm von, 24
Heraclitus
    and first word, 11
    and historical process, 17
    logos in, 12
    and role of philosophy, 17
    and unmediated experience, 13, 14
hermeneutics, 64–5, 77n6
    aesthetic versus philosophical, 76
    approach to, 56–7
    and art, 68–9
    emphases in, 70
    and history, 70
    and objectivity, 78n14
    as philosophical method, 67, 69, 78–9n15
    and philosophy, 74, 75–6
    as practical philosophy, 65
    as scientific methodology, 67
    see also interpretation
Hertz, Heinrich, 111
    influence of, on Wittgenstein, 99
    and model of time, 110
Hesse, Mary, 66
highway of despair, 146
Hintikka, Jaakko, 115
Hintikka, Merrill, 115
historians
    interpretation by, 148
    and recollection, 138, 139–40
    scientists as, 149–50
historical consciousness, 146
historical engagement, 53–5
historical narrative, objectivity in, 151n3
historical process
    and Anaximander, 17
    and Heraclitus, 17
    of philosophy, 16–17
historical tradition
    abuse of, 55, 88–91
    cyclical return to, 27
    law as, 72–4
    philosophical uses of, 57, 68, 74, 75
    in religion, 57
    in theology, 57
'Historiography of Philosophy: Four Genres' (Rorty) (1984), 48

history
  abuses of, in philosophy, 83, 85–91
  being versus meaning in, 69–71
  comprehended, 146
  continuity in, 50
  conversation with, 80n25, 83, 128
  cultural, in present, 150
  as discipline, 39
  erasure from, 136, 137, 138–9, 140–1, 142–3, 145, 148
  and forgetting, 85, 136–7, 140–2
  and Gassendi, 116
  genetic code as, 150
  and hermeneutics, 70
  and Hume, 116
  importance of, to all disciplines, 38–40
  injustice of, 1–5, 13–17
  intellectual, 9–10, 26, 74
  and law, 71–4
  and metaphysics, 17
  methodology in, 138–9
  narrative in, 148
  partial forgetting in, 139
  perspectivalism in, 136
  and philosophical insight, 16
  of philosophy *see* philosophy, history of
  philosophy as conversation with, 74–5
  philosophy in margins of, 16
  versus progress, 39–41
  and recollection, 136, 142, 148
  recovery of, in philosophy, 44
  redemption of, 17, 27
  reflective engagement with, 76
  remembering in, 140–2
  reweaving narrative of, 50, 54, 139–40, 146
  roles of, 39–40, 82–5
  in social sciences, 42
  suppression in, 140
  and truth, 49–50, 55
  winnowing and selection in, 85
  see also past
History of Western Philosophy (Russell) (1945), 92, 104
Hocking, William Ernest, 102
Holocaust, 139, 147
Homer, and myths of origin, 75
homme de lettres, 86
humanism versus science, 38, 41–2, 56, 116
Hume, David, 103
  and caricature, 91
  and false precision, 116–17
  and history, 41, 116
  and irony, 117
  in margins of philosophy, 117
  and mathematics, 116
  morality in, 35–6
  renewed interest in, 37
  and science, 116
  and Whitehead, 92, 93, 128
Husserl, Edmund
  disciples of, 85–6
  and *epochē*, 11
  and philosophy as science, 34
  renewed interest in, 37
  repudiation of history of philosophy by, 49
  and unmediated experience, 10, 12
hyle, 12

idealism
  absolute, 22, 23–4
  decline of, 22, 23–4
  German, 21, 52
  versus realism, 11
image
  ontological standing of, 64
  versus thing in itself, 64
immortality, and recollection, 134, 145
Imperial College (London), 101
Imperial College of Science and Technology (London), 126
incompleteness
  of being, 83, 87
  of God's nature, 133
  of history, 77n3, 136, 146
  of meaning, 144
  and privacy, 87
  sense of, 146
Incompleteness Theorem (Gödel), 115–16
India under colonial rule, 71–2
injustice of history, 5
  and Anaximander, 15–16, 17
  and Beneke, 25–6, 141–2
  and existence, 15
  and metaphysics, 17
injustice of history, rectification of, 16–17
  and Beneke, 25–6, 141–2
  through recollection, 146, 151
interpretation
  aesthetic versus philosophical, 65–9
  as answer, 65
  and art, 69, 70, 74
  and constitutional law, 72
  as conversation, 74
  for Gadamer, 65–6
  by historians, 148
  individual freedom in, 69
  of law, 65, 71–4
  and literature, 65, 66, 69, 74
  and philosophical uses of historical traditions, 74
  and philosophy, 66–7, 69, 74, 75
  and poetry, 65, 66, 69, 74
  and questions, 69
  of rabbinical law, 72–4
  in theology, 65
  and truth, 69
  see also hermeneutics
interpretation, errors of, 85–91
  caricature as, 88–91
  discipleship, as, 85–7
  exegesis as, 87–8
  hagiography as, 88
irony
  and Hume, 117
  and Moore, 120
  in philosophy, 88, 115, 116, 118–19
  and Whitehead, 120
  and Wittgenstein, 118, 120

James, Henry, 66
James, William
  and experience, 131
  marginalisation of, 33
  and Russell, 92
  and unmediated experience, 12
  and Whitehead, 92
Janik, Allan, 98, 99
Japan, 146
  war crimes by, 136, 139
Jeremiah (prophet), 16
Johnson, Allison H., 134
Joy, Lynn Sumida, 27, 38, 41

Joyce, James
  experience in, 19n12
  myth and imagination in, 11, 19n12
justice
  in Anaximander, 15–16
  and being, 15
  and existence, 15
  and experience, 14–15, 16
  and nonbeing, 15
Justinian Code, 71

Kafka, Franz, 98
Kant, Immanuel, 30, 32, 100, 103
  categories of understanding in, 130
  morality in, 35–6
  renewed interest in, 37
  and Whitehead, 101, 113, 128
  and Whitehead's metaphysics, 93
Kant und die Epigonen (Liebmann) (1865), 22
Kenya, under colonial rule, 71–2
Keynes, John Maynard, 111
Kierkegaard, Søren, 37
Kimball, Bruce, 4
Kirk, G. S., 8
Kline, George L., 70, 106, 134, 143–4, 153n12, 153n14
knowledge
  desire for, 14, 146
  and language, 114
  versus memorisation, 86
  and narrative, 84
  and perception, 130
  philosophy of, 22–3
  in positivism, 12–13
  theory of, return to, 22
  and unmediated experience, 14
knowledge industry, 31, 34, 112
Köhnke, Klaus Christian, 23, 24, 147
Kraus, Karl, influence of, on Wittgenstein, 98
Kritik der reinen Vernunft (Kant) (1781), 32, 101
Kuhn, Thomas, 34–5, 36, 41, 42, 82, 112
Kundera, Milan, 136, 137, 143, 145
  and forgetting, 137, 138, 146–7

Lange, Friedrich, 22, 24
language
  common, 120
  and knowledge, 114
  and Moore, 116
  ordinary, 127
  and philosophy, 113, 115
  theories of, 113
  use of, to order the world, 11
  and Wittgenstein, 115, 117–18
law
  adaptation of, and context, 71–3
  being versus meaning in, 71–4
  and historical tradition, 71–4, 75
  interpretation in, 65, 71–4
  and precedent, 57
  rabbinical, 72–4
  and reflective engagement, 76
  and social context, 71
Lehrer, Keith, 47
Leibniz, Gottfried Wilhelm, 104
  and preestablished harmony, 131
  renewed interest in, 43
  and Whitehead, 92, 128
Liebmann, Otto, 22
Linge, David, 67–8
literature
  history of, 39–41
  interpretation in, 65, 66, 69, 74
  narrative in, 37
  passionate engagement in, 55
  and philosophy, 66
  transitions in, 55
Lives and Opinions of Eminent Philosophers (Diogenes), 29
Locke, John, 103
  renewed interest in, 37
  time in, 103
  and Whitehead, 93, 103, 128
logic
  of Beneke, 22
  false precision in, 116–17
  and metaphysics, 9
  and Moore, 116
  in philosophy, 115
  repudiation of, 127
  and Russell, 116
  and Whitehead, 115, 126
  and Wittgenstein, 99, 117–18
logos
  as first word, 11
  in Heraclitus, 12
  transition to, from *mythos*, 55–6
Loos, Adolf, 98
Lotze, Hermann, 2, 52
Love's Knowledge (Nussbaum) (1990), 66
Lowell Lectures (Whitehead) (1925), 128
Luckmann, Thomas, 36
'Ludwig Wittgenstein, A Biographical Sketch' (von Wright) (1954), 112–13, 114
Lyotard, Jean-François, 37

Mach, Ernst, 100
  and decline of philosophy, 37
  and history of philosophy, 33, 44, 47, 54
  and history of science, 41, 42
MacIntyre, Alasdair, 17, 30, 49, 82
  marginalisation of, 33
  master narrative in, 51
  and narrative in philosophy, 50–1
  and philosophy as science, 43
  and philosophy of history of philosophy, 48
  theory in, 100
McTaggart, J. M. E., 101, 106, 107
Mahler, Gustav, 99
Maimonides, 30
Malcolm, Norman, 113
Malinin, Vladimir, 137, 138
marginalisation
  and anger, 16
  by dominant intellectual movements, 25–6
  in Enlightenment, 117
  in history of philosophy, 1, 54, 85
  as injustice, 5, 15–16, 25–6
  of intellectual movements, 25–6, 27
  process of, 16
  in science, 27
Marx, Karl, 37
master narrative, 5, 17, 18, 51, 54
  definition of, 51
  function of, 51–2
  of Hegel, 16
  in MacIntyre, 51
  and Newtonianism, 51
  in philosophy, 51
  in physics, 51
  and progress, 51

master narrative *(cont.)*
  in science, 51, 52
  see also narrative
mathematics
  false precision in, 116–17
  and Frege, 116
  and Gassendi
  history of, relevance of, 30
  and Moore, 116
  and philosophy, 115
  and Russell, 116
  as subdiscipline of philosophy, 32
  and Whitehead, 115, 126
matter
  and mind, 155n24
  past in, 149–50
Matter and Memory (Bergson) (1896), 148, 149
Maxwell, James Clerk, 100
meaning
  and being, 70, 153n14
  versus being, 69–74, 76, 79n20, 143
  and past, 143–4
memorisation, versus knowledge, 86
memory
  cosmos as, 149
  failure to obliterate, 147
  and forgetting, 138
  and history of philosophy, 145
  past as, 144–5
  physical, 155n24
  preempting, 141
  in psychoanalysis, 79n20
  recovery of, 145
  and research method, 138–9
  search for, 147
  see also forgetting; recollection; remembering
metaphysical homelessness, 69
metaphysics, 107–11
  Cambridge tradition of, 109–10
  definition of, 17
  and experience, 105, 120
  as first philosophy, 8
  grounded in experience, 112
  and history, 17
  history of, relevance of, 30
  and history of philosophy, 9
  and injustice, 17
  and logic, 9
  and Newtonianism, 100
  opinions about, 102
  origins of, 9
  presuppositions in, 77n3
  renewed interest in, 43
  speculative , 22, 23–4, 127
  systematic, 43
  as therapy for incoherence, 100–1
  and Whitehead, 93, 100, 107–11, 126
  Whitehead's definition of, 117
  and Wittgenstein, 107–11
  Wittgenstein's definition of, 108–9
Metaphysics (Aristotle), 51
Microcosmus (Lotze) (1856–64), 52
Mill, John Stuart, 21, 52
  and Beneke, 21–2
  empiricism of, 21
  and German philosophy, 21–2
  influence of, 22
  morality in, 35–6
mind
  and matter, 155n24
  and unmediated experience, 14

modelling, role of, 110
modernism
  and Moore, 120
  and philosophy, 120
  and Whitehead, 120
  and Wittgenstein, 120
monads, in Whitehead, 129
Monet, Claude, 62
  philosophical interpretation of works by, 66
  subjects of, 62–3
  temporal passage in paintings by, 62–3
Montaigne, Michel de, 4
Moore, G. E., 12, 101
  and analytic philosophy, 98, 126
  and common sense, 116, 120
  and Enlightenment, 120
  and history of philosophy, 30, 49, 104
  and importance of reason, 118–19
  and irony, 115, 118–19
  and language, 116
  and logic, 116, 127
  and mathematics, 116
  and ordinary language, 127
  and sense-data theory, 131
  and Wittgenstein, 108, 114, 120
morality
  in Mill, 35–6
  and Wittgenstein, 119
Morgan, C. Lloyd, 33
music
  history of, 39–41, 66–7
  passionate engagement in, 55
  progress versus history in, 39–41
  transitions in, 55
musician, creation of worlds by, 67
Musil, Robert, 98
myth
  and first word, 11, 14
  of origin, 9, 75
  and philosophy, 8–10, 16, 17
  and presocratics, 90, 95n14
  and unmediated experience, 11, 13, 14
  in Vico, 11
'Myth of Er', 145
mythology
  in Joyce, 19n12
  versus philosophy, 5
mythos, transition of, to *logos*, 55–6

Nabokov, Vladimir, 66
narrative, 49–52
  in arts, 37, 39–40, 48, 64, 69
  changes in, 2, 3, 4
  completeness of, 136, 146
  effect of, on past, 70–1
  evaluation of, 50–1
  hagiographic, 88, 140
  historical, revision of, 139–40
  history as, 1, 2, 4, 17, 38–40, 48, 49–50, 148–51
  incommensurability of rival, 50–2, 54, 69
  and knowledge, 84
  in literature, 37
  marginalisation in, 3
  by marginalised persons, 1, 6–7n1
  master *see* master narrative
  objective versus subjective, 50–1
  objectivity in, 151n3
  official, 140
  omissions in, 3, 139
  and past, 148

and philosophical method, 2
in philosophy, 49–52, 58n10, 84
in Plato, 84
by privileged persons, 1–2
in psychoanalysis, 70–1
as reflective historical engagement, 75
religious text as, 73
revisions in, 139–40
reweaving of, 50, 54, 70, 139–40, 146
in science, 37
structure of, 50, 51–2
superior, 51–2
as triumph over suffering, 146
and truth, 49–50, 51–2, 59n12, 84
National Gallery of Art (Washington, DC), 62
naturalistic fallacy, 119
Nature
in Whitehead, 108
and Wittgenstein, 108
neo-Kantianism *see* philosophy: neo-Kantian
Neurath, Otto, 113, 115
Neville, Robert C., 134
Newton, Isaac, 93, 110
and Whitehead, 128
Newtonianism, 100
fallacy of misplaced concreteness in, 100
and Mach, 100
and master narrative, 51
metaphysics in, 100
replacement for, 102
and Whitehead, 93, 100, 102, 109, 128
Nicholas of Cusa, 3
Nichomachean Ethics (Aristotle), 51
Nietzsche, Friedrich, 50
appreciation of, 2, 37
bad historical consciousness in, 6, 6n6, 38, 83, 88
and decline of philosophy, 37
and passion in philosophy, 54
and passionate engagement, 55
and Wittgenstein, 98
nihilism, 43, 46n20, 54
nonbeing, 15
nous, and unmediated experience, 14
novelty, 130, 132
Nussbaum, Martha, 4
and hermeneutics, 66
and literature as philosophy, 27
and return to history of philosophy, 48

Oakeshott, Michael, 103–4
object (past), 129
object, and passage of time, 105–6
object, enduring, 126, 130, 155n24
object, eternal, 129
and actual occasion, 130
definition of, 130
and experience, 131–2
and God, 132
versus objectified occasions, 130
ordering of, 133
and *res verae*, 131
oblivion, consignment to, 25–6, 137, 143
oblivion, loss to, 5, 85, 140
of events, 142–3
as historical process, 15, 16–17, 25–6, 85
of intellectual movements, 25
recovery from, 85, 134, 140, 149–50
occasion
actual *see* actual occasion
becoming of, 105

of experience, 129
and feelings, 131
ordinary, and flux, 131
and past, 131
perishing of, 105, 129
as quantum, 133
On Certainty (Wittgenstein) (1969), 18, 108
ontological past, location of, 143
Ontological Principle (Whitehead), 129, 130
ontological status of past events, 142–5, 147–8, 149, 152n10
ontology
of events, 106–7
of images, 64
of present and past, 106
of time, 106–7, 129
see also being
order
and experience, 132
ideal, 132
ordering of time
process of history as, 17, 26
redemption from oblivion in, 151
ordering principles, search for, 12–13
organism, philosophy of, 128
origin, myths of, 9, 75

Parmenides, 9, 13
Pascal, and Wittgenstein, 98
past
alteration of, 70–1
being of, 143–4
defined, 105–6, 143, 148
desire to change, 137
erasure of, 142–3
event *see* event, past
and forgetting, 136, 137–8, 144–5, 148–9
location of, 149–51
in McTaggart, 106–7
in matter, 149–50
meaning of, 143–4, 149–50, 153n14
as memory, 144–5
narrative's effect on, 70–1
ontological grounding of, 144–5, 147–8
as perishing, 144–5, 147
persistence of, 145, 153–4n15
and present, 105, 106, 132
in present, 50, 148–51
recollection of, 148
reconstruction of, 68
reinterpretation of, 70–1
transmission of, 141–2
in Whitehead, 106–7, 129, 143
see also history
Peirce, Charles Sanders, 131
and experience, 11–12
firstness of, 11, 12, 14
secondness of, 12
thirdness of, 11, 14, 132
perception, 132
act of, 148
and causal efficacy, 131, 132
and knowledge, 130
and presentational immediacy, 132
and thing perceived, 148
in Whitehead, 132
perfectibility, progress towards, 117–20
perishing
definition of, 105
of occasion, 129

perishing, perpetual
  history of philosophy as, 16–17
  time as, 103, 105, 153–4n15
permanence, versus change, 127
Perry, Ralph Barton
  idealism versus realism of, 11
  and sense-data theory, 131
Phaedrus
  as disciple, 56, 86
  and explanation versus understanding, 56
Phaedrus (Plato), 86
phenomenology
  influence of, on philosophy, 13
  of Monet, 62
  and unmediated experience, 12
Phenomenology of Spirit (Hegel) (1807), 16, 26
  absolute knowing in, 133–4
  and forgetting, 145–6
philosopher
  as celebrity, 86
  as dreamer, 16
  history studied by, 17
  interpretation of world by, 67, 75, 76, 84
  marginalisation of, 26–7
  versus rabbinical scholar, 57
  and recollecting, 145
philosophical insight, 16
philosophical interpretation, versus aesthetic interpretation, 65–9
Philosophical Investigations (Wittgenstein) (1953), 18, 108, 113
Philosophical Remarks (Wittgenstein) (1930), 118
philosophical thinking
  task of, 13–17
  underlying notion of, 8
philosophical uses of historical traditions, 48, 50, 57, 74–5
Philosophische Bemerkungen (Wittgenstein) (1930), 118
philosophy
  abuses of history in, 83, 85–8
  and academic politics, 24–5, 26, 34, 118
  and aesthetics, 66, 69
  antiprogressive, 21, 50, 140
  applied, 27, 37
  and art, 65–6
  audience for, 85
  of being, 103
  caricature in, 36, 89, 90–1, 92, 94n12
  as civic education, 4, 6n8
  combative, 5, 24–5, 26, 42, 89–91
  and common sense, 116, 117, 120, 127
  and consensus, 24, 36
  as conversation , 2, 4, 5, 36–7, 44, 50, 54, 69, 74–5, 76, 84, 92, 93, 107, 114
  and cosmology, 93
  death of, 37
  definition of, 8, 9, 89
  disciples in, 56, 85–86
  as discipline, 32, 33, 34–5, 38, 44
  disciplines spun off from, 32
  epistemological turn in, 113
  ethics in, 115
  exegesis in, 87–8
  and experience, 8
  false, 91, 11
  false precision in, 116–17
  first principles in, 9
  fragmentation of, 36
  goals of, 34, 57, 100–1
  and hermeneutics, 74, 75–6
  and historical narrative, 3–4, 56
  historical process of, 16–17
  and historical tradition, 48, 50, 57, 74–5
  as history, 44
  history's role in, 82–5
  idealist, 36, 52
  inclusion in, 37
  and injustice, 3, 5, 15–16, 17, 25–6, 146, 151
  and interpretation, 2–3, 69, 74, 75
  irony in, 115, 116, 118–19
  and knowledge, 8–9, 12, 13, 14, 22–4, 39, 44, 48, 59, 60n25, 84, 86, 116, 119, 130, 132
  and language, 52, 113, 115
  of law, 49–50, 57
  versus legal reasoning, 57
  and literature, 4, 27, 37, 66
  as living tradition, 57
  logic of, 115
  marginalisation in, 1, 2, 11, 16, 25–7, 32, 54, 85, 86–7, 125
  and mathematics, 115
  metaphysics as first, 8
  method of *see* philosophy, method of
  movements in, 1–3, 25–6, 27, 525, 89
  and myth, 5, 8–10, 16, 17
  and narrative *see* narrative
  neo-Kantian, 21, 22–5
  new beginning in, 50
  normative conception of, 4–5
  origins of, 8–10
  passionate engagement in, 53, 54–5
  perennial questions of, 33
  and poetry, 4, 66
  positivist, 27
  post-analytic *see* philosophy, Continental
  practical, 4, 27, 33, 65
  as preparadigm science, 36
  private, 83–5
  progress in, 32–3, 34, 39–41, 42–3, 89
  public, 4, 6n8, 83–5
  redemption of, by history, 5
  as reflective historical engagement, 74–6, 91–3
  reform of (Descartes), 119
  in research institution, 31–2
  as rhetoric, 91
  role of, 2, 4, 26–7, 100, 108–9, 145
  and science, 100
  as science, 25, 30, 32, 34–5, 38, 82, 89, 90, 108–9, 115
  systematic, 23, 34, 43, 102, 108–9, 126
  as therapy for incoherence, 100–1
  thinking about versus thinking with, 8–10
  and time *see* time
  transitions in, 55
  and truth, 60n25
  twentieth-century, 99–104, 126
  universality in, 16
  work of, 5, 8–9, 17, 26–7, 33, 34, 57, 67, 75, 84, 89, 117, 145, 147
  in the world as we find it, 17
  see also philosophy, history of; *see also under branches of philosophy*
philosophy, American, 104, 130
  and history of philosophy, 47
  and privacy, 88
philosophy, analytic, 99, 126
  and history of philosophy, 36
  British, 98, 99, 100, 101, 130
  decline of, 27
  hegemony of, 44

history of, 4
  problems with, 66
  rise of, 32
philosophy, Anglo-American
  consensus in, 36
  and history of philosophy, 47, 82
  interpretation by, of Whitehead, 102
  interpretation by, of Wittgenstein, 99
  origins of, 126
philosophy, British, 104, 130
  analytic, 98, 99, 100, 101, 130
  caricature in, 90
  empiricist, 117
  language in, 113
  and Whitehead, 104, 107, 113–14, 130
  and Wittgenstein, 98, 99–100, 113–14
philosophy, Continental, 18, 37
  approach of, 103–4
  exegesis in, 87, 88
  and history of philosophy, 103–4
  rise of, 27
  and Whitehead, 103–4
philosophy, Enlightenment, 3, 116–20
philosophy, German, 3, 21
  antispeculative, 21–2
  bad historical consciousness in, 88
  decline of, following 1848, 24–5
  divisions in, 23–4, 25
  exegesis in, 87, 88
  factions in, 21–2, 23
  idealist, 21–2
  and Mill, 21
  political influences on, 140
  repression in, 21, 22, 23–4
  and Revolution of, 1848, 24
  speculative, 21–2
philosophy, history of, 23–4
  alternative versions of, 1–5
  ancient Greeks in, 3
  appropriate uses of, 91
  and Aristotle, 84, 85, 89
  attitudes toward, 81–2
  and called-thinking, 9–10
  canonisation of, 54
  and caricature, 35–6, 40–1, 48–50, 54, 58, 82, 88–91, 92, 104
  and Carnap, 30
  and Collingwood, 30, 44
  as common ground, 35
  conceptions of, 47–57
  and Continental philosophy, 104
  continuity in, 50
  as conversation, 4, 36–7, 44, 50, 54, 57, 69, 74–5, 76, 84, 92, 93, 103, 107
  cultural shifts in, 26
  and Danto, 44
  and discipleship, 85–7
  engagement with, 9, 53–5
  examination of, 4–5
  exclusion from, 1–2
  first principles in, 9
  and Gadamer, 67
  German-language, 3
  and Hacking, 44
  and Hartshorne, 89
  and Hegel, 44
  and Heidegger, 44
  and historical context, 58n9
  versus history of art, 48
  versus history of science, 48
  importance of, 5, 66–7, 82, 83, 84, 85–7

inclusion in, 1–2
incompatibilities in, 54
and interpretation, 25, 56–7
loss to oblivion, 16–17
and MacIntyre, 44
marginalisation of, 1, 3, 29–30, 32, 35–6, 54, 56, 83, 85
master narrative in, 52
and memory, 85, 140, 145
method of, 10
and Moore, 30, 104
movements in, 49, 53
narrative in *see* narrative
and new beginning, 3–4, 49–50
ordering of time in, 8, 13–17, 25–6, 55–6, 151
partial forgetting in, 139
as pedagogical tool, 29
as perpetual perishing, 16–17
philosophy as conversation with, 93
philosophy of, 48–9, 50, 68
and Plato, 84, 85
privilege in, 54
progress in, 49, 54–5, 82
and Putnam, 44
and Quine, 10
recovery of, 29–44
and Reichenbach, 30
rejection of, 32–3, 49, 54, 83, 87
relevance of, 30, 82
return to, 44, 47–48
role of, 9, 29, 51, 59, 81–93, 103–4, 125, 148
and Rorty, 44, 50
and Russell, 29, 30, 89, 92, 104
and Schlick, 30
and Smith, 44
study of, 8–9, 27
and Taylor, 44, 50
transcendence in, 50
and truth, 49–50, 84, 89
uses of, 48, 50, 57, 74–5, 97n28
value of, 29–30
and Vienna Circle, 30
views of, 8–9
and Weiss, 86–7, 89
Western perspective of, 3
and Whitehead, 86–7, 92, 113–14
work of, never completed, 69, 76, 77n3, 78–9n15, 153n14
philosophy, method of
  of Aristotle, 51, 59, 84
  combative, 26, 42, 89–91
  hermeneutics as, 67, 69, 78–9n15
  and narrative, 2
  proper, 3–5, 10, 25, 26, 31, 32, 34–6, 41–2, 48, 67–8, 81–93, 108
  reflective historical engagement as, 81–93, 103–4, 125, 148
  scientific, 32, 34, 35, 36, 58–9, 67, 104, 116–17, 148
  and truth, 84
  of Whitehead, 112, 125
  in Wittgenstein, 108
philosophy, process, 15, 102, 105–6, 110
  exegesis of, 127–33
  value in, 15
philosophy, Renaissance, 3, 30, 93
  conflict of, with science, 38
  integration of, with other disciplines, 33
  method in, 90–1, 116
Philosophy and the Mirror of Nature (Rorty) (1979), 36–7, 43, 47, 55

physics
    history of, relevance of, 30
    master narrative in, 51
    as subdiscipline of philosophy, 32
    and Whitehead, 102
Pinsent, David, 99, 113
Planck, Max, 99, 100
Plato
    caricature of, 36, 94n12
    and disciples, 86
    and forgetting, 145
    method of, 84, 85, 90
    and myths of origin, 75
    and passion, 54, 55
    philosophical positions of, 90–1
    rejection of, 4
    relationship of, with Aristotle, 89–90
    and Whitehead, 93, 113
    and Wittgenstein, 113
Platonic Forms, 90, 95–6n15, 127, 148
Platonic universal, eternal object as, 130
poet, creation of worlds by, 67, 75, 76, 83, 84–5
poetry
    history of, 66-7
    interpretation in, 65, 66, 69, 74
    and philosophy, 66
    private worlds in, 83
Poincaré, Henri, 100
political science, 32, 42
Pols, Edward, 11
Popper, Karl, 151n3
Portrait of the Artist as a Young Man (Joyce) (1916), 19n12
positivism, 117
    history of, 25
    and knowledge, 12–13
    rise of, 22
    and *Tractatus*, 118
    and Wittgenstein, 118
Posterior Analytics (Aristotle), 50, 57, 59
pragmatism, 12, 13
Prague Spring, 138
precision
    and progress, 117
    repudiation of, 127
    and Wittgenstein, 117, 118
prehension, 129, 132
    negative, 16–17
    positive, 128
    theory of, 128
present
    definition of, 105, 106–7
    and future, 105
    in McTaggart, 106–7
    and past, 105, 106, 132, 129
    past in, 50, 148–50
    in Whitehead, 106–7
presocratics, 89–90
    and myth, 90, 95n14
    origins accounts by, 9
    as preoccupied, 16
    reflective engagement with, 75
    search by, for order, 12
    thinking about, 8, 9
    thinking with, 8–17
    and unmediated experience, 10–14
Price, H. H., 52
Principia Ethica (Moore) (1903), 119

Principia Mathematica (Whitehead and Russell) (1910–13), 101, 108, 125
    logical space in, 104
    and progress, 119
    as scientific philosophy, 115
Principle of Concretion, as actual occasion, 131
Principle of Relativity (Whitehead), 129
Principle of Relativity with Applications to Physical Science (Whitehead) (1922), 101, 126, 129, 133
privacy
    and discipleship, 85
    as error in philosophy, 13, 81–5, 87, 88, 92
process
    and actual occasions, 129
    and being, 130
    and injustice, 15
    quanta of, 128
    versus substance, 127
    and value, 15
Process and Reality (Whitehead) (1929), 92, 93, 102, 103
    actual entities in, 128
    actual occasions in, 128
    as conversation with history of philosophy, 92, 93
    cosmology in, 109
    editorial problems with, 125
    feelings in, 128
    God in, 133
    influence of, on philosophy, 125
    objects in, 130
    origins of, 127
    perpetual perishing in, 105
    relativistic geometry in, 133
    reputation of, 134
    spacetime in, 104, 133
    structure of, 128–34
process philosophy, 127
    exegesis of, 128–34
process theology, 133
Proem (Parmenides), 9
progress
    and Bloomsbury circle, 119
    evangelism for, 43
    versus history, 39–41
    and master narrative, 51
    and Moore, 120
    in philosophy, 32–3, 39, 42–3, 89
    and precision, 117
    repudiation of, 43
    and Russell, 119
    in science, 117
    and Whitehead, 120
    and Wittgenstein, 120
Proust, Marcel, 4, 66
psychoanalysis, 70–1
    as analogy for recollection of past, 146–7
    being versus meaning in, 70
    memory in, 79n20
psychology, 32, 42
Pure Reason, limitations on, 130
Putnam, Hilary, 103
    and history of philosophy, 44, 47–8
Pythagoras, 16
Pythagoreans
    memory training by, 17, 145
    and objective immortality, 145
    and recollection, 146, 146

Index 177

quanta, 128, 129
quantum experience, 106
quantum mechanics, 127
quantum of experience, 126, 133
'Question Concerning Technology' (Heidegger) (1954), 64
questions
   and history, 84
   and interpretation, 69
   search for, 64–5
Quine, Willard V. O., 103, 134
   and history of philosophy, 8–9, 10, 33, 47

rabbinical interpretation, and reflective engagement, 75, 76
Raven, J. E., 8
realism
   decline of, 52
   direct, 11
   and history of philosophy, 35
   versus idealism, 11, 92
reason
   importance of, 118–19
   and Moore, 120
   in quest of Good, 119
   and Whitehead, 120
   and Wittgenstein, 120
recollection
   and Augustine, 145
   and existence, 149–50
   and forgetting, 138, 146
   and history, 136, 142, 145–6, 148
   and immortality, 134, 145
   and injustice, 146, 151
   preempting future, 141
   reasons for, 138
   and tyranny, 146
   and Whitehead, 145
   and wisdom, 146
   see also forgetting; memory; remembering
reflective historical engagement, 52–3, 74–5, 76, 95
   legal interpretation as, 76
   as philosophical interpretation, 74–5
   as philosophical method, 81–93, 103–4, 125, 148
   philosophy as, 74–6, 91–3
   and rabbinical interpretation, 75, 76
   by Whitehead, 93, 125
Reformed Subjectivist Principle (Whitehead), 105–6, 129
Reichenbach, Hans, 32
   and history of philosophy, 30, 49, 54
   and scientific philosophy, 43, 115
   and time, 105, 107
relativity, general
   Einstein's theory of, 101, 126
   Whitehead's theory of, 101, 125–6
remembering
   act of, 148
   and consciousness, 142
   deliberate, 143
   and existence, 142
   and location of past events, 142
   and thing remembered, 148
   see also forgetting; memory; recollection
Renaissance
   humanism versus science in, 3, 38, 93
   philosophy in, 3, 30, 33, 38, 90–1, 93, 116

repression
   definition of, 137
   political, 24, 137, 142, 146
   in psychoanalysis, 71
Republic (Plato)
   forgetting in, 145
   ontological standing of representation in, 64
res verae
   and actual entities, 105
   definition of, 105
   in Descartes, 129
   and eternal objects, 131
   see also actual occasion
revolution
   in academia, 34, 37, 43
   in science, 93, 100, 102, 125–34
Revolution of 1848 (German states), 24
rhetoric, philosophy as, 91
Rilke, Rainer Maria, 98
Rise of Neo-Kantianism (Köhnke) (1986/1991), 23, 24, 147
Rise of Scientific Philosophy (Reichenbach) (1951), 32
Rorty, Richard, 103, 134
   and caricature, 91
   and decline of philosophy, 37
   and doxography, 88
   and hermeneutics, 66
   and history of philosophy, 33, 44, 47, 48, 50, 55
   and literature as philosophy, 27
   method of philosophy of, 4, 91
   and narrative in philosophy, 50–1
   and systematic metaphysics, 43
Rouen Cathedral, West Façade (Monet) (1894), 62
Rouen Cathedral, West Façade, Sunlight (Monet) (1894), 62
Russell, Bertrand, 12, 125
   and analytic philosophy, 98, 126
   books by, 104
   and caricature, 89, 92
   and common sense, 116
   and history of philosophy, 29, 30, 49, 54, 89, 92, 104
   influence of, on Wittgenstein, 99, 114
   and language, 116
   and logic, 116, 127
   and mathematics, 116
   and metaphysics, 127
   in modern philosophy, 4
   and progress, 119
   and scientific philosophy, 115, 116
   and sense-data theory, 131
   and Wittgenstein, 118
Ryle, Gilbert, 54

Sadi Carnot, Marie François, 63
saying, versus showing, 110–11, 112
Schelling, Friedrich, 33
Schleiermacher, Friedrich, 16, 22, 67
Schlick, Moritz
   and history of philosophy, 30
   and philosophy as science, 43, 115
Schneewind, Jerome, 3–4
Schoenberg, Arnold, 99
Schopenhauer, Arthur, 21
Schrödinger, Erwin, 100
Schulte, Joachim, 108, 118

science
    and common sense, 117
    and Gassendi, 3, 38, 42, 116–17
    historical narratives of, 56
    versus humanism, 38, 41–2, 56, 116
    and Hume, 116
    marginalisation in, 48, 51, 53, 93, 100, 102, 109, 110, 128
    master narrative in, 52
    narrative in, 37
    passion in, 53
    and philosophy, 25, 30, 32, 34–5, 36, 38, 42, 82, 89, 90, 100, 108–9, 115
    philosophy of, 126
    privileging of, 38–9, 44
    and progress, 39–41, 48
    reason in, 59–60n18
    reform of (Galileo), 119
    revolution in, 93, 100, 102, 125–34
    in social sciences, 42
    theories in, 100
science, history of, 59–60n18, 93
    and Collingwood, 41
    and Hacking, 41, 42
    versus history of philosophy, 48
    and Hume, 41
    importance of, 41
    and Joy, 41
    and Kuhn, 41, 42
    and MacIntyre, 41, 42
    narrative in, 50–1
    relevance of, 30, 82
    and truth, 84
    and Whitehead, 102
Science and the Modern World (Whitehead) (1925), 92–3, 101, 128
scientific discovery, logic of, 102
scientific revolutions, 125–34
    history of, 102
    narrative in, 52
secondness (Peirce), 12
semantics
    and Moore, 120
    and Whitehead, 120
    and Wittgenstein, 120
Sen, Amartya, 41
Seneca, 3
sense-data, 12, 130, 131
sense-perception, 132, 134
Sherburne, Donald W., 134
showing, versus saying, 110–11, 112
Skinner, Quentin, 69
Smith, Adam, 31
Smith, John E., 33, 34, 37
Social Construction of Reality (Berger and Luckmann) (1966), 36
social sciences
    history in, 37, 41–2
    as science, 32, 42
sociology, 32, 42
Sociology of Philosophies (Randall) (2000), 28n6
Socrates, 30, 56
    and disciples, 86
    and myths of origin, 75
    and passionate engagement, 55
Sophocles, 37
Soviet Union
    archives of, 146
    political prisoners in, 137, 139
    purges in, 138–9

space
    in Einstein, 104
    logical, 104
    in *Principia Mathematica*, 104
    in Whitehead, 104
    see also spacetime
Space, Time and Deity (Alexander) (1920), 133
spacetime
    of Einstein, 104
    evidence of Big Bang in, 149
    linearity of, 104
    in *Process and Reality*, 104, 133
    of Whitehead, 10
    see also space; time
Spencer, Herbert, 52
Spinoza, Baruch, 30, 103, 148
    renewed interest in, 43
    and Whitehead, 93, 128
Stalin, Josef, 138–9, 146
statement, as answer, 64–5, 77n3
Stoics, 3
Strauss, Leo, 56
Structure of Scientific Revolutions (Kuhn) (1962), 34–5, 36, 42
subject (present), 129
    versus object, 129
    and passage of time, 105–6
Subjectivist Principle (Descartes), 106, 129
substance, versus process, 127
suppression
    of Beneke, 137, 140, 142
    in history, 136–7, 140, 142
    of history, 44, 139–40, 142, 143, 146
    of original thought, 88
    reasons for, 140
symbolic reference, and unmediated experience, 14
System of Logic (Mill) (1843), 21

Talmud, 73–4
Taylor, A. E., 36
Taylor, Charles, and history of philosophy, 44, 47, 50, 55
temporal activity, 126
temporal experience, 127
temporal passage, 153–4n15
    as arrow, 106
    experience of, 104, 105–6
    in Monet's paintings, 62–3
    as perpetual perishing, 103
    in philosophy, 104
    from present to past, 142
    quantum experience in, 106
temporal relation, of subject and object, 129
temporality
    of events, 127
    in Whitehead, 104
Thales, 14, 16
theory, 10–11, 100
thing in itself, 64, 69
thinking
    and being, 9
    and evil, 9
thirdness (Peirce), 11, 14, 132
Thomas, Dylan, 15
Three Rival Versions of Moral Enquiry (MacIntyre) (1990), 59n12
Timaeus (Plato), 93, 103
time
    arrow of, 105–6
    asymmetry of, 105, 106

in Einstein, 105
epochal theory of, 105
and experience, 107, 109
and flux of historical events, 154n18
as illusion, 107
injustice in the margins of, 1–5
modelling of, 110
as moving image, 107
as mystery, 107
object in, 105–6
passage of, 103, 107, 109
as perpetual perishing, 105, 153–4n15
and philosophy, 14, 104
in relativity, 126
subject in, 105–6
and understanding, 14, 68
and Whitehead, 103, 104, 105, 108, 109
and Wittgenstein, 109
see also spacetime
time, ordering of , 8, 25–6
in Anaximander, 13–17, 151
in Monet exhibit, 64
in philosophy, 55–56
in relativity theory, 104
in Whitehead, 121–32
Torah
as historical tradition, 76
interpretation of, 72–4
Toulmin, Stephen, 98, 99
Tractatus Logico-Philosophicus (Wittgenstein) (1922), 99, 107–8, 126
in history of philosophy, 114
misreading of, 118
and positivism, 118
and progress, 119
propositions in, 110
as scientific philosophy, 115
structure of, 112
Trinity College (Cambridge), 98, 101
truth
and context, 55
definition of, 84
and history, 49–50, 55, 84
and history of philosophy, 89
and interpretation, 69
and narrative, 49–50
and philosophy, 60n25
and Whitehead, 115
Truth and Method (Gadamer) (1960), 67–8, 69, 70
'Two Dogmas of Empiricism' (Quine), 36
tyrant, 147
erasure of history by, 137, 138–9, 145, 148
and forgetting, 142–3, 145
and recollection, 146

Über Gewissheit (Wittgenstein) (1969), 114
understanding
and being, 70
categories of, 130
versus explanation, 56, 61n31, 86
as participation in tradition, 68
past and present in, 68
and time, 14, 68
university
culture of disciplines in, 30–1, 32, 38, 41
division of, into individual disciplines, 24–5, 30–2, 33, 34, 38, 39, 41
as knowledge industry, 31, 34
as research institution, 31
role of students in, 31

specialisation in, 30–1
as teaching institution, 31
University College (London), 101
University of London, 101, 126

value, 15
values, models for, 111
Van Gogh, Vincent, 55
Verene, Donald Phillip, 11
Vico, Giambattista, 3, 30, 50
and caricature, 90–1
and *fantasia*, 11
marginalisation of, 33
myth and imagination in, 11
renewed interest in, 37
Vienna Circle
and history of philosophy, 30
influence of, on Wittgenstein, 99
and philosophy as science, 43
Vlastos, Gregory, 134
von Humboldt, Alexander, 31–2, 45n6
von Wright, Georg Henrik, 112–13, 114, 116

war crimes, 136, 137, 146
Waterloo Bridge, 62, 63
Waterloo Bridge, Gray Day (Monet) (1903), 62, 63, 64–5, 66
Waterloo Bridge, London, at Dusk (Monet) (1904), 62, 63, 64–5, 66
Waterloo Bridge, London, at Sunset (Monet) (1904), 62, 63, 64–5, 66
Waterloo Bridge paintings
being versus image in, 64
being and meaning in, 70
interpretation of, 63, 64–5, 69
organisation of exhibit of, 62, 63, 64
Watermark (Brodsky) (989), 62
Weininger, Otto, 98
Weisse, Christian Hermann, 24
Weiss, Paul, 81, 82, 134
and actuality, 83
caricature by, 89
and disciples, 86
and history of philosophy, 86–7, 89
and privacy, 87, 88
Wheelwright, Philip, 8, 14
Whitehead, Alfred North, 9
academic interests of, 102
academic training of, 112
and analytic philosophy, 98, 126
audience for, 102
biographical sketch of, 101
and Bradley, 92
career of, 101–2
and causality, 109
and common sense, 117, 120, 127
and Consequent Nature of God, 17
consternation over, 102
as Continental philosopher, 103–4
conversation of, with history of philosophy, 103
cosmology of, 109, 111, 125
cultural betweenness of, 111
cultural context of, 104
and Descartes, 128
and disciples, 86
early versus late, 102, 104, 114, 116, 117–18, 119, 126–7, 133
education of, in philosophy, 93
enduring object of, 155n24

Whitehead, Alfred North (cont.)
  and Enlightenment, 120
  as expatriate, 111
  general relativity of, 101, 133
  Gifford Lectures of, 93, 101, 103, 125
  God in, 108, 109
  at Harvard University, 126
  and history of philosophy, 86–7, 92, 102, 113–14
  and Hume, 128
  idealism versus realism of, 11
  importance of, 91–2
  influences on, 93, 100, 103
  interpretations of, 128–9
  irony in, 115, 118–19
  and James, 92
  and Kant, 101, 113, 128
  and language, 127
  legacy of, 134
  and Leibniz, 128
  and Locke, 128
  and logic, 115, 127
  marginalisation of, 26, 33, 108, 125
  and mathematics, 100, 115
  and metaphysics, 18n9, 104–11, 117, 126, 127
  and models, 110
  monads in, 129
  Nature in, 108
  and Newton, 93, 100, 128
  and past, 129, 143
  perception in, 132
  philosophical method of, 112, 125
  philosophical style of, 104
  and philosophy as conversation, 92–3
  philosophy of, as science, 109
  philosophy of being of, 103
  philosophy of time of, 103
  and Plato, 113
  process in, 15
  quanta in, 129
  and quantum mechanics, 127
  and reason, 118–19
  and recollection, 145
  and reflective historical engagement, 93, 125
  Reformed Subjectivist Principle of, 105–6
  renewed interest in, 37, 43
  reputation of, 102, 134
  and role of philosophy, 100
  and science, 100
  and sense-data theory, 131
  space in, 104
  spacetime in, 109
  and speculative philosophy, 126
  and Spinoza, 128
  symbolic reference in, 14
  temporality in, 104, 109
  theory in, 100
  time in, 104, 105, 109
  and truth, 115
  in twentieth-century philosophy, 99–104
  unorthodox interpretations by, 103
  and Wittgenstein, 107–8, 111–12
  World in, 108
  writing style of, 111–12, 127–8

Whitehead, Evelyn, 103
Whose Justice? Which Rationality? (MacIntyre) (1988), 59n12
wisdom, and recollection, 146
Wittgenstein, Ludwig, 98
  academic training of, 112–13
  and analytic philosophy, 126
  and British philosophy, 98
  and Cambridge, 98, 99
  and cosmology, 109
  cultural betweenness of, 111
  cultural context of, 104
  early versus late, 108, 110–11, 114, 116, 117, 118, 119
  and Enlightenment, 120
  and ethics, 99, 119
  as expatriate, 111
  and false philosophy, 118
  and God, 122n27
  and Good, 119
  and history of philosophy, 113
  importance of, 98
  influences on, 98, 99, 114, 120
  interpretation of, 98–9
  and irony, 115, 118–19
  and language, 113, 114, 115, 117–18
  and logic, 99, 117–18, 127
  metaphysical homelessness of, 99, 104
  and metaphysics, 107–11
  and modelling, 111
  and Moore, 108
  and morality, 119
  and Nature, 108
  and ordinary language, 127
  philosophical method in, 108
  philosophical style of, 104
  and Plato, 113
  and positivism, 118
  and precision, 117, 118, 127
  propositions of, 110
  and reason, 118–19
  and role of philosophy, 100, 108–9
  and Russell, 118
  and scientific philosophy, 115
  and time, 109
  and Whitehead, 107–8, 111–12
  and World, 108
  writing style of, 111–12
Wittgenstein's Vienna (Janik and Toulmin) (1959), 98, 99, 112–13, 117
Woolf, Virginia, 4, 66
word, first, 11, 84
World
  in Whitehead, 108
  and Wittgenstein, 108
world as we find it, 5, 17, 67, 116, 132
World War II, atrocities in, 136, 139
writer, creation of worlds by, 75, 76, 84

Yuasa, Ken, 136, 138

Zola, Émile, 64
Zweig, Arnulf, 23, 28n5

EU representative:
Easy Access System Europe
Mustamäe tee 50, 10621 Tallinn, Estonia
Gpsr.requests@easproject.com

www.ingramcontent.com/pod-product-compliance
Lightning Source LLC
Chambersburg PA
CBHW070358240426
43671CB00013BA/2550